MINDBRAIN, PSYCHOANALYTIC INSTITUTIONS, AND PSYCHOANALYSTS

MINDBRAIN, PSYCHOANALYTIC INSTITUTIONS, AND PSYCHOANALYSTS

A New Metapsychology Consistent with Neuroscience

Antonio Imbasciati

KARNAC

First published in Italian in 2015 by FrancoAngeli srl as *Nuove teorie sul funzionamento della mente*

Translated by Joan Rundo

First published in English in 2017 by
Karnac Books Ltd
118 Finchley Road
London NW3 5HT

Copyright © 2017 by Antonio Imbasciati

The right of Antonio Imbasciati to be identified as the author of this work has been asserted in accordance with §§ 77 and 78 of the Copyright Design and Patents Act 1988.

All rights reserved. No part of this publication may be reproduced, stored in a retrieval system, or transmitted, in any form or by any means, electronic, mechanical, photocopying, recording, or otherwise, without the prior written permission of the publisher.

British Library Cataloguing in Publication Data

A C.I.P. for this book is available from the British Library

ISBN-13: 978-1-78220-515-9

Typeset by Medlar Publishing Solutions Pvt Ltd, India

www.karnacbooks.com

CONTENTS

ABOUT THE AUTHOR vii

INTRODUCTION ix

CHAPTER ONE
Psychoanalysis and psychology 1

CHAPTER TWO
Cognitive sciences, psychoanalysis, neuroscience 13

CHAPTER THREE
The origins of the mind: prejudices, ideologies, and science 29

CHAPTER FOUR
Neuropsychic development and the relational formation
 of the mind 59

CHAPTER FIVE
Transgenerationality and Perinatal Clinical Psychology 73

vi CONTENTS

CHAPTER SIX
A new metapsychology congruent with neuroscience   89

CHAPTER SEVEN
The Institution: doctrine and ideology   181

NOTES   211

REFERENCES   221

INDEX   233

ABOUT THE AUTHOR

Antonio Imbasciati (www.imbasciati.it) is a full member and training analyst at the Italian Psychoanalytical Society, and Professor Emeritus of Clinical Psychology in the University of Brescia. He has written over sixty books and over 300 papers on experimental psychology, clinical psychology, and psychoanalysis. Since 1978 much of his work relates to the complex relationship between psychoanalysis with experimental psychology. His pioneering protomental theory (elaborated in *Constructing a Mind*) provided a critical analysis of Freud's metapsychology and its consequences for the ideological development of psychoanalysis. He outlined a new metapsychology in in his book *From Freud's Witch to a New Metapsychology: How Our Mind Functions*.

INTRODUCTION

In this most recent book of mine, I have collected and tried to summarise the ideas that have matured in my long experience, as a psychoanalyst and, at the same time, experimentalist researcher and then teacher, trainer, and director of a university institute, to integrate with the different sciences of the mind. Over the years, my intention has been to systematise, integrate, and possibly unify the various theories on the origins and functioning of the mind, which in psychoanalysis, although they have been produced over a hundred years, are still mixed up and confused, resulting in epistemological and general cultural inadequacy. In my lifetime, the field of psychoanalysis has been the one in which I have most passionately seen the scientific limits implicit in the Institutions which explicitly aim to develop the science founded by Freud a century ago. It is the same everywhere, though: the Institution, as Jacques said, works against the Organisation.

Now that I am reaching the end of my career, in this book I have wanted to indulge in a freer critical expression of what, in my opinion, limits the development of research in psychoanalysis, less so in the excellent clinical practice, but more in theory, or rather the theorisation, and in the integration in the current general scientific panorama. Psychoanalysts, in their traditional associations, have remained isolated, with respect to the other sciences of the mind, and recently, have been wary of neurosciences.

Today neurosciences approach the problems of unconscious affectivity, the traditional hunting ground of psychoanalysis, but they do so with other means (biotechnologies) and using another language. Here I outline a critical examination of Freud's Energy-drive Theory, which takes on the characteristics of a *monstre sacré* in the religiousness which can be noted underpinning the spirit of the psychoanalytic institutions. This spirit is accompanied by a confusion between the different and often incompatible psychoanalytic theories: a mere example is the contradiction between the Freudian vision of a mind driven by endogenous forces which clash with external reality and the relational theories (from Klein, to Winnicott to Bion and many other more recent authors) which describe mental functioning as constructed in relationships and by relationships. I believe I can blame the poor social image that psychoanalysis has earned in the past few years, with other scientists and then in the general public, on this confusion of theories and haughty withdrawal into a single presumed orthodoxy.

At present, psychoanalysis seems to be in the midst of a serious crisis: on the level of its therapeutic application, it no longer seems to meet the new social needs of patients and therefore their demands, whilst on the theoretical level it no longer corresponds to sufficiently scientific criteria. An ex-President of the IPA, Otto Kernberg, has predicted the suicide of the psychoanalytic institutions.[1]

During the course of my life I have gradually devoted myself to the theoretical and epistemological disorder, working on integrating psychoanalysis, experimental psychology, developmental psychology, cognitive sciences, attachment theory and now neurosciences. In this framework, I have developed a new metapsychology, different from the one conceived by Freud one hundred years ago, in work which remains fundamental for psychoanalysis: *On Metapsychology* (Freud, 1915), in which the master conceived the explanation of drive for the functioning of the human mind. This "explanation", although it has been the object of criticism for about fifty years now, still remains within the institutional competence of psychoanalysts, even though it appears to be in contrast with the development of clinical psychoanalysis.

Emphasising the great gap between the clinical progress of psychoanalysis and its theoretical backwardness, vagueness, and confusion, from the 1980s onwards I outlined my protomental theory and more recently a new metapsychology which can be congruent with neurosciences. These innovations, like those by other scholars, do not appear for the time being to be easily assimilated by the institution, and are kept in obscurity, while the explanations of Freud still appear as holy icons, to be preserved and worshipped. The "mindbrain", the name I use in this book, seems alien from the central interest proposed and almost prescribed by the institution, which seems to want only clinical psychoanalysis, clinical cases and therapy! Yet Freud said (1923) that psychoanalysis was much more, and that the therapeutic result was to be considered secondary. I therefore believe that studying how the human mind functions is important as well as its relative therapeutic application. The genius of Freud has to be developed, not preserved like a precious relic.

In this book, I have outlined a theory on the origins and functioning of the mind, in new terms which are psychological and at the same time comparable with that we know today from neurosciences, in particular with reference to what they have recently been studying on unconscious emotions, subjectivity and intersubjectivity: the "affective neurosciences". This outlines a new and different conception of the unconscious: an unconscious of neural mnestic structures. A mnestic trace, an engram, instead of drive: implicit memory, the memory of ways of functioning, memory that cannot be verbalised, which challenges the clinical practice of the talking cure. The problem of the relationship between the mind and the brain is discussed in this framework.

I also emphasise here the need for a new type of training for psychoanalysts, who to date have been trained for talking cures, in the perspective of a future competence for non-verbal communication and a scientific study which is no longer directly focused on the unconscious but on the skills acquired or that can be acquired by the consciousness, first of all that of psychoanalysts who aim to understand the unconscious. This new training may not only renew psychoanalysis in integration with other sciences for the progress of research into the human mind, but also find new therapeutic strategies that are more in line with the needs of patients in the current changed social climate.

I hope that this book can act as a stimulus for all my colleagues who from different vertexes study how the human mind works, and first and foremost for all psychoanalysts, often held back by the fear of tarnishing the genius and the work of the master. In this framework, the multiplicity of practices and techniques that aim to cure mental suffering can be clarified, in sufficient knowledge of the psychophysiology of the mind, which precedes the therapeutic intervention and which implicitly guides it without warping the humanity of each intersubjectivity.

CHAPTER ONE

Psychoanalysis and psychology

A different historical development

Scientific psychology, which came into being at the beginning of the nineteenth century, more than half a century before psychoanalysis, gradually divided into different psychological sciences. Today most of these have become official with their respective names in the legislative systems in different countries. Psychoanalysis, on the other hand, although having been differentiated, but in a less definable way and without official names or recognition and in a somewhat "diluted" way in the confusion between old and new, as we will see, has not been included, in present-day culture, in what are properly called "psychological sciences", either as a whole or in its various schools. Now that the debates on its scientific nature have ended, today, many—obviously first and foremost psychoanalysts—consider psychoanalysis a "science", characterised by its specific method, as is appropriate for every science, but its connotation at many cultural levels remains clearly separate from that of the "psychological sciences" and nowadays from what is better termed "sciences of the mind", understanding the latter in the word "mind" as the impact of the more recent neurosciences.

At the popular level, psychoanalysts and psychologists are confusedly assimilated (*cf.* below section "The psychologists") in the figure that used to be called a "shrink". In this single and all-comprehensive image, at the level of pseudo-culture, we can catch a glimpse of the idea rooted in every human being of being able to understand the minds of others. It is true that a child, throughout its development acquires what has been called "theory of mind" (Baron-Cohen et al., 1993) or also what was understood within the concept of metacognition, or indicated as the ability to decipher the expression of the emotions of its peers and their relative intentions, seized in the motricity of the system of mirror-neurons (Ammaniti & Gallese, 2014), however this ability is absolutely not comparable with the training acquired in the methodology of psychological sciences, or the scientific abilities of a psychologist, even more so of a psychoanalyst. Furthermore, the aforementioned acquisition by children is not acquired in the same way by all individuals, nor in adults is it developed in the same way: an example of this is the alexithymic dimension (Porcelli, 2014). Yet many adults and even cultivated people seem, in their attitudes, to consider it equivalent to the skill of a specialised professional: as though everyone were "psychologists". What we find at a popular level, more than a capacity is a claim, motivated by narcissism in a conception of consciousnessism (*cf.* Chapter Three).

Demonstrative in this respect is the common occurrence whereby, in any discussion that concerns psychological issues, everyone feels entitled to intervene and give their opinion, even contrary to that of the professionals of the subject: this would be surprising if the professional were a doctor or a lawyer, but is commonly observed for the psychologist. Everyone effectively feels, at least a little, they are psychologists. I believe that this attitude, which is not very conscious, is the emotional foundation in which the confusion that reigns in popular knowledge on the sciences of the mind has its roots, especially where the affective-emotional processes, a specific subject of psychoanalysis, are concerned. The secret appeal of penetrating the feelings of others comes into play here.

Beyond these considerations, with the relative emotive reasons, as far as the different connotation of psychoanalysis compared to other sciences of the mind is concerned, its different historical development must be considered. In the collective cultural conception, this has separated psychoanalysis from the other more "classic" psychologies. Psychology, introduced embryonically in universal philosophical speculation, and in the West codified by medieval theology,[1] was included in pedagogy in the eighteenth century but its effective foundation in experimentation, favoured by the positivist spirit, did not come about until only the nineteenth century. Physiologists such as Helmholtz, Weber, and Fechner opened up the way for the first "laboratory", in 1878, of Wilhelm Wundt, professor of both philosophy and physiology at the University of Leipzig. Scientific psychology developed from this matrix in its various articulations, especially in France and in English-speaking countries.

In Italy, "experimental psychology", with its first scientific laboratories, dates back to 1905, with the first university competitive examination[2] sponsored by neurologists, neurohistologists and anthropologists, which gave rise to the first three chairs named this way: in Turin, for Kiesov, in Rome for De Sanctis and in Naples for Colucci; in 1922 these were joined by that of Padua, for Benussi, soon succeeded by Musatti (Lombardo, 2014). The fascist climate, in its idealist spirit, slowly suffocated and then suppressed "experimental" psychology and its first university chairs: the one established in 1925 at the Catholic University of Milan with Agostino Gemelli survived, as it was Catholic and private. After the second world war, it would not be until the competitive examinations of the 1960s that once again there would be chairs and laboratories of psychology, with the start of the rapid boom that led to the establishment of the specific degree in psychology in 1972.

The historical course of psychoanalysis was, on the other hand, totally different and outside the academic institutions. Freud had started from psychiatry, i.e., from psychopathology instead of physiology and I believe that this is significant for the evolution of psychoanalysis up to the present day: focused on the cure more than on research into how the mind works. Although the master in one passage said that he had never really felt he was a doctor (Imbasciati, 1983b) and despite his definition of psychoanalysis (Freud, 1923a), the training of psychoanalysts as it was gradually regulated from the 1930s onwards, remained focused on the cure, as we will see later (*cf*. Chapter Three). What psychoanalysts still call "research" today is a mere confirmation of the efficacy of the cure depending on innovations in the technique and personal training of the individual analyst. The spirit of psychoanalysts has remained alien to Freud's original intention of research focused on the functioning of the mind, relatively independently of the interpersonal effects of the cure.

4 MINDBRAIN, PSYCHOANALYTIC INSTITUTIONS, AND PSYCHOANALYSTS

Other historical factors have contributed to the divarication between psychoanalysis and the other sciences of the mind. In the first place, the clinical discovery by Freud of an unaware mind, the unconscious, collided with the entire philosophical tradition whereby the mind should have coincided with what the individual feels and knows about himself, or with his consciousness: psychology was by antonomasia psychology of the consciousness, i.e., it based its verification on what a human individual, as a conscious being, could consciously confirm. A "mind" beyond consciousness was not conceivable, nor was this considered a subject for investigation, but it was understood as an a priori fact and a natural quality that was the same for all human beings. The neurologists of the time also agreed with this in full. It was in medical circles that Freud was first defeated, even resoundingly, which forced him to prudence. He consequently cultivated his discovery privately together with a close circle of pupils. This is how the "Wednesday group", later the "Vienna Psychoanalytic Society", started and the first study centres, again privately, developed in Germany, and to a lesser extent in France, England and Russia, until the first world war and just afterwards.

The fundamental historical event that marked the fate and development of psychoanalysis once and for all was the rise of Nazism, which in central Europe destroyed the original centres at the hub of development of this "Jewish" science. After 1927, communism then stifled and ultimately wiped out psychoanalysis from the Soviet Union, where it was undergoing important developments. A decisive fact in my opinion was the flight of the German psychoanalysts, almost all Jewish, to the United States. These "first" analysts, settled into theoretical and clinical positions which today have been superseded, who had also been forced to flee without having been able to complete their training, found themselves in the over-facilitating climate of a free country but virgin in terms of psychoanalysis, where moreover their past as victims of persecution helped them to proliferate rapidly without having to submit to more selective reasons for training. Against this background, they re-founded the International Psychoanalytical Association (IPA) in 1946, based on an eminently practical, medical and medicalised spirit, focused essentially on treatment, with underlying economic motivations. They made up for these defects with continuous references to Freud, with little criticism of what the master had written half a century earlier. The charter of the IPA, which is still in force, to which all the different national societies, including the European ones, adhere, defines psychoanalysis as "the theory of Freud" without it ever being specified, even today, what "theory" means (Imbasciati, 2013a), distinguishing it from method, technique, treatment or effective discoveries on how the mind works (*cf*. Chapter Three). This way, the scientific status is still anchored to the whole work of Freud: this has meant blocking it, to at least hindering its evolution, as every science, in order to be one, evolves, and a century has passed since Freud's work (*cf*. Chapter Six).

Psychoanalysis effectively has a rich and complex history and a great has been written about it. It is not my intention here to outline it, except to point out those elements which I think are significant to give the reasons I highlight in this book for the current situation of the relations between psychologists and psychoanalysts.

Psychoanalysis in Italy

In Italy, the organisation for the training of psychoanalysts and the development of psychoanalysis—Società Psicoanalitica Italiana, SPI—agreeing with, continuing and subjected to the IPA rules, after a first embryo in 1935 that was immediately aborted with Fascism, came into being in the 1950s and gained relative autonomy[3] in the 1960s. In that period, Psychology, from the school of Father Gemelli (the only university chair which remained active throughout the Fascist period), developed far more powerfully, and was followed by the collateral Schools of Metelli in Padua, and of Valentini in Rome. In Milan, Cesare Livio Musatti,[4] who in the meantime (1946–1955) had become increasingly qualified as an expert in psychoanalysis[5] was given the chair again: he was the first president of the newly established SPI and he held this position for several mandates.

In Milan, Musatti offset Gemelli in frequent and regular seminars at the two Universities, the Statale (State University) and the Cattolica (Catholic University), where they debated general topics of psychology, whilst Musatti prudently kept psychoanalysis to himself as a private activity, just as the SPI also remained private. In actual fact, despite the political correctness, Musatti and Gemelli had opposing positions, from the scientific point of view and regarding their ideological background.[6] During his long lifetime, including in academically powerful positions, Musatti never promoted any chair for a psychoanalyst, even though they may have had experimental skills. His academic pupils who had also become psychoanalysts were called "the children of the left side of the bed". There was a famous competitive examination for a second chair in Milan, where the examining board, of which Musatti was the president, turned a trio into a duo,[7] excluding Musatti's favourite and multi-competent pupil.

He actually discouraged his academic pupils from even starting out on the road of psychoanalysis, and those who had also become psychoanalysts never enjoyed the support of their master. In public, Musatti had specified that the two paths could be in conflict with one another. It was rumoured that Musatti wanted to keep the double competence only for himself. There was a lot of gossip about this, by psychoanalysts who, I think, were unable to evaluate the political prudence of Musatti. There continued to be very reactive attitudes full of grudges in the SPI for "university professors" in a deeply rooted idea that the best psychoanalysts had to be exempt from contamination by academia.[8] During my psychoanalytic training, I was advised on several occasions by my supervisors to stop my concomitant university career—and being a "university teacher" was the cause of several obstacles in my progression in the SPI.[9]

On the other hand in the 1970s and 1980s, there developed, especially in Europe, a heated debate against psychoanalysis, conducted on several fronts (Imbasciati, 1984, Chapter Three). Philosophers and epistemologists, famous like Popper, or even Hook and Grünbaum, accused psychoanalysis of not being scientific. The "Catholics" accused it of propagating a subversive conception of the human person that was deterministic and pansexualist. The majority of experimentalist academics also held that psychoanalysis was not scientific, often without knowledge of it, like the philosophers and also the majority of psychiatrists. The attack on psychoanalysis, global in scope, made the psychoanalytic organisations take up a staunchly defensive position, in an institutional spirit[10] of danger/defence: they closed up to a totally internal development, in a syndrome of a citadel under siege as it was defined. This caused, on the one hand, an effective progress in methods and therefore in clinical psychoanalysis, on the other the psychoanalytic milieu excluded theoretical contributions by other psychological sciences. Psychoanalysis became increasingly regulated, until it also excluded those psychoanalytic currents deemed "unorthodox".[11] This "orthodoxy" embarked on the road of a religious spirit, in absolute and total fidelity to the original teachings of Freud, with the consequence that even today nothing is thrown away of what the master wrote a hundred years ago, including those theoretical hypotheses which today are contradicted by the progress of the other sciences; moreover, these theories were judged by Freud himself as provisional hypotheses (Imbasciati, 2013b).

In Italy, perhaps more than elsewhere, the SPI gradually became isolated. The attack brought about anguish in the collective of the Institution and defence in the Organisation.[12]

The worldwide controversies against psychoanalysis lost some of their impetus in the 1980s and 1990s. In the USA, psychiatrists opened up to the contribution of psychoanalysis, perhaps too pragmatically, with wariness by the IPA and exclusion of talented scholars (such as Sullivan) from the "qualified" milieu of psychoanalysis. Psychoanalytic initiatives also flourished in Italy in the psychiatric milieu (which a few years later were swept away by the progress of psychiatric drugs) but which received little support and appreciation from the SPI. In this last circle, those contributions which could open up to the other sciences of the mind were branded by the laconic opinion "it may be useful but this is not psychoanalysis." Conversely, in the European IPA citadel, there were scholars who revolutionised Freudian psychoanalysis or, to put it better, revolutionised clinical practice taking care not to consider and therefore contradict the original theory. We only have to think of the revolution started by Melanie Klein[13] and her school, and then the more discreet revolution of Donald Winnicott and, in the last place, the so-called third revolution of Winfred Bion.

These revolutions, to which we owe the progress of current psychoanalysis, were however limited to clinical psychoanalysis, overlooking the theoretical aspects. Accepting pluralism (Wallerstein, 1988, 1990) in the IPA is still discussed today, but this tolerance has often concealed avoiding having discuss the different theoretical positions: by wishing to preserve the old and the new in veneration of the master, what is "theory" and what the very term "theory" even means and what clinical is, with the relative "discoveries" and what the progress of the "Method" is, has not been clarified (Imbasciati, 2013a).

The psychologists

The wave of psychology graduates started in the 1990s, following the establishment of the specific degree in 1972: today there are more than one hundred thousand of them. Many of these "youngsters" had chosen to do a degree in psychology because they had heard something about psychoanalysis which had aroused their curiosity. This was based on that feeling mentioned earlier, of wanting to enter the souls of others, and they had been fascinated by this. However, they found very few teachers competent in psychoanalysis in the universities, which was the result of this isolationism of the SPI and the aforementioned prejudice against academic psychoanalysts; there were quite a few analysts who entered academia but then left it due to the malaise with respect to the SPI. The students would more frequently come across teachers who were clearly against psychoanalysis, who disqualified it or, worse still, lecturers whose knowledge was almost always of a mystified psychoanalysis or was not up to date. Some currents vaguely related to psychoanalysis were developed in the 1990s and early 2000s and became Schools of "psychoanalytic psychotherapy" or even "psychoanalysis" but they were outside the SPI. In the meantime, the SPI practised a very strict selection, although unfortunately misleading, while a law on the professional practice of psychotherapy was passed. These different Schools were sometimes "serious" enough, although in my opinion the training given was always clearly of a lower quality that than of the SPI but sometimes much lower. Then there were Schools that in practice were organised to make money out of the students, giving them the official "piece of paper" so that they could register on the special list of Psychotherapists with the Association of Psychologists which had been established in 1989. The legal regulations on these Schools would have been good, as for all the rights on paper in Italy, but just as with many laws in this country, the relative application required complex and detailed checks and therefore resources to implement them. The resources dried up, the regulations were in practice eluded and the Schools took advantage of this, becoming easy ways to get a diploma against payment.

The SPI continued to remain isolated: its behaviour with respect to the legislation on the profession of psychologist with the relative rules for the practice of psychotherapy was paradigmatic of this. There was the problem of distinguishing, in the general name of "psychotherapy" the various types of psychotherapy, for the relative schools that had qualified and, above all, distinguishing psychoanalysis, considering that in the SPI it was stated with conviction that one thing was psychoanalysis and psychotherapy was something else, even though "psychoanalytic" (I recall the "This is not psychoanalysis!"). The bill, after a very lengthy and controversial gestation (Blandino, 2012)—the first graduates were in 1976—had finally been taken over by Adriano Ossicini, a member of the SPI and who in the meantime had become a senator. He had prepared a law that was favourable for psychoanalysts, distinguishing between psychotherapy and psychoanalysis, and mentioning the SPA-IPA. This bill was to have saved the specificity of psychoanalysis and would have protected it in the IPA (at that time well established with about ten thousand members) and it would also have preserved the SPI from what was to happen in the following years, with the progressive laxness of application of the rules in the recognised Schools as qualifying for practising psychotherapy. If it had been discussed competently, it could also have contemplated naming the various and different psychotherapies (cognitivist, behavioural, systemic, gestalt, and so on), thus avoiding, or at least limiting, the chaos that ensued (Imbasciati et al., 2008). Ossicini, in total clarity, submitted his text to the Executive of the SPI, which wanted to call a special Extraordinary Assembly in 1987. Ossicini's proposal was rejected by the majority. I can clearly remember that tumultuous half-day. At the time I was only an Associate member (*cf.* note 9) and I did not have much authority. "Lively" arguing went on and the only underlying motive that could be identified was the (collective, unconscious, institutional) anguish of being contaminated by a state system which would have opened up the "besieged citadel": this anguish was defended by the illusion that such a citadel could survive and develop (in times that had changed?) and that the SPI could have continued to prosper as a private association. The honest Ossicini was on that occasion really, in my opinion, ill-treated. He withdrew and—in 1989—a law that was totally disastrous, was passed.

The aforementioned illusion disappeared in a few years, with the effects of the boom in the psychotherapeutic "market", operated through the authorised Schools: by rules, as mentioned, that were not applied and perhaps not applicable. It was then that the SPI made another decision which was also, in my opinion, dictated by institutional anguish: it asked for the training to become psychoanalysts to be recognised as a School of psychotherapy. In vain quite a few members, and I was amongst them, pointed out the disqualification of such a recognition ("Do we give a diploma in accounting to graduates of the Bocconi University?") proposing on the other hand that the SPI separate its training from a School run by the SPI itself, which could apply for recognition, or that any state recognition of a School of psychotherapy be distinguished from its being associated with the Society and the IPA. The decision that was taken (by a very close majority) disqualified, at least in the popular imagination, the figure of the psychoanalyst, assimilating it with any other psychotherapist from the gradually increasing number of recognised diploma "mills", attended by the majority of Psychology graduates, the number of whom was also greatly increasing. This meant that those who had taken a decade to be trained in the SPI ended up having the same diploma as others who had obtained it in three years and in questionable ways. The psychoanalysts, who are so fond of recalling that psychoanalysis is a science, thus ended up as craftsmen: craftsmen of value, in the middle of many small artisans, who can be identified only by the "gut" of the user. And, what is worse in my opinion, psychoanalysis increasingly concentrated on treatment and not on research—research into how the human mind works.

Nevertheless, amidst the fragmentation and degeneration of psychotherapeutic psychologists, a few isolated scholars, oddly enough in the despised universities and outside the SPI and IPA, cultivated research into cognitive sciences, with worthwhile experimental research, at various levels and with different approaches and today, neurosciences, or rather, affective neurosciences, according to the successful term of Panksepp (2012). Psychoanalysis has thus continued to remain outside the progress of the other sciences of the mind. Even today, compared with neurosciences which are working on affections, feelings, emotions, subjectivity, and relational skills that makes humans mature (*cf.* Chapters Three and Four), the majority of psychoanalysts are indifferent, or even diffident, and ignore the necessity to bring themselves up to date.

This phenomenon is supported by a last unfortunate consequence of the various unruly transformations of the Degree in Psychology (the dozens of different short degrees), in the current degeneration of university education as a whole (Imbasciati, 2013b): hundreds or even thousands of "psychologists" are being churned out who, as well as having a training that is definitely very poor, have the mirage of an idealistic psychoanalysis. The more intelligent then turn to the SPI: if they are admitted, but the selection is questionable, they are able to practise the profession of psychoanalyst well (high quality craftsmanship) but without having, given that the "citadel is finished", a basic methodological training, and so they are handicapped with regard to neurosciences. If they are not accepted, they turn to some other qualified School, where often their illusions are fuelled by mystifications. Other graduates, who are not so clever, or more clever in another sense, go straight to the easier Schools. They will be psychotherapists.

A negative consequence, or at least a limiting one, weighs on the future of psychoanalysis. The psychologists[14] who become SPI members have an excellent professional training at the level of clinical psychoanalysis, but, as they do not have the methodological bases of General Psychology,[15] end up by becoming excellent craftsmen, valid for the treatment, but without being able to have (as craftsmen usually do not have) sufficient openness to effective scientific research in the functioning of the mind, hence in neurosciences. The poor social image of psychoanalysis in the current general scientific panorama also starts from here (Imbasciati, 2013b, 2013c). The "faith" in Freud, which seems to hold them together, turns out to be treason to that Freud who said he did not feel much of a doctor, but much more a scientist (Imbasciati, 1983b).

In the current chaos it seems that recently the SPI organisation is waking up again—but perhaps not yet the old establishment of the IPA.

CHAPTER TWO

Cognitive sciences, psychoanalysis, neuroscience

Psychoanalysis and cognitive sciences: a prejudicial separation

For decades, psychoanalysis and cognitive sciences developed in mutual ignorance, or even contempt. There is an enormous amount of literature on these subjects which I do not think can be suitably reviewed here. I will therefore restrict myself to setting out the personal considerations that I have made in my lengthy experience, simultaneously as a psychoanalyst and experimentalist psychologist, university teacher of general psychology and then of clinical psychology.

Psychoanalysis came into being a few decades after experimental psychology, but its development and above all its cultural success was far quicker than that of the psychological sciences which were gradually differentiated from the common matrix of experimental sciences cultivated in universities. Psychoanalysis, on the other hand, arose from a "private" initiative: its spread and then its subsequent development were fostered by the uproar that very soon, then in the long term, surrounded the statements by Freud with adverse controversies about the discovery of an unconscious psyche that conditions human actions and even corporality. The Freudian innovation revolutionised what psychology was deemed to be at the time: the investigations into what appears to the consciousness of the individual. It was taken for granted *a priori* that the "mind" consisted of what an individual was aware of; the individual was considered the only and direct intermediary, on condition that he was in good faith, of what in his mind could make him think and act; his sincere introspection was considered truthful about what took place in his mind and how it worked. This conception still continues today at popular level: it remains since people have in mind a simplistic, rudimentary and reductive idea of what thought is; they have lucid, precise and narratable thought in mind, at least to the extent that it appears so to the individual. At the time, this idea was deemed scientific. For everything that could appear more uncertain, almost nebulous—less conscious we would say today—like feelings and affects, the ancient and ambiguous term of "psyche" (=soul?) started to be used, for purely descriptive reasons, but without precise scientific grounds. For Freud as well, who discovered the unconscious, the consciousness remained the pivot of the mind. He was convinced that everything should and could have become conscious, except supposing some obstacle or other to its becoming conscious (Imbasciati, 2013b). Throughout the nineteenth century, "psychology" was by antonomasia the psychology of the consciousness. Speaking of an "unconscious" sounded like a contradiction due to the unanimous conviction of the truthfulness of one's consciousness. Consciousness and knowledge were considered synonyms: it was argued that, if something were not conscious, it could never have been known. So, what Freud was interpreting would have been based on what?

The uproar surrounding the controversy (not least that on infantile sexuality) thus attracted a large number of scholars: his opponents publicised his enthusiasts and both spread psychoanalysis in the world, both by demonstrating its therapeutic or at least mutative potential and due to the fascination of this new "medical" practice which gave the figure of the therapist a halo of mystery and even more so due to the explanations made by the master in his *On Metapsychology* (1915) in which a revolution in the dominant sexual habits could be proudly sensed.

These factors established a network of followers, who very quickly became organised in a close-knit association (the "Vienna Society of Psychoanalysis" which soon became the "International Psychoanalytical Association" IPA). The opposition of its members to the medical and philosophical and psychological culture of the time against the continuous attacks of an authoritative "scientific" level gradually became a haughty isolationism with respect to all the developments that were taking place for the other sciences of the mind. On the other hand, the latter did not have the discoveries that had power in the media equal to those spread by psychoanalysis. The isolationism of the psychoanalysts, on the other hand, meant that they did not keep up with the studies and research in experimental sciences. Even today, many psychoanalysts, regarding fundamental notions such as perception, learning, and memory, not to mention cognition, have remained at those that Freud had; a century of difference in the progress of the other psychological sciences. From isolationism there was a slide towards ignorance and from there towards a collective climate of proud persecutionism.

Psychoanalytic science, as psychoanalysis soon liked to define itself, appeared as deeply and essentially different from all the other sciences, psychological and otherwise. The instrument of investigation was entirely in the mind of the operator who, although a scholar and perhaps an excellent one, was nevertheless subject to comments and conclusions that were totally subjective. The training of this mind, however more specifically and strictly documented by the rules on training established by the IPA, was nevertheless not convincing.

In addition, the "substance", the precise object of study of psychoanalysis, was affects, moreover, the ones not felt or declared by the investigated individuals, indeed often strongly negated. Who could guarantee their existence? Furthermore, their possible genesis and action could be attributed to something completely different, compared to what Freud wanted to explain with his metapsychology. In my opinion, this is where the deep-rooted and prejudicial idea of all Western cultures intervened: the essential separation between cognition and affection (and also with respect to "volition").

Cognition, in our tradition, was very clearly considered "natural", as an automatic event in the brain of homo sapiens, except in the cases in which its nature was deemed compromised, by some known or mysterious cause (illness, demon, head injury). Its development, from child to adult, was deemed an equally natural consequence of the brain. There appeared to be nothing else to investigate. On the other hand, feelings were considered equally as natural, but secondary to a real "mind", which could therefore be attributed to what began to be called the "psyche": this term aimed to differentiate (Imbasciati, 1991) what was thought could cross over into overwhelming passions, which still could and had to be moderated and managed by the "mind", in particular by the "free will" in the human being. Therefore "feelings" were as though extraneous to the "mind", simply interfering with the latter. Psychoanalysis, by discovering that a part of what could not be denied as mental was however unconscious, ended up essentially investigating feelings. By explaining the unconscious mind with the invention of the drive theory, Freud then considered feelings as conscious events, "psychic representations" of drives which were essentially unconscious (Pulver, 1971). Speaking of "psyche" instead of directly of the mind, indicated a part which, although not denying that it was also "mind", did not consider it fully as such: the real mind was the consciousness, and its essence and activities were understood (*a priori*) as made up, essentially, of cognition, but this was understood as natural work of the brain; whereas feelings were attributed to the more "uncertain" part which was referred to by the term "psyche".

The assumption that the mind was natural and the predictable consequence of having a brain (that of homo sapiens) meant that psychoanalysis did not pay much attention to investigating cognition—as it appeared clear and obvious, as though the brain were the simple transmitter of the command of the real to the consciousness—and concentrated rather on that part of the "mind which is not properly the mind", called psyche and which had to do with feelings. Psychoanalysis thus evolved as the specific study of affectivity. Freud made an intelligent attempt to connect it with neural functioning (Freud, 1895) but, failing to explain the relationship with respect to his theory of drive and at the time not having sufficient knowledge of the functioning of the brain, he abandoned this line of research. The evolution of psychoanalysis continued to concentrate on feelings and the original idea, if they had to be conscious, was tacitly neglected, considering feelings in practice as the effective protagonists, also unconscious, of the "psyche". A more detailed investigation about the connection with the Freudian concept of "psychic representatives of the drive" was neglected, to avoid contradicting something the master had said (*cf.* Chapter Six) and hence his theory of drive. Under the aegis of this tangled[1] (in actual fact not specified for unconscious reasons of the psychoanalytic collective) concept of "psyche" and of the consequent adjective "psychic" which differs from "mental" but still concerns the mind, psychoanalysis became separated from the study of cognition.

The study of small children has shown today that feelings *are* (their) cognition: therefore affectivity is cognition (Imbasciati, 2005b). This is, however, a recent acquisition (*cf.* Chapters Three and Four): cognition and affectivity remained different domains for decades, entrusted to two different sciences and were considered so very different from one another that one could ignore the other. Christian theology made no small contribution to the aforementioned concepts, and the distinction between *res cogitans* and *res extensa* decreed by Descartes (Damasio, 1994: *Descartes' Error*) put a very particular seal on this in the sciences of the time.

From theology to Descartes

For centuries in the West, from Augustine of Ippona to Thomas Aquinas, cognitive skills had been considered the specific activities of the intellect, which was an emanation of the spiritual soul, infused by God in every man. The affects were "the flesh": the will, also a divine attribute of man, had to prevail, on condition that, in the spirit, God was "prayed to" to be able to dominate it, at the cost of mortifying it in ways which today seem cruel to us.

Descartes believed he could clarify and settle the more complex debates which took place, amidst convictions for heresy, abjuration or burning at the stake—and he succeeded!—with his distinction between what belongs to the spirit, the *res cogitans*, and what belongs to matter, the *res extensa*: a division of power, between theologians and scientists. The latter were to study only matter. "Thought" was safe, the *res cogitans*, the intellect, mainly of the divine soul, was for the theologians.

What happened in the centuries immediately following? Progress in anatomy and then in physiology showed that the mind had a *res extensa* in the brain. This seemed to be the same for everyone, and characteristic of the "nature" of homo sapiens; this way cognition could continue being considered, if not exactly divine by infusion of the soul, nevertheless "natural" for man, and for all men: it was the job of neurologists to describe it and of theologians to explain the "why" of this nature. In any case, cognition was the natural function of the brain.

Moreover, the human brain appeared to be very different from that of animals. It also "appeared" identical for every man, just like the so-called intelligence, i.e., the cognitive skills; these "appeared", to the means of observation of the time, the same for all men, in the so-called

18   MINDBRAIN, PSYCHOANALYTIC INSTITUTIONS, AND PSYCHOANALYSTS

mental faculties; if anomalies were found, evident with respect to what had been identified in these "mental faculties", they were attributed to some compromise of the material nature of the brain. Just as external events could compromise the natural function of each organ, the same was thought for the brain: in medicine the—dichotomic—concept of normality and pathology, and of cause (*noxa*) of the latter, was applied. It took more than a century to be free of this idea and the liberation is not yet complete (Imbasciati, 2008b).

With the developments of genetics, it was believed that confirmation of the natural nature of human cognition in the natural function of the brain as dictated by the human genome would be found. The fact was— and it was realised a long time afterwards—that those "functions" of the mind's activities, to be attributed to the brain, had been identified on the grounds of what appeared to the common observer, who highlighted them and differentiated them according to what seemed natural to distinguish in his introspection, in other words according to what its function of consciousness showed him. Functions, believed natural and really distinct from one another, were thus distinguished and psychiatrists classified them: language, thought, orientation in space and time and so on. For each of these it was thought that their physiology could be identified in corresponding functions to be located in the brain.

The above division (very rough, in actual fact) as it appeared to the consciousness of the individual as well as to that of an observer who too commonly "observed" was deemed obvious, just as it was obvious to consider the brain in the same way as other "organs" of the body. Today, we know that this is not the case: the brain is a very close-knit network of neural connections that is anything but "given" and stable, as for the structure of the other organs, but its micromorphology and its consequent functioning is in continuous construction, transformation, and reconstruction, whilst what had been labelled "mental functions", as identified above, are none other but global epiphenomena as they appear to the introspection of an observer belonging to the culture of half a century ago, i.e., who believes in what seems obvious in consciousness.

These conceptions are still alive, even in cultivated people today. The spirit of localisation of what "appeared" to be a mental function dominated for over a century in neurology, and unduly in psychiatry and psychology. It was only when the means of observing the psychic were far more perfected that it was understood that the identification of these functions was so rough as to make them appear identical for all men, normal ones of course, without seizing in full the merely statistical meaning; it was acknowledged on the other hand that by isolating finer and more specific functional performances, each individual was different from all the others. Moreover, philosophers had already guessed that each person has a mind of their own: nobody's mind works like someone else's. There was, however, a struggle to connect this crucial notion with the studies on the brain (Imbasciati, 2005b). Today we know that, if the brain appears macroscopically the same for everyone, at microscopic, physiological and functional levels, nobody has a brain that is the same as someone else's. Consequently, nobody's mind is the same as anyone else's (Imbasciati, 2013b).

This led to the diatribes on the so-called brain/mind problem, on their reducibility of each other, almost a resurrection of the ancient dilemmas on spirit/matter, soul/flesh and *res extensa/res cogitans*. It was not until the advent of epigenetics that with the documentation of molecular biology on the continuous constructions and transformations of the neural networks following experience (Cena & Imbasciati, 2014; Imbasciati & Longhin, 2014), medical culture has begun, in the past few years, to recover the conceptions that many years ago the cognitive sciences, with experimental–psychological methods instead of biological ones, had contributed to clarifying the functioning of the mind. Cognition—adequate global perception of the real world, we could say and we could thus globally consider "the mind"—is absolutely not produced by a passive imprinting of experience in the brain, as if it were a faithful recorder, the memory of which is automatically transformed into effective operability nor can it be reduced to those rough distinctions inherited from the diagnostics of psychiatric tradition, which it is pointless to look for in localisations of the brain, nor can it be reduced to the distinctions, although very useful, worked out by tests in the study of intelligence, which only state the outcomes of cognition which has taken place, and not the processes that produce it. Cognition is, on the other hand, the result of a complex and continuous personal process which changes in time: its complexity starts in the psychophysiology of perception. It is not a simple process of a sound and video recording sent to the brain (*cf.* Chapter Three) but the automation of progressive learning, in the first days of life of the baby. Cognition, even more so, is the result of automations of learning: functional, not of contents. Before learning "contents", i.e., images, notions

20 MINDBRAIN, PSYCHOANALYTIC INSTITUTIONS, AND PSYCHOANALYSTS

and concepts, the brain, i.e., the mind, has to learn how to function: to learn progressive and increasingly articulated ways of functioning, i.e., of learning more. All this is purely individual. The mind of each individual works in a different way from that of everyone else, as experience or primary functional learning has been different for every single child. Each brain has learned its way of learning. All this is anything but conscious!

Each person has their way of "knowing", their cognitive strategies, which they apply, not only depending on the individual problem to be solved, but also depending on the interpersonal context in which it takes place. For some time now, the cognitive sciences have studied the individual differences in cognition and brought to the light how under every thought, conviction or idea which appears crystal-clear, lucid and simple to the individual, there may be other connections, which can be made explicit in the cognitive–behavioural therapeutic techniques. When made explicit, these change the mental structure of the individual by bringing into the cognitive light what had been underlying. Psychoanalysts can say they are made aware, except to specify that the relative degree of unconsciousness from which they have been extracted is not precisely that of the real unconscious; and that underneath this, psychoanalysis studies something quite different. What? Psychoanalysts themselves, in general, speak about the relation between the analyst and the patient, but they do not yet know how to explain it well; but in the most recent studies, especially those which are integrated to a certain degree with neurosciences, today we can answer that it is the "emotions": of course, not those felt by the individual nor perhaps those interpreted by the analyst.

Psychoanalysis has grasped the importance of the emotions in the cognitive processes and not as an interference (as was believed) in an otherwise natural process, but in relation to all the effective processes of the mind; however, it is presumed too easily in psychoanalysis that these can be translated into words. The neurosciences come to our rescue, showing how before any mental development the brain has to first develop, i.e., learn (from the primary infantile experience) "primordial feelings" (Damasio, 1999): these concern one's identity, the sense of one's actions, the sense of self, of one's continuous "knowing" as well as acting, of one's feeling an agent of what one perceives, knows, understands and does. We could say of all of one's "remembered present" (Edelmann, 1989) in the relationship with other human beings, which can never be eliminated. The aforementioned "feelings" are the result of neural connections which were formed in early infancy following the experience that the child may have: i.e., they are learned.

Psychoanalysis reached this active and personal conception of experience as a matrix of cognition after the 1960s, with the spread of the works of Bion (1962) but the integration with the past of psychoanalysis is still laborious, and it is even more so with neuroscience.

The isolationism of the psychoanalysts

Individuality and the very singularity of the cognitive processes of a person speak of learning: not of contents but of different functions depending on the individual. This squashes the conception which is still widespread today that functions which are the same for everyone depend on a preformed brain. The brain is built up with experience (Imbasciati, 2006a, 2006b) and this is active learning, i.e., the processing of information by a pre-existing functional system. This is not the nature-brain of homo sapiens, but it is itself an individual construction based on experiences, built up from the foetus and at its maximum evolution in the first two years of life. This is where infant research and neuroscience come on to the scene.

The former documents how all the mental functions, including the "affective" ones, are gradually built up in the foetus-child relationships with the mother and caregivers (their different functional structure depends each time on the type of relationship which is built up with the neuromental structure of the caregiver) and also shows the forced nature of the distinction between affect and cognition (Imbasciati, 1991) and how feeling belongs fully to the "mental" (the small child "knows" with what we will later call affects) as well as the primary nature of the emotional in establishing the subsequent cognition understood *sensu strictiori*. The neurosciences demonstrate the biological reality of the continuous construction and reconstruction of synaptic networks, which takes place depending on interpersonal processes according to the emotional level which is generated at biochemical level with the consequent learning. It is obvious repeating that it is a question of learning functions, but not of contents. It is a learning of progressive functions by neural work (processing) of coding/decoding transformation and construction of the relative memories; as "memory"—today this is understood—is the continuous construction and reconstruction of processes of functional mnestic traces throughout each experience (Siegel, 1999; Damasio, 1999; Alberini, 2012).

It is worth recalling here how what is meant today by "emotional", translated into Italian as *"emozionale"* does not coincide at all with the more usual Italian adjective *"emotivo"*, i.e., it has nothing at all to do with the fact that the individual can feel emotions: this latter event is mere appearance of consciousness and may be completely missing from what really happened emotionally, with relative effects of learning/ memory at a totally unconscious level, i.e., in the brain. It is exactly this way that "we learn", really. Infant research, in its successful association between attachment theory, psychoanalysis and experimental psychology, is successfully integrating psychoanalysis with cognitive science (here I mean "of cognition") in the light of neurosciences.

The integration of neurosciences with epigenetic studies tells us that the brain generates the mind and its activity generates the brain, in a continuous circular feedback throughout a human's life (Imbasciati & Longhin, 2014, Chapter Twenty One).

Returning to the essential "diversity", at last contested today, of psychoanalytic science with respect to other sciences, it is worth noticing the importance of historical and political events. We have already talked about the separation between feeling/cognition which characterised all of Western culture and the related identification of the mind with consciousness: it seemed taken for granted, simple, natural and obvious that what the individual knows about thinking could enlighten how his thought takes place and is structured. Külpe (1883) studied at length the introspection (of individuals) to try and understand how the mind could work. In actual fact, what the individual "thinks he is thinking" or feels or anything else, is only the epiphenomenon, which is changing, misleading, and final of a whole series of mental processes in which he has no consciousness whatsoever. As far as affects are concerned, their appearing to the individual's ability of consciousness as more blurred, hazy and at times uncertain or contradictory in his very conviction, compared to the lucidity of his much more convinced cognitions, has meant that culture has kept it separate from what is called cognition. Indeed, Panksepp (Panksepp & Biven, 2012) states that every affect, even a primordial feeling, present even in animals, is not only a form of knowledge, but also an elementary form of consciousness.

Did philosophy and religion codify the aforementioned separation to avoid uncertainties? Individual and collective anguish? Probably: when

Freud started to deconstruct the equivalence of mind/consciousness, he felt the danger of it. Freud perhaps tolerated it (1895) but he could only protect himself from it by inventing his theory of drive, which his pupils still consecrate as "truth".

Another historical reason which in my opinion is important for the perpetuation of such a contradictory conceptualisation throughout the development of psychoanalysis, is to be considered in the image of an opposed psychoanalysis superimposed on that of the persecution of the Jews. The vast majority of psychoanalysts were Jewish; at the time when there was the greatest contestation of scientific (or pseudo-scientific) controversy, at the same time a political image of the Jew as "different" ("*Untermensch*") took shape and was really persecuted. The controversy against psychoanalysis became superimposed in the soul of psychoanalysts (and all the Americans who welcomed them) with the persecution of the Jews, as though it were the persecution of a science because it was different. This had, in my opinion, its effects on the soul of psychoanalysts and from here on the soul of their institutions, in producing the isolationism of psychoanalysts, if not their latent aversion for the other sciences of the mind, ignoring their relative progress. Isolationism—we could say barricading themselves—in their science, not following the progress of other sciences. This fact, added to that whereby psychoanalysts essentially study affects, led to them remaining anchored to the old conceptions of a cognition that was completely different from affective processes, i.e., considering cognition as a predictable natural and simple event and therefore believed only conscious, due to the brain. It was therefore to be neglected, as an object extraneous to the more real "psychology of the deep", of which, in the neglect of and consequent ignorance about cognition, there remained that offered by psychoanalysis in its study of the "unconscious". This is the "psyche" which would have had little to do with the brain as some psychoanalysts who oppose neurosciences still think. The sciences of cognition did not interest psychoanalysts and the training of analysts went in this direction.

Lastly, the absolute and dominant prevalence of doctors amongst the officially organised psychoanalysts meant that, focused on the treatment more than on research[2] and cut off from contemporary academic psychological culture cultivated in non-medical faculties, they accentuated the isolationism of the psychoanalytic community (IPA, International Psychoanalytical Association), which ignored what experimental psychology, the cognitive sciences in particular, were developing in the meantime, on the clinical level as well.

Bowlby, a psychoanalyst, was marginalised from the IPA, as he had started an experiment (or rather an experimental observation) outside the psychoanalytic setting, then deemed untouchable. Even today, most psychoanalysts are not acquainted with basic psychology. As far as cognition is concerned, the continuation of the idea that it is a "natural" process and not a skill learnt by the brain, has fostered an implicit thought in the community of psychoanalysts that cognition is an exclusively conscious process except for "pathologies" which may compromise it,[3] and therefore outside the area of interest of psychoanalysis. This recurrent and underlying idea is fostered by ignoring the complexity of the processes that lead to the different levels and moments of consciousness (Liotti, 1994); consciousness is also conceived by the majority of psychoanalysts in the popular old way, as a natural and simple process, in the dichotomy between conscious/unconscious. In this dichotomy, the object of study of psychoanalysis remains only the unconscious, identified with the feelings and these are considered of a different nature from cognition, instead of focusing on consciousness itself; indeed, on the various abilities of consciousness (Imbasciati, 2014b).

In all truthfulness, it has to be said that the positions mentioned have never been defined by writings that clearly proposed them; it has always been a question of underground collective movements, as often characterise the inertia of the Organisations due to the spirit of the Institution (Jacques, 1955). There are scientific articles, including in official journals of the IPA, which have tried to identify psychoanalytic models that could contextualise the cognitive processes (Imbasciati, 1989b) proposing to psychoanalysts a better study of perception and memory, however they have had no effect on the vast majority of psychoanalysts, engaged exclusively on a therapeutic professionalism.

The separation between affect and cognition

Underneath these historical vicissitudes, there is the deep-rooted conviction of the West (stereotype and prejudice, as social psychologists would say) that affect is something different from cognition, The same idea underpins the delay with which the cognitive sciences approached the study of feelings, emotions and the interpersonal, so that for many decades they considered the contributions of psychoanalysis, as well as unreliable, "secondary" compared to real, experimental research into the cognitive processes; moreover these are considered as separable from affects, which are elements deemed insufficiently controllable in experiments.[4] This idea also underpins the consideration of the discoveries of psychoanalysis, not in the effectiveness of an interpersonal clinical practice that changes people through a reciprocal and unconscious communication of affects (which are themselves unconscious) but according to the theoretical propositions of the explanations that Freud gave of them (Oedipus and Energy-drive Theory): these explanations are fascinating, invented by Freud (who was, however, well aware of their "witchcraft": Imbasciati, 2013a) and, reified by the epigones as though they were "discoveries", offered easy bait for objections, criticisms, destructive controversies of other authoritative scholars, and the neglect that the cognitive sciences showed at length for psychoanalysis as a method of investigating affects.

The isolationism of psychoanalysis and their exclusion of the study of cognition as it was believed the work of a "natural" and preformed brain, have produced in the psychoanalytic institutions the on-going idea that cognition was an exclusively conscious event; therefore, that it had nothing to do with the study of the unconscious, which was the object of study of psychoanalysis. This was in spite of all the studies which had been taken for granted for some time on cognitive strategies, which presuppose unconscious and individual mental work which precedes and produces every conscious result or in any case operating cognition.

Conversely, the concept of the unconscious is effectively present in cognitive sciences, *mutatis mutandis*, but it is not related with the psychoanalytic models, as the cognitive scientists know it only through the primitive Freudian model, which is easily linked with that energetic reification of the affects, which is established in psychoanalysts following the "sanctification" of Freud's metapsychology (Imbasciati, 2013a; Imbasciati & Longhin, 2014, Chapter Six). This means that the majority of psychoanalysts cannot conceive how a mind outside the consciousness can work (exist!) without being referred to that affective functioning which they explain by keeping it separate from cognition.

Fortunately, the neurosciences (neuropsychoanalysis) are dismantling the above misunderstandings and quite a few psychoanalysts, especially younger ones, are also becoming competent in the other sciences of the mind. The activity of the brain is essentially outside the consciousness, which is only a pale, misleading and subjective epiphenomenon if it.[5] The unconscious exists, but not like a driven elf in the mind. The mind is itself *essentially* unconscious. The comparison between the different conceptualisations of mental events is indispensable today. Neuroscientists are currently studying how some consciousness is formed; elsewhere (Imbasciati, 2014b) I defined it the future object of study of psychoanalysis.

Even though with the reciprocal hesitations of prejudices and the reciprocal cultural scotomata, cognitive sciences and psychoanalysis began to grow closer to one another from the 1970s and 1980s onwards, albeit with suspicion and caution. The cognitive sciences, addressing the study of the emotions, that is the interpersonal, and psychoanalysis turning from objectual theory to the current conception of the mind as generated by learning in interpersonal relationships, governed by the primary ones of the foetal and neonatal period. In this change of direction by psychoanalysis, infant research was fundamental in showing, irrefutably in the eyes of all scholars of opposed dogmas, that the first cognition of homo sapiens and the matrix of every subsequent cognitive capacity is what happens in the perinatal period, carried out by the communication of affects between the child and mother/caregivers (Imbasciati & Cena, 2010; Imbasciati, Dabrassi, & Cena, 2011). Today we know that this communication is what really organises the brain (Schore 2003a, 2003b), mediated by communications which above all are non-verbal in precise and individual semiotics (Stern & BCPSG, 1998, 2005, 2007, 2008).

Attachment study, experimental methodologies, infant (neonatal–parental) psychoanalysis and cognitive sciences have converged into infant research, and the neurosciences have consolidated their integration and ability of integration. We have an example of this in the studies by Bucci (1997, 2001, 2009). Neurosciences are consolidating this, in particular in my opinion, with the study of experiences which form the identity in the subjectivity of the individual self (Damasio, 1999). To my way of thinking, in this process of integration, more than speaking of the contribution of cognitive psychology in the dialogue between psychoanalysis and neurosciences, I think it is useful to consider the more complex, intriguing, controversial, and slow progress, equally distributed, of the different orientations of infant research with the respective methods in the study of the human mind.

The further progress of epigenetics, still under way, is still to set its seal. This offers a solution to the problem of the reciprocal relations between brain and mind: the latter is the functioning acquired by a brain and therefore we can state that the brain generates the mind, but the mind, in turn, in its functioning generates continuous new experiences which give further opportunities for learning to the brain; we can therefore say that the mind regenerates the brain. There is a reciprocal feedback. This circuit has a transgenerational scope (*cf*. Chapter Three).

CHAPTER THREE

The origins of the mind: prejudices, ideologies, and science

A naive organicism

To approach the topic of how the human mind originates and develops scientifically and organically as we will do in Chapter Four, I believe that some popular prejudices should first be explained in this chapter. These prejudices come from ideologies of philosophical but also scientific history on the investigation of the mind, which are still upheld by illusions alive in the unconscious background of the Western collective imagination.

Today everybody is ready to say that the mind depends on the brain and to clarify the way this is done, attempts are made to specify that it depends "on having a brain"; and a normal brain. If we go to further investigate what this common-sense conviction means, uncertainties, confusion, contradictions, and reductionisms emerge. Is the mind perhaps the product generated by the brain? How? Is the mind the way the brain works? The mind of men is not the same for all. What about the brain then? What on earth is a "normal" brain? Normal for everyone? What does normality of the mind consist of? What is the "functioning" of the brain? Since I am convinced that it is me who directs my thoughts, i.e., my mind, is it me that commands the functions of the brain? Or is it

30   MINDBRAIN, PSYCHOANALYTIC INSTITUTIONS, AND PSYCHOANALYSTS

the brain that commands me?! Does mental pathology depend on an ill brain? How? What are the causes?

Many other questions may arise if we reflect diligently and patiently on those notions which at first sight appear clear: perhaps because they are too simple.

That the brain is indissolubly implied with the mind is a notion that is anything but ancient: until the end of the fifteenth century it was believed (except for some intuitions by a number of philosophers) that brain was necessary to secrete "pituita", phlegm, and that the fulcrum of life, including mental life, was the heart. "Mental life" is a modern expression; until a few centuries ago, people talked about the spirit or the soul, whether divine or animal, and indeed the etymology of "animal" says a great deal (anima=soul). In human beings it was a question of intellect, as an abstract entity from which cognition derived—here is the *res cogitans*—distinguished by an *affectio* and a *volitio*. That the head was the vital fulcrum had been shown for some time by wars, which human beings have always fought between themselves, but that this depended on its content was not known, as shown by a certain folly in the surgery of head injuries. More obviously, the heart appeared the centre of life, of all life, but the notion that the brain governed its functioning is recent.

Philosophical speculation, based on the ability to reflect on what the individual can feel in himself—today we say based on his consciousness—seemed to sufficiently clarify what the human mind was. It took a number of centuries for a different investigation to open up different horizons. In the slowness of this historical evolution, in my opinion there are three ideologies that can be identified, fuelled by three illusions of the human collective imagination.

I will start by what currently seems the most widespread conception, which can be called naive organicism.

Having ascertained that the brain is indispensable for the life of animal beings, certainly the "superior" ones, gradual anatomical discoveries in the sixteenth, seventeenth and eighteenth centuries, mostly derived from surgery (head injuries) showed the need for the brain to be intact to guarantee all those so-called intelligent functions which characterise the human being, as they were compromised by brain injuries. As many of these compromised functions, even evident, highlighted in psychiatry, were not accompanied by anatomical injuries, at least macroscopic, the causes of the alteration were looked for at a closer level that was histological and of precise areas in the brain. The expectation

THE ORIGINS OF THE MIND   31

was to find in which specific parts of the brain the individual mental functions were generated or at least governed and which it seemed obvious to distinguish, for the purpose of better identifying the causes of any alterations of those functions, At the end of the eighteenth century, neurophysiology came into being. In analogy with the general medical model (natural rule dictated by genetics compromised by some cause or other: the "*noxa*"), for each function of which a certain homogeneity was recognised at the level of common logic—for example, language, motricity, thought, memory—the localisation in the brain was sought.

In this logic, the underlying idea that brain meant intelligence came into play, without there being too much concern about analysing what the term "intelligence" or the even more general "intellect" meant, and without distinguishing it from other general terms called intuition, often connected with "feelings". No consideration was given to how all affects, emotions and passions were connected with the brain: they were all attributed, actually with little definition and therefore roughly, to other factors such as upbringing. The conception of the *res cogitans* (*cf.* the previous chapter) played its role in the idea that the functions considered the main ones of the brain, had to be attributed to "cogitating" or cognition, hence to the all-inclusive concept of intelligence.

Research into the presumed functions of the brain was thus oriented towards considering sets of human manifestations which appeared to be connected with intelligence. Thus, a distinction started to be made between memory, language, logical reasoning, spatial and temporal orientation and so on, with various labels which are still used today by psychiatrists. These labels can be useful for epidemiological classifications but say nothing about a more detailed operational meaning as is shown today by studies in experimental psychology and more advanced neurology.

The localising research by neurophysiology between the nineteenth and the twentieth centuries therefore considered the "functions" as dictated by common sense. Today we know that these labels do not each represent a precise function, but are final results, each of myriad processes and therefore of functions, which are intertwined with one another (and those of a group which originates a certain apparent result to those of another group) with an outcome that appears unitary only in the final performance of an individual. Unitary categories appear only to an approximate common logic, in superficial observation as can be made in the majority of adult individuals. In children, and the more they are younger, this categorisation proves to be inapplicable, although a "mind" can be considered. It therefore has no sense to look for the correspondence of a superficial categorisation in a biological mechanism, as there could be, for example, in the function of ventilating and oxygenating the lung, or the purifying of the kidney, or that of the motility of a muscle. In other terms, it was seen that the brain could not be considered in the same way as the other organs studied by medicine. Its functions as they appeared to the evaluation at first sight of any person could not be seen as the equivalent of physical laboratory data similar to those obtainable on the lungs, kidneys, muscles and so on.

The attempt at localisation based on the functions as considered above, lasted for a long time in neurophysiology, and it was pursued at length, like a destination that had to be reached. The characteristics of an illusion of a scientific nature which was expected to be final, can be seen, pursuing the ideal of the existence of a natural law of the functioning of the brain, just as for the lungs or the stomach or for other organs. Therefore, the causes that had compromised it, in its variations towards abnormality, had to be found. As in many cases, although the instruments of research were becoming more refined, a cause was not found that could be responsible for the alteration from the normal—understood according to the traditional concept of a "natural" law—an explanation was looked for in the rules of nature, i.e., in genetics. From the time when Mendel discovered the hereditary nature of different characters in the same species, genetics had in the meantime developed for all living beings: the recourse to genetics could explain the alternations of the norm. In this course of scientific thought, the consolidated medical paradigm came into play, according to which every organ or part of it had a precise function and any possible deviance with respect to what was found in most individuals was considered an "alteration" attributed to some cause which must have "altered" the norm laid down by nature. This is the paradigm of the dichotomy of normality/pathology and of the "defect" that causes the pathology which, valid in medicine, has proven misleading if applied to the psychic and the neurological (Turchi & Perno, 1999; Imbasciati, 2008b, Chapter Nine).

The expectation of finding precise locations for all the functions attributed to the brain agreed with the concept according to which it was believed that the human brain, like every other "organ" of the body, was determined by genetics in its morphology and functioning: finding an anatomically identical brain for all individuals of the same species and identical in its circumvolutions as well as in the first histological findings, should have been evidence of an identical functional development for all humans. This is how "normal" individuals appeared; all men, on the other hand, with respect to those "functions" as they were intuitively considered, appeared identical in their manifestations. The problem, as was subsequently shown, was that those "functions" were arbitrary classifications, which covered widely different characteristic aspects of each individual person.

Starting from these bases, a completely "organicistic" conception of the mind was consolidated on the scene in the nineteenth century and the early part of the twentieth by studying the relative organ, the brain, in its various parts. Based on anatomy, histology and genetics, the mind as it was made up of the functions considered that way at that time, had to be the expression of the brain. By applying the medical model, a normal brain should produce a normal mind: any variation had to have a cause, a pathogenic *noxa* of normal development or a genetic variation.

This organicist conception soon found two levels of objection. To philosophers, accustomed for centuries to reflecting on the mind with the mind, it appeared extremely reductive that the mind was produced by the brain: the brain-machine (as it could be considered at that time) could not be reconciled with what man thinks about himself as a thinking being. The machine conception also negated the capacity of self-determination, free will and volition. On the other hand, the rise of psychology, with its experimentation, completely disrupted the fact that the mental "functions" were those that intuitively (at psychiatric level unfortunately still used) had been identified. The so-called mental functions identified according to an intuitive cataloguing of the performances of a normal adult turned out to be vast, composite, and basically arbitrary categories and could be taken apart into very many (an infinite number?) more elementary functions: the very concept of "function", if identified according to what it had appeared logical to catalogue and group into what a "normal" adult man—in reality the standard man—showed he was capable of doing or saying, proved to be inconsistent and useless when it could be analysed better. On the other hand, the expectation of finding precise locations in the brain that explained the so-called mental functions on the basis of an extension of the medical model of the "brain" organ, proved to be increasingly complex; a possible location in the brain that turned out to be involved, explained the relative pathology by a deficit, not the function itself.

It therefore had to be concluded that that function was performed by several zones. On the other hand, the differences between various individuals could be observed in increasing detail, as the instruments to record the behaviour of the single individuals and above all the differences, even minimal but existing, of their mental performances were perfected: experimental psychology, study of children, psychometrics and testology proved it. How could this be explained, presupposing a "normal" brain and therefore the same for everyone? What could be invoked to explain the highly individual variability between individuals of the mind of homo sapiens? Above all when the continuum was identified between individual variations and eccentric behaviour up to those defined "pathological".

Lastly, how could human variability in terms of affects and emotions be explained? How could the fact that human beings can become overwhelmed by passions without realising it, except afterwards, be explained? And how can they be led to behave in ways that they did not want and do not want and did not even know they had? How can this be reconciled with the concept of the mind as made up of intelligent "functions"? The organicistic conception was thus challenged in its simplistic and mechanistic aspect.

However, variously modulated, it still persists, in the common understanding, almost following the illusion that with the sciences that study the brain what appears as an enigma in the mental functioning of human beings can be known and therefore dominated.

An ideological element can be recognised in this persistence: the desire to be able to know and therefore in some way dominate the elusiveness of the reasons of much of human conduct. This neurobiological illusion also appeared able to solve an age-old philosophical dilemma: "I do not do the good I want to, but the evil that I don't want to." The reflection of Augustine of Ippona was the subject of important theological debates in the Middle Ages. An ideal organicism then seemed to be able to dissipate the anguishes of ancient dilemmas: by studying the brain, it will be possible to explain the uncertainties, the doubts and contradictions shown by human conduct.

This organicistic ideal collapsed in the face of scientific discoveries and finer observations of human conduct. Yet it exists in many, especially at popular level, as a simplified ideology.

It is true that the investigation with which a given performance, or its absence, is correlated with given areas of the brain is useful, especially as it is conducted today, i.e., by checking all the multiple areas concerned and which of these are indispensable for that function. There is a huge amount of literature, including from the present day in this regard, which is increasingly specific and sophisticated. However, the usefulness depends on the fact that until now we have not had any other instruments, compared with those to record the activation of neural areas following specific performances or any deficits. In reality, the possibility of carrying out a given function does not depend on the fact that those areas "produce" it, but that they are implicated in interconnections between various neuronal groups, of those and other areas. We know today that it is the synapses, and not the neurons, that are the origin of a given functioning, and that these can vary from one individual to another: "we are our synapses" (Le Doux, 2002), we are our connections, our "connectome" (Seung, 2012). Our instruments are not investigating, for the time being, the connections: they only allow us to see which microzones are activated, or are activated the most. Scholars know it, but at popular level it is believed that it is those parts of the brain which carry out certain functionalities. As for the fact that for certain performances we find confirmation in certain areas for almost all individuals, this may presuppose, not a natural destiny of that part of the organ, but an experience common to all individuals. The genic expressiveness "deposits" it in certain circuits, of which we see only some neuronal zones activated (*cf.* Chapter Four).

The mind independent of the brain: the illusion of the consciousness

After the ideal of an easy organicism had collapsed, discussion started on what was to be understood by mind, and mental processes. The philosophical tradition of the West has rooted in it the idea that the mind corresponds to what we can think logically, rationally and fairly lucidly or do intelligently to solve a very wide variety of problems in their practical application. In this context, precisely in the exercise of these faculties defined this way, the conviction of being the author of one's own thought automatically emerges. Much of philosophical speculation postulates free will on this basis. A tradition of Thomistic derivation had besides postulated volition, alongside cognition and affects (affection)[1] as the three spheres of the psyche. Spiritualism of a religious origin went very well alongside philosophical ideal, which supported the primacy of a mind, as defined above, to work well for the development of an ordered civilisation. The first development of psychological sciences assumed an analogous conception of the mind, in basing its investigations on the account of the subjects and their performances. The first experiments which started the construction of mental tests were developed on this basis.

This idea of mind was however invalidated by the assertion, with psychoanalysis, of a notion of the unconscious mind; what we think is in reality what it appears to us that we are thinking; what appears clear, lucid and "cognitive" to us is in reality what the ability of consciousness allows our introspection at that moment (Imbasciati, 2005b). The most recent psychoanalysis has emphasised how the activity that appears conscious is a minimal part of totally unconscious work. Experimentation, on the other hand, has discovered the fallacy of conscious memories, the continuous transformation of recollections and memory as a whole and subsequently the implicit memory, which can never be rendered conscious in any recollection. The neurosciences have shown how the vast majority of our brain works beyond any consciousness (Schore, 2003a, 2003b).

Experimental psychology, psychoanalysis and neurosciences thus extend the concept of mind, on the basis of the progressive and on-going discovery of functions which were previously ignored or hastily considered extraneous to the "mind", i.e., the functions labelled as affective-emotive. A new connection between mind and brain is also ascertained. The acknowledgement of even minimal individual differences, challenging the previous concept of "mental functions" (beyond those which could be roughly labelled as "normal" functions, in reality simply found in the majority of individuals and therefore equivalent only to a statistical average) tells us that each person has "their" specific functions: what previously had been labelled as "mental function" (a label which unfortunately continues in present-day psychiatric culture) is an arbitrary categorisation, which in actual fact involves infinite functions, different for each individual, just as the variability of the mind possessed by each individual is infinite.

Wanting to connect the brain to this variability, we would have to assume that every minimum variation in the mind has an equivalent variation of the functions of the brain: this is accepted even by those who maintain that we should study the mind independently of the brain. The event acknowledged, of an infinity of mental functions to which

THE ORIGINS OF THE MIND   37

the same number of brain functions ought to correspond, has thus perturbed the primitive concept of brain localisation. This meant that any localisations were considered in a more articulated and complex way, i.e., regarding more zones and more circuits of neural connections.

In this picture there appears again a new organicistic conception which can be seen under the name of genic expressiveness. The human genome is the same for everyone, but the genic expression is individual: this saves the individuality of every mind. The number of genes of each individual is insufficient to justify the infinite variability. This is why genic expressivity was studied and is studied; each gene can "express itself" differently depending on the circumstances of development of the individual, i.e., of his experience.

These studies, taken as a whole, were then given the name of epigenetics. The two names—genic expressivity and epigenetic factors—both indicate that each experience can involve learning which modifies the neural connections, and therefore some (and perhaps many) functions, as shown by recent discoveries (Schore, 2003a, 2003b). We can therefore say, more simply, that what is learned from experience modifies the brain. What for the time being has been discovered concerns molecular processes of the memory. The processing in the brain representing learning reaches, in most cases, the DNA or the nucleus of the neuron (= of neurons) where the molecular chains which form the genes (= genome) bring about a protein synthesis which determines a "transcription" (transcriptome) to the cellular cytoplasm of the neuron, therefore to the relative RNA, which, in turn, produces new synaptic proliferations, i.e., new functional networks (connectomes). These recent discoveries modify the original naïve organicistic conception.

We can say that the whole mind, which has experience, modifies the brain, and that in its turn, due to these developments, the brain modifies the functioning of the mind, and with this the ways of having experience. The age-old problem of the mind/brain relationship is thus solved in a feedback circuit: the mind generates the brain which in turn generates the mind. Considering the foetal start of development, this can also be rendered, by reading the circuit inversely: the brain generates the mind which continuously generates the brain which will come about (see Figure 2 in Chapter Four).

What we know today about mind/brain relationships has had a long and laborious prior scientific, cultural and ideological journey. In the lasting yet latent conception that the mind has to be considered independently of the brain, the infinite variability of the human being has posed quite a few difficulties in the face of an inevitable obligation of connecting it in some way with the brain. The conception, according to which we ought to study the mind independently of the brain reveals a "consciousnessist" presupposition, preserved even when confronted by the discovery of non-conscious mental events: they have been called, not surprisingly, "psychic" using "psyche" as a term with a very different meaning from that of "mind". It has continued to keep affectivity separate from cognition or has coined other terms, such as character, temperament and others, to exclude in some way what was mismatched with certain presuppositions, defined at the start for this concept, from the concept of mind.

In reality, the desire to be able in some way to keep the illusion that the consciousness is the master of the mind, introduces an ideological element, which is rationalised in creating the new terms of psyche and others. The differentiation between cognition and affectivity still continues, even in cultivated milieus. It has now been a century since neurologists discovered how what was called affectivity was to be put into relation with certain parts of the brain. The functions of the mesolimbic brain and the dependence of the endocrine system on this have gradually been highlighted. Today we know that the whole of the right brain, as well as the mesolimbic parts, and also much of the left brain, as well as all the centres below the median line of the encephalic trunk, continue to work beyond all consciousness, with processes that we can make coincide with what was called affectivity. The right brain is engaged in governing affectivity, in the non-verbal communication between people (Schore, 2003a, 2003b), in the functions which most determine the complex conduct of human beings. Present-day psychoanalysis, on the other hand, on the clinical side, has elucidated how the base of thought, in the broad sense, as well as that thought which appears to the consciousness, proceeds from processes that have been labelled as affective: the work of Bion should be considered. The affects are in the first place unconscious, sometimes ineffable (see the etymon) and what the individual consciously feels—the affects and the emotions—are a negligible, as partial and misleading, epiphenomenon of the emotional work of our brain. Today we have realised—preceded by the neurologists—that we have to study why the consciousness is formed and how it functions (Imbasciati, 2014d; Cena & Imbasciati, 2014) and not for what the individual concerned can feel and report, but for how

THE ORIGINS OF THE MIND   39

it comes about that all the psychic—today we say mental—work is transformed, when it forms what the individual feels; and how it comes about that the conscious result can be missing, or totally different from what at unconscious level is processed as "thought", as well as because the consciousness is not a natural faculty or the same for everyone—a notion dear to philosophers—but an ability that can vary from one individual to another and in the same individual it can vary from one moment to another, especially from the situation of the type of relationship which in that moment the individual has with others (Liotti, 1994, 2001; Imbasciati, 2005b).

The resistances to admitting the organic components at the basis of the conception of the mind, and therefore a radical opposition to considering the organic, the neural, as well as a subtler opposition to everything that derives from the consideration of the unconscious mind, seem to derive from a philosophical heritage that puts consciousness at the centre of the mind: perhaps no longer a substantiality of mind and consciousness but at least a centrality of the consciousness in the functioning of the mind. Not even Freud was immune from this fundamentally consciousnessist presupposition, when he stated; "*Wo es war soll Ich werden*" (Where was the Id there will be the Ego) (Freud, 1933a; Imbasciati, 2013b, 2013d); we should then be suspicious of an ideology based on the illusion that comes from feeling our own masters, with our own consciousness: the illusion of consciousness.

Consciousness and the illusion of omnipotence

Progress, by both psychological sciences and neurosciences, has shown that what was intuited under the name of affects is much vaster and different from what appears to the consciousness of the individual; it is also, by full right, "mental". The continuous and incessant activity which engages most of the whole of the brain (including at complete rest or sleeping) is today recognised as "emotional" and takes place beyond any consciousness and is the basis of all neuromental processes. The concept of mind today is very different from the one we have been accustomed to by philosophical tradition. Not only do we include all the affective-emotive functioning that was labelled under the adjective of psychic, understood as different from "mental", but also everything that the psychiatric categories continue to call character, or temperament, or anything else. We also include the implicit meaning of every

40 MINDBRAIN, PSYCHOANALYTIC INSTITUTIONS, AND PSYCHOANALYSTS

human action, in the interactions, in interpersonal relationships, in what today is called (and studied from the neural point of view) sense of self, or subjectivity, as well as in our decisions and in our very will. Neuroscience has shown how everything that was indicated by various names—which, to tell the truth, are very often inaccurate—implies a global functioning of the brain which can today be neurologically identified in the basic emotional functions: the basis of what could appear to the individual a "mind" in the narrow sense, or at least felt at some level of consciousness.

We are our emotions, say authors like Siegel (1999) or Damasio (1999).

Everything that governs all human conduct and the very functions of the body—psychosomatic—is modulated by the brain: modulated or dependent? Generated or "constituted"? This is an age-old debate, still very much alive, which arises here: about to what extent the mind can be identified with the brain, or considered only two sides of the same event. There is an enormous amount of literature on this and it is full of controversial positions, At the centre of the misunderstanding there is, in my opinion, understanding or rather underpinning, that the brain is predetermined by nature or by genetics, which currently has been proven to be totally false: the brain develops through the experience of the individual and this does not depend simplistically on the external circumstances the individual goes through, but by how he processes them; in other words by his mind in the course of development. The strictly organicistic position—the mind is generated by the brain—has been superseded today, thanks to the discoveries on how brain and mind develop reciprocally, influencing each another (*cf.* Chapter Four), not simply two faces of the same event seen from different vertexes of study, but two events that are reciprocally and closely connected with one another and interacting between one another. These discoveries have not yet been assimilated however, and the opposite positions (could we say emotive?!) continue about an organicism as opposed to a "mentalist" protest, which still today advocates the conception according to which the mental must be studied exclusively with psychological instruments. Even many psychoanalysts support this position. Under the current lasting divergences and even more in the past diatribes, the illusions, stated at the beginning, combined in a single reason, can be glimpsed. Even today many scholars, especially philosophers, find it hard to recognise that the mind does not coincide with what appears "thought" (or cognition) to (intelligent) conscious introspection and to

THE ORIGINS OF THE MIND   41

what can be expressed in suitable verbalisations. The illusion that may underlie this is the deep-rooted idea, also Western, that the mind is at our disposal, that we can govern it, in good and evil, truthfully rather than falsely; if not exactly with our knowledge, at least with some psychological artifice, for example with psychoanalysis.

In my opinion, this is a hidden ideal of omnipotence. Psychoanalysis, in its most present-day developments on the asymbolic unconscious, connected with the implicit memory, shows how the consciousness expressed by verbalisation, intrinsic in the interpretation of the analyst, acquired in an equally verbalised way from the patient, counts for very little. If anything, it is the ineffable (in the etymon of the term) "something more" (Stern & BCPSG, 1998) delivered "inside" the verbality but not denoted by this, that gets something across: something indefinable, precisely because it is ineffable—passes from the implicit memory of the analyst to the implicit memory of the patient. The non-verbal, which in psychoanalysis today is deemed a more effective mutative agent and what cannot be verbalised, also passes through the non-verbal.

Psychoanalysis today establishes an impossibility to regulate—or dominate—one's own mind, even with the aid of psychoanalysis, if we use only what classic psychoanalysis would make conscious by words. In other terms the verbalised unconscious is not sufficient. Regulation, along the personal psychoanalytic journey, takes place from an unconscious to another unconscious: *Affect Regulation and the Repair of the Self* says the title of a work by Schore (2003a). Yet a dream remains, an illusion of omnipotence, which is found, paradoxically in parallel, in the organicist conception. The latter, although it says that the mind depends on the brain, subtly cultivates the idea that neuroscience can succeed in the future in manipulating it adequately: usefully or criminally? Is this a science fiction? (Cena & Imbasciati, 2014, Chapter Two). In our culture it seems that admitting—really—what we know jointly from psychoanalysis (i.e., that the introspective radius of our consciousness may be extended but never totally) and from neuroscience (i.e., that the (right) brain is our arbitrator unbeknown to us), encounters considerable resistance: it dethrones man from feeling he is his own master. The omnipotent illusion of the organicist position, far more subtly cultivates a similar omnipotent ideal: beyond appearances so that will and free will are negated, as the research of Libet (Wegner, 2003, *cf*. Merciai & Cannella, 1999) would anticipate, the dream is to discover how to

42 MINDBRAIN, PSYCHOANALYTIC INSTITUTIONS, AND PSYCHOANALYSTS

manipulate the machine of the brain to be its master. But we could suspect: masters of the minds of others.

Infant observation to prove the adult's illusions wrong

Until some forty years ago, it was thought that babies, not considering the foetus, did not have a mind and that this was formed through laws of nature together with and following the acquisition of language. Learning was thought about only for this latter conquest, of a specific language learnt from the person caring for the child. For all the other types of learning—perceptive, motor, recognitive and others—although known to those who worked with babies, it was not considered learning; everything represented development in the first year of life was considered a growth attributable to nature: it was thought that genetics regulated all this development. Nor on the other hand was it clear what was to be understood by "mind" and whether or not it could be attributed to a baby. Furthermore, the concept of learning was understood from an adult point of view, as intentionally learning notions to "put into the head". The attribution of neonatal development to genetics was maintained by the concept of neurological maturing: the brain was believed to develop according to the genetic make-up and then the mind would be formed. In this framework, any mental anomaly found was attributed (= genome) to some cause (the "*noxa*") which would have "spoiled" (Imbasciati, 2008b) the development of the brain.

This mechanistic-like conception proved to be groundless to the point of scaling down the very concept of maturing and, in my opinion, no longer justifying the term itself. We know today that the nerve tissue "matures"—in the proper sense—during the embryonic development and in the foetal development, but in a decreasing way: until in the first days of life we only have the myelinisation of the nerve fibres. There is effective "maturing" only in these early periods, to be attributed to the genome of homo sapiens. Starting from the fourth–fifth month of pregnancy and then more and more, we know today that it is experience that modulates, up to determining after birth, the development of the brain, or in other words the connections that progressively make it function.

Experience conditions the dendritic proliferation, the neural connections, selects specific neural populations and discards others, sometimes even eliminating them. In this way the macro-morphology of the brain is determined by the genome, but the micro-morphology, the histology, and above all the functioning depends on experience. A fundamental consideration is that it is not a question of experience understood generically, on the model that the exercise consolidates the organ, but the type of experience that the individual can have: this is different for every child, and also for every foetus, so that the construction of the way with which that individual brain and therefore every individual mind can function, will be different. The idea that any pathologies, serious or mild, are to be attributed to causes that have interfered with the normal development also collapses; "normality" is to be understood only in the statistic sense, a part from particular cases in which any traumatic factors, sometimes genetic, have been identified. In the vast majority of cases, what was defined a "normal" mind development refers to the average developments observed. Any "abnormality" is actually an "anomaly" (see the etymon) i.e., a deviance from the average that is more accentuated than usual, so that it is noticed.

This change in knowledge, compared to the original idea that the whole of development was entrusted to nature or at least to the "nature" of that individual, that is the changed concept of "maturing", are due to the progress of the clinical and experimental techniques of observation, both of the foetus and of the baby and then of the child. From the first intuitions of the psychoanalysts, to the observational techniques of Bick (1964) to those on the foetus by Ianniruberto and Tajani (1981) to all the studies derived from the attachment theory, to the most modern techniques of neuroimaging (Schore, 2003a, 2003b), we know today that experience "constructs" the brain and that a specific experience constructs a certain brain. Therefore, the mind of each single individual is determined by the relations that are offered to the single child by its caregivers (Imbasciati & Margiotta, 2005, Chapter Eight; Imbasciati, Dabrassi, & Cena, 2011, Chapters One & Four). In the relationship, messages are passed from one individual to the other, delivered by non-verbal media which, received, decoded and processed by the incipiently functioning neuromental apparatus of that child, structure its brain. The type of structure and therefore the functioning which is constructed in that individual brain depends therefore on: a) the neuro-mental structure of those individual caregivers; b) their relative functioning at that time; c) environmental circumstances that foster or hinder looking after the child; d) the neuro-mental structure at that time of life that has formed in that child following its previous experience, which conditions the type of processing of what it receives. The four aforementioned factors determine what the child will process from the information that reaches it and, thus processed, will be integrated into the functions which up until then have been structured in its brain. The fourth factor deserves special attention.

The problem of the structuring processing of what may have been received is extremely complex (*cf.* Imbasciati, Dabrassi, & Cena, 2011): here we can mention how its results can be positive, in the sense of fostering the construction of a mind with an adequate, excellent rather than negative functioning, because it constructs a mind that is more or less dysfunctional, more or less deviant from the norm up to what is said to be a "pathology". The theme, stated between the two polarities, rises up in the degree and in the type of optimality of the caregiver's mind, in the circumstances in which the communication takes place and in the degree of attunement between the two "dialoguers" (non-verbal, it should be recalled). In semiotic terms, the emitter must emit signifiers (= signs which carry a meaning) that must be coherent and congruous, so that they can be coded by the receiver, who may become able to decode in their meaning in order to be able to answer them: if this happens, the receiver can answer with congruous signifiers (= i.e., delivering a meaning of an adequate answer) to what has been received, i.e., the coding that has been done, and at the same time suitable for that done by the emitter, so that he can also respond adequately and so on and so forth. The emitter obviously has to have sufficient abilities, as well as possibilities to decipher the progressive signifiers, in order to be able to respond in turn congruously, so that the receiver (child) can in turn decode (= understand!). This is the degree of attunement in the semiotics of reciprocal signifiers.

In essence, experience does not consist of the real events in which the baby lives and grows, but in the result that is structured in the functioning of its brain, and its mind, as the result of the continuous non-verbal interpersonal dialogue, according to the above schematisation. Having schematised it in semiological terms (emitter, receiver, coding, decoding, signifier, meaning, vehicle) can, I think, be useful to the reader to debunk his consciousnessist assumptions. Or, as it concerns non-verbal signals that every person spontaneously emits without realising, the reader can understand how the adults who look after children are not aware of them and also how unintentional and involuntary they are.

THE ORIGINS OF THE MIND   45

The caregiver who wants to "be an actor" with the intention of wanting to be a "good caregiver" will without any doubt produce a failure, as he or she will not be able to express the unconscious interior automatism that is necessary for effective attunement of the dialogue. Those caregivers may perhaps be able to effectively mimic, but the baby will never be able to play along with similar person, who ought to recourse to a fiction because he does not have the inner ability to understand what the child is expressing and, above all, he ought to recourse to a fiction because he does not have the ability to understand what happens in himself when he has not understood what the child was expressing; i.e., when he ought to recourse to conscious intentions and to acting to do what in actual fact he is not capable of doing. In other words, an insufficient structure of the caregiver is at stake here. We could say that we cannot lie to babies; not even unconsciously.

In conclusion, a baby grows, in the brain, according to how the adults looking after it shape it, and they shape it according to what they "are", not according to what they think or want. This truth is, in a certain way, terrible, for the responsibilities of those who want to generate a new homo sapiens.

In the picture outlined, the mind and brain are not two different "things", nor is it sufficient to define them as two different sides of the same event: they are two situations which reciprocally activate one another. One is the biological apparatus that is functioning, the other the function (the functions) carried out at that time. The peculiarity is that the function continually modifies the apparatus that carries it out; one does not depend on the other, nor does the other depend on the former, but the fact that the brain depends on experience (the experience "with others" which depends on what the other are like) i.e., on the functioning until then acquired as a "mind", and this in turn derives from that brain as it is structured and at that time in function. It is this reciprocal interaction that structures the child's brain, which is being structured: in "*statu strutturandi*".

What has been outlined here reveals the illusion, or better the ideology, both of those who remain attached to the bitter end to genetics (including epigenetics?! Cena & Imbasciati, 2014, Chapter Three) and of those who remain in the dark prejudicial roots of a mind-consciousness that is the master of their fate.

What is the fate of men? Which one, in this continuous feedback, which, above all, depends on those of the people encountered and

46 MINDBRAIN, PSYCHOANALYTIC INSTITUTIONS, AND PSYCHOANALYSTS

above all on caregivers, conditioning its future development. This opens up the problem of transgenerationality (Imbasciati, Dabrassi, & Cena, 2011) as we will see further on.

A baby's brain learns

Recent developments in neuroscience, on the basis of the results made possible by neuroimaging techniques, have confirmed, with the evidence of experimental sciences, what psychoanalysis had clinically observed for some time, and theorised after the work of Bion. The mind is developed by a continuous process of learning from experience; the famous *Learning from Experience*, the title of this author's best known book (Bion, 1962), indicates with the "from" what is described above, i.e., that it is not real and external experience that builds up the mind, but a processing of what is learned. This learning always passes through a relational experience and its processing depends on the type of relationship that is established. These conclusions were obtained by Bion in the psychoanalytic relationship and helped to clarify how complex and deep this relationship was, and how varied it was in conditioning what the analysand learns; it also clarified how this learning is unconscious. All Bion's work is focused on observing the ways with which the unconscious elements are transformed and processed in the analytic encounter. This opened up the way to considering the unconscious essentiality of all learning and how all this is the foundation of every process of growth of the mind. What Bion found in the analysis of adults was used to study what happens in children. Infant psychoanalysis developed this way, in the treatment of children, including infants, together with their parents. It was discovered how the effect of relationships is not revealed only in the analytic relationship, with the child or with the adult, but in any relationship; that of a parent with their child is, in particular, not simply transformative, but structuring. This is how the mind an individual is structured, starting from the earliest periods of its life. Today neurosciences confirm that this is how the brain of a child, or a future person, is structured: by the type of relationships possible with respect to the abilities of the person looking after them.

The developments of attachment theory, in the psychotherapeutic application to children with their parents, have proven in another way the essentiality of the quality of the relationship in determining mental structures that are decisive for the individual's future (Imbasciati,

Dabrassi, & Cena, 2011). Infant research, continuing the experimental legacy of developmental psychology, has shown the convergence with respect to the other approaches mentioned above: the mind is built up on and from relations. Neurobiologists, lastly, have shown how what had been observed by clinicians of different backgrounds and methodologies, could be demonstrated in the brain. The best-known book by Siegel is entitled *The Developing Mind* (1999). The relational experience, i.e., what passes from one mind to another in a relationship, establishes, transforms and increases the functional structure of the brain, depending on the "quality" of the relationships.

The mind, therefore, does not develop by nature, nor does the brain develop by the genome of homo sapiens, but both develop by the experience that the individual obtains from the people that looked and look after them. This "obtaining" or, to put it better, processing is of fundamental importance in the early periods of life, starting from foetal life. The foetus learns from the voice of its mother, from her movements, the noises and above all the biological humours that the brain—the mind—of the mother spreads in her body. The baby learns as the development of the sensory organs lets it organise the afferences in sets which have a meaning. For a long time this learning was not recognised at scientific level: the idea of learning as well as that of the mind remained prisoners of the Western philosophical tradition and even more of the consciousnessist ideology, which claimed reducing both mind and learning to what appears to the consciousness of adults and their illusion of volition.

In actual fact, the learning we are talking about here, and that has been discovered as fundamental, is a comprehension that is neither verbal nor can it be verbalised, but is a learning essentially of emotions. The consciousnessist illusions also dominate for this last term: in the common understanding, "emotion" means what the individual feels is happening inside himself, and even people who should be informed, at least rudimentarily, on what the human psyche is, slip up on this idea. The term "psyche", used with a semantic aura different from mind, is used to conceal the conviction that a mind-consciousness ought to exist, indeed that the consciousness is the mind, although perturbed by something to which another name is given. Affect? Feeling? Passion? Character? Or, in any case, psyche other than mind. All these are terms which say how man-consciousness by self-idealising himself protects himself from realising that the mind—and today, we know, his brain—works unknown to him; and makes him do things that he would not

48 MINDBRAIN, PSYCHOANALYTIC INSTITUTIONS, AND PSYCHOANALYSTS

even like to think about. And yet he thinks: because thought is, in its first and essential place, involuntary and unaware, and only a small part of it, often mistaken, reaches the consciousness.

When psychoanalysis, about a hundred years ago, said that there were unconscious affects and that there was an unconscious that made man act, there was enormous opposition, so that even Freud had to invent his metapsychology to explain to his contemporaries that there were (there "had" to be) drives and repression to have the idea of the unconscious accepted (Imbasciati, 2010b, 2011a, 2011b, 2012a, 2013b), and to add the corrective that this unconscious could perturb the consciousness but that with the instrument of psychoanalysis the latter could subjugate it again. *Wo es war soll Ich werden* (Freud, 1933a, p. 190).

Today we know that the mind is primarily and essentially unconscious, that at its origin there is a learning of emotional functions, that "emotion" is an essentially unconscious process that only sometimes appears, distorted, to the consciousness of the individual, that emotion, understood this way, is the basis of every other mental function, including what is called thought, and that this foundation, which was at the origin of the structuring of the infant's mind, continues to be present and operating in all new learning, by the baby and the child and the adult, and at every development of that individual's mind.

It is of "that" individual as the relational experience which generates the first structures which in turn form all further learning is unrepeatable for each individual. It is due both due to all the possible changes of the relationships from which it generates in time, (from the environment in the situation of mental functioning to every instant when the caregivers relate with "that" child), and for the way in which the mind, even incipient, of that baby, works (because this is how it has learned until that moment). Therefore, the baby will process in a specific way what it obtains from the relationship of that moment, and lastly for all the subsequent experiences which that child, then as an adult, will process, throughout all the other relationships in its life, which will be added to and modify to some degree what had been structured.

The developments of attachment theory, combined with (experimental) developmental psychology and with infant psychoanalysis, have been integrated into the series of clinical and experimental research which go under the name of infant research. This convergence has increasingly enlightened both the concept of "relationship" with what it can transmit, depending on the almost infinite ways of functioning, and

THE ORIGINS OF THE MIND   49

how this structures the mind of the foetus, the baby, the child, the young boy and the future adult individual in the early moments of human life; and, in the last place, how all this functions beyond the consciousness and the intentions of its unaware protagonists.

The contribution of the neurosciences

Today the neurosciences have confirmed the above with the evidence of the technological instruments at our disposal. The relationship structures the brain. The brain is originated for this and by this experience. The old concept of neurological maturing has greatly changed, to the extent that keeping the name is questionable: "maturing" implies the concept of a process determined by nature, by genetics as was said last century. In actual fact, only the macro-morphology of the brain is determined by the genetics of homo sapiens, but the micro-morphology, the physiology and the functioning are generated by the experience of that single individual.

Experiences overlay very early on and with a gradually preponderant effect the genome and the relative protein synthesis that produces the first neural connections in the foetus: the relative afferences, received, then perceived, coded and processed by the system operating at that time, reach the brain by entering into the protein synthesis that generates the synapses, so that they, i.e., the neural circuits that form the functioning of that brain and therefore of that mind, depend on the type of experience as it is recorded that way, in the biology and the physiology of that brain. The mind is the whole of all the functions of a brain however it is observed: with neurobiological instruments or in the behaviour of the individual, and—for what it is worth—in what its consciousness "knows" about its own subjectivity.

We have to specify here again for quite a few readers that when we talk about brain and mental functions, this does not mean at all those crude labels that psychiatry on the one hand and philosophy—in actual fact consciousnessist speculations—on the other, coined, for example, language, character, temperament, humour or reasoning, logic, will, control or others. Function is every micro-functionality of each circuit or neural population, put into relation with possible but not necessary manifestations in the individual, on condition that these are observed carefully and competently. By using semiotic and at the same time psychophysiological terms (which can help understanding what experience, processed in the mind, is translated into internally in the

50   MINDBRAIN, PSYCHOANALYTIC INSTITUTIONS, AND PSYCHOANALYSTS

many and varied ways as described), and to better understand what happens here beyond the consciousness, I will clarify the concept of "representation" (Imbasciati, 1991, 2013b).

This is the psychological term used to describe what represents the various and subsequent aspects of external reality inside their interior reality, including their corporal reality, which are being processed in an individual (always beyond awareness). It is not representation meaning an image that can be more or less faithful of objects, similar or at least corresponding to how these appear to the perception of external reality (this is a naïve conception made by the consciousness) but those codes representing the various statuses and stages of the progressive transformations and organisations which undergo the afferent inputs along the way; from the sensory (and internal) receptors to the brain, and there the further processing with which elements of meaning are constructed, building up the mind. It is also the "representations" of each individual, even minimal, functional capacity that has been structured in new neural connections. Damasio (1999) speaks of "maps", organised in the brain to represent external reality, corporal reality at every instant of the biological state of each part of the body and that of the neuromental functions themselves which are active at every instant (= subjectivity).

In this respect, throughout the years of my research, I developed my Protomental Theory (Imbasciati & Calorio, 1981; Imbasciati, 1994, 1998b, 2006a, 2006b) which I am now proposing as a new metapsychology (Imbasciati, 2013b). Here I used the term of "engram",[2] to indicate what is being progressively formed (and in an increasingly articulated way) in the brain—new synaptic connections—to represent each progressive functional capacity generating (or "representing") any mental element (also new functions) whatsoever, beyond not only awareness, but above all beyond the possibility of representing describable "objects". This means beyond any ability to be verbalised: all these engrams form implicit memory, i.e., essentially function memory (Imbasciati, 2006a, 2006b; 2013b), which are neurologically "represented" by "engrams" (given in all likelihood by neural networks), which represent the possibility of generating as many mental elements (cf. Chapter Five). Implicit memory is therefore the emotional structure that has been constructed.

The neurosciences have confirmed today and detailed how the emotions are the first and fundamental form of cognition: originally, in the baby and the child, and throughout the life of man. An impressive amount of literature (part of which bears the name of neuropsychoanalysis) is

THE ORIGINS OF THE MIND   51

continually elucidating new discoveries. Scientists such as Kandel, Siegel, Damasio and Schore—to mention only a few—are producing works which will remain fundamental in the history of the discovery of the mind. Here, by continuing to emphasise the relational origin of the mind and all its developments, or the essentially social nature of homo sapiens, I think I should say something more specific about the concept of memory. It is not the crude psychiatric-consciousnessist categorisation that makes memory coincide with the recollection, nor the finer categorisation that psychologists have drawn up (long or short term memory, recognition, re-evocation, working memory and others: *cf.* Imbasciati, 1986, vol. 2, Chapter Seven), but specifications relating to the current state of psychoneurobiological research. The memory is in the first place essentially unconscious, indeed, much of the memory—called implicit—has never been re-evocable in any way because it cannot be verbalised. It is sub-symbolic or asymbolic memory (Bucci, 1997, 2001, 2007a, 2007b, 2009). All mental functioning is memory: every minimum construction of any circuit of neural connections has to remain, in order to be able to function, at least until that function is not further articulated: it is therefore memory that is continuously transformed, by each new experience.

Every minimum representation (Imbasciati, 2013b) which is built up forming "mind", is memory. We are our memory and above all the implicit one, about which we "know" nothing but which inhabits us. It all comes from experiences of relationships: genetics gives us the hardware and experience the most sophisticated software. The action of the genetic make-up of an individual—and here we are already in the individual variability—is subjected to all the "epigenetic" influences which due to the infinite situational combinations of experience modifies its expressivity (Cena & Imbasciati, 2014). Each individual, in their "mindbrain", and from here in their body, is "singular" and unrepeatable.

The experience of the "mindbrain" and the future of civilisation: which transgenerationality?

Mind and brain are an inseparable unit. We can say that the essence of a human being is his "mindbrain". From the vertex of neurobiological sciences, with the relative instruments and competences, and from the vertex of psychobiological sciences, here too with specific instruments and skills, different aspects can be seen, which are currently proving that they can be integrated, as the two points of view are compared and the relative skills of those who study them interlock and are integrated. However, there remains in the common understanding, but also in scientific circles, the tendency to "forget" the unitary nature of which today we have proven knowledge. I believe that this tendency can be an expression of a drifting—inevitable in the human mind—to "turn away" from uncomfortable and disappointing knowledge to more pleasant fantasies, such as those which until not very long ago were maintained by ideologies that had developed on the basis of incomplete knowledge. I am referring to what I have tried to describe in the first two sections of this chapter.

The comfortable fantasy dictated by the illusion that possessing a consciousness that provides us with knowledge and control over ourselves, and that our conscious thought can excogitate technologies that will allow us to dominate them, is part of our archaic heritage of those primitive and omnipotent ideas, mediated by the indifferentiation between our interior baby and our equally omnipotent internal mother who provides for everything. There are still people today, even learned ones, who think, or even maintain, that the mind is something different from the brain, so that in this separation the mind gains priority (= "I am the one commanding my mind") except for the unfortunate eventuality in which the brain affected otherwise, from the outside or by nature (genetics) can disable the mind (for example, the concept of pathological mind or even of a mind that falls ill).

There are also people who in the wake of hard sciences think that everything depends on the brain, but that human genius, i.e., the mind, with technopharmacology, can guide it in the best way and "heal" it if necessary. If in sufficiently learned people the aforementioned drifting into fantasy can be criticised and therefore modified, at the level of common thought there still remains today the relative convictions that are formed as ideologies. The first, less cogent, permeates above all those who are concerned by the fate of humanity, in the current gigantic change of habits and the social crisis which holds us in its grip at a global level, and concerned about possible violence, or other passions being triggered off, they are occupied therefore by a moral and social question, very often supported by stronger traditional religious ideologies. The second, on the other hand, much more widespread, is currently flaunted by all the mass media: the neurosciences, of which

THE ORIGINS OF THE MIND   53

those who organise the media usually know very little, are idealised and almost deified to show us a better future, where all diseases can be defeated, including mental diseases and even the minor disorders of minds that cannot stand suffering.

This eschatological prospect is often accompanied by scenarios straight out of science fiction; in actual fact they are terrifying because, if on the one hand the curative use is presented, on the other the possible manipulation of brains is imagined. This could be done for criminal purposes; this last vision is presented by the mass media as fiction, just as in fiction films truculent images are shown to push away a real understanding of them, only the first vision, the optimistic one, is foisted off as feasible. In actual fact, criminal use of these, for the time being, fictional scenarios, is not implausible (Imbasciati, 2013a).

Beyond possible or impossible manipulations of the assimilation of specific experiences, the fact is that experience, which today we know is the matrix on which the mind is constructed, does not depend on our will: it happens to us. That this comes to us from our parents is a point of anguish. They are powerless in turn, in that they do not have the possibility of transmitting to us an experience for a better construction of our mind as they would like. Insufficient parents, or ones who are not very sufficient, or with neuromental structures that are fundamentally dysfunctional, will produce children who are rarely better than themselves: it is not through any fault of their own. Their impotence is not easily acceptable by their offspring: the anguish of a "bad mother" looms high. The anguish of the uncontrollable that looms over us and the paranoid grudge for parental figures who feel guilty is then split—in the specific psychoanalytic meaning of "splitting"—to seek the perspective of a refuge in an immediate, tireless although temporary, liberation from anxiety. However, we also forget what could really happen in a worse future, if today we do not think of what we could do to prevent the problems of tomorrow. In other words, there is a transgenerational circuit between parents and children and the children's children, with a domino effect: parents who, by their misfortune or that of their parents, have had a deficient construction of the emotional base of their mind, will produce and raise children who are unlikely to be any better. There may easily be a vicious circuit that gets worse and worse. The impossibility of repairing the defects of the implicit memory that has structured the foundations of the unconscious emotional functioning, only through the good educational intentions of an adult, is a pious illusion, destined to be successful very occasionally. On the other hand, this adult should be helped, their poor capacity serenely recognised and this parent should benefit from psychotherapeutic aid.

However, even in the case of parents who are sufficiently suitable to make the mind of the children grow well, economic, social and cultural factors may intervene which prevent them from having enough time to transmit to the children their good psychic abilities. The negative transgenerational circuit can therefore take place and become worse. In all these cases, the future of the generations to come should be considered. I am referring to the preventive treatment that we could try to organise for all parents, as well as for all those who look after children. I am talking about the possible organisation of care of Perinatal Clinical Psychology which I studied at length with colleagues (Imbasciati, Dabrassi, & Cena, 2007; Imbasciati & Cena, 2010; Imbasciati, Dabrassi, & Cena, 2011; Cena, Imbasciati, & Baldoni, 2010, 2012). The integration that is being implemented between the different therapeutic applications of the different psychological sciences, and of these with neurosciences, could allow general care, for expectant mothers, parents and all caregivers, covering all the family and social situations that appear at risk for the children as future individuals, as well as to reinforce the parenting skills of all parents so that they can produce better children; and that at the same time works to prevent all the social and economic situations that may threaten or weaken the construction of children's minds. Work like this requires resources: for politicians, the cost for this currently appears unsustainable. In actual fact, the cost, if correctly calculated, would be less than the cost of treating all those who are marginalised, the mentally ill, criminals, drug addicts and all the others for their whole lives in various institutions, treating them when it is now "too late": ideologies also come into play here.

In conclusion to this unsolved social problem, which I believe threatens the whole of humanity, a diagram that has previously been published (Imbasciati, Dabrassi, & Cena, 2011) can, I think, be useful to act as a memorandum of how far the different sciences of the mind, psychological and neurobiological, are in agreement on warning us of our transgenerational fate.

THE ORIGINS OF THE MIND   55

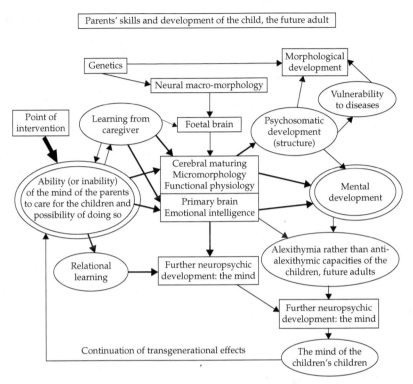

Figure 1. Transgenerationality and intervention point. Diagram by A. Imbasciati and L. Cena, 2011.

The diagram shows how various factors condition each other in modulating a child's development, both physical and, underlined, neuropsychic, producing future individuals who in their turn will pass on to their children what their brain has learned during their relational life. The direction of the arrows shows the direction of the connection and their thickness indicates the intensity of the conditioning. The diagram highlights in its intertwining the transmission of the relational skills as a vehicle of a more global transmission from one generation to the next. In the centre of the diagram, we can see a schematisation of the formation of the primary, foetal and neonatal brain, conditioned in its structures, not so much by genetics, responsible for the neural macro-morphology, but by the quality of the learning from the caregivers and in particular by their relational skill of good care (on the left in the figure). The quality

56 MINDBRAIN, PSYCHOANALYTIC INSTITUTIONS, AND PSYCHOANALYSTS

of structuring modulated this way will mean that the brain of this child can be capable to varying extents of further relational learning through-out its future life (below-centre in the figure). If, in this transmission, good caring abilities, i.e., good relational, anti-alexithymic abilities, are delivered, they will be transmitted to the children, who will in their turn be able to look after the children they have when adults (children of the children, below-right) and therefore generate an improving trans-generational circuit. This circuit could however also come about in the negative. On the left, the diagram shows where to focus a suitable work of prevention and care that can improve the transgenerational domino effect and avoid risks of negative evolution of the population. At the top, the diagram shows how greatly the genetic make-up conditions the corporal morphological development and the development of the brain, but the latter only for its macro-morphology. Going down towards the centre of the diagram, we can see how the foetal brain and increasingly that of the baby, owe their micro-morphology and func-tional physiology (cerebral maturing, once ascribed to genetics) to the experience drawn from learning from the caregiver (on the left) and this owes its quality in particular to the ability of the parents' mind for good care, and the possibility of doing it. The brain structured this way conditions (on the right in the diagram) both the psychosomatic development and the very psychosomatic structure that will regulate it and which will then modulate physical development and vulnerability to diseases (top-right) and above all the mental development. A par-ticular role in this maturing is played by the structuring of the primary brain (emotive) which today has proven to be extended to the whole of the right hemisphere of the brain, and how this conditions, in the individual that becomes an adult, the all his neuromental development (centre-bottom). The structuring of the primary brain is responsible for the anti-alexithymic[3] (relational) capacities of the child, who therefore as an adult will, precisely for this reason, be able to transmit it to his own children (transgenerational effect, children of children, bottom-right). This effect will condition the degree of future parents' ability to raise their children excellently instead of deficiently (or pathologically) follow the arrow along the bottom of the diagram that leads from the left and then goes upwards.

Transgenerational effects are in a cascade: parents who are not opti-mal and precarious socioeconomic situations contribute to producing weak children with a precarious psychic structure and at the risk of further events in their adult lives which aggravate these situations. These children, when they are adults, will not be able to generate in their turn children with good mental structures and so on in the children of their children in a worsening vicious circle. In particular, as shown by the developments of attachment theory, the reflective ability of adults will progressively be compromised (Fonagy, 2001; Fonagy & Target, 2001; Fonagy and coll., 2003), accentuating the alexithymic traits and the avoiding attachments; this will be particularly harmful for their children, as it entails the lack of the parental capacity to understand the signs of help and contact of small children and therefore there is no possibility of an attuned dialogue which constructs their minds (Imbasciati, Dabrassi, & Cena, 2011). Unfavourable social conditions will complete the ill-fated work.

Preventive and therapeutic care for the perinatal period, for all couples that can have children, can interrupt the vicious circuit and create the conditions for an improvement in the transgenerational cycle. Similarly, care for all parents, including those who fortunately have adequate mental structures, may further improve their parenting skills and therefore obtain generations of children who are further well equipped: to face up to the adversities of adult life, but above all to improve their own children even more, so that a virtuous circuit of better psychic structures raises the average situation of a population. The fate of a civilisation is indeed perfected or the worst is avoided. However, voluntaristic ideologies, or better still, fanciful ones, can prevent the delicate feat, as important as it is concealed and long term. A "moral" work in the scientific sense, will not be easy. Illusions, of consciousness and volition, may suggest that things are going well until "pathologies" are encountered, and in this case there will again be the belief that they can be remedied. Following this last inauspicious concept which comes from a medicalistic ideal omnipotence, we will have generations of logopaths,[4] who will not be able to express their suffering. Silence will fall on the horizons of the future.

CHAPTER FOUR

Neuropsychic development and the relational formation of the mind

Preconceptions and prejudices

For years it was believed—and unfortunately the idea still lives on in popular culture—that the foetus and the baby, and the child in his first years of life, developed according to the laws of nature, the nature of homo sapiens, governed (as we had become accustomed by the acculturation of the last century) by genetics. After the first two years of life, the progressive importance of upbringing was considered, deemed as having the greatest impact between the ages of seven and fifteen. The development of all those skills called the "mind" was conceptualised this way, as well as what was called, to differentiate it, "psyche", by distinguishing affectivity from (supposedly) mere cognition, and from "character"; and also from what has been distinguished from the latter as temperament; or by other names, such as "mood", personality, passion, tendencies, motivations, or other terms (*cf.* Chapter Three).

None of this is confirmed by current sciences. The various names shown above are only labels due to incomplete, or even ideologically traditional knowledge of what the human mind really is, of what is today called by that term if connected with the brain, and how the latter develops. These labels are misleading, as they do not correspond to precise entities that can be scientifically identified; the names are not entities, they are not "things", but only the invention of words, by which we try to conceive of a concept, with the intention of understanding reality. If, as this understanding progresses, more useful concepts are coined and indicated by other names, the old concepts, with the old terms, should be abandoned; they are not "discoveries" (Imbasciati, 1994, 1998b, 2013b) but instrumental inventions, which can be superseded by better ones and therefore no longer used. The reality of how human behaviour originates has been seen today to be far more complex than according to the attempts to conceptualise it by philosophy, then pedagogy with their concepts, and then again by the first biological sciences, genetics, neurology and medical sciences in general, and also psychology, until a few decades ago.

Therefore, the misleading categories of our tradition have to be cleared from our minds, in order to be able to accept the current scientific discoveries without distortions.

These can be summarised as follows, in line with the current state of knowledge:

1. Every biological function is modulated by the brain. Every organ functions in its own specific way but this may vary, up to the point of pathology (in extreme cases even in its morphology, as for cell reproduction) by the brain. This absolutely does not mean that we can modify our bodies, as considered in point 7: brain does not mean our will or conscious intention.
2. The macro-morphology of the human brain is determined by the genome, but its micro-morphology and even more so its physiology (= functioning) are structured according to an individual processing function determined by the experience of each individual subject. Nobody has a brain that is the same as someone else's.
3. The cliché that for a normal mind the brain has to be "normal" is wrong and misleading. There is no such a thing as a normal brain, in other words normal by nature: each brain is structured by each single experience. The "normal" of common language refers, very approximately, to a brain that has structured itself so that it can enable those mental expressions and that behaviour which appear average for all adult human beings.

NEUROPSYCHIC DEVELOPMENT AND RELATIONAL FORMATION   61

4. Experience never corresponds exactly to external reality or, to put it better, to what we perceive as the external reality surrounding an individual and that we think the latter perceives it exactly as we perceive it. Experience as per point 2 is the end-product of a work that each individual brain carries out on the afferences it receives from the external and internal sensorial apparatuses. This work is not the same for everyone: all the information is processed according to a type of processing that depends on how that particular brain can function at that time.

5. The experience that has the greatest impact on structuring the brain depends on the emotional level (neither too much nor too little, biochemistry tells us): this means that the vast majority of the information that structures the brain comes from inter-human relations. It is these, and the more intimate they are, that generate the adequate emotional level. The neural network that is structured this way depends on the emotional structure of each of the two or more brains that relate to each other when they communicate. The processing as in point 2 is therefore the result of what passes through the brain of an individual and how he has processed it in the context of their communications, as well as in all the human contacts he has and will have. This processing belongs to what we nowadays designate as mind.

6. The aforementioned processing and therefore the structuring of the individual brain, starts as early as in the foetus, probably at the end of the fourth month of pregnancy, has its greatest impact in the first eighteen months of the child's life and nevertheless continues throughout life. The brain is structured above all through the experiences of early infancy, but it is continuously being restructured in time, depending on the processing of the experience drawn from the continuous inter-human communications throughout life, above all those of a suitable emotional level.

7. Every single detail of all the behaviour of an individual is governed by the brain. Therefore, everything that is termed character, temperament, affect, passions or by any other name depends on the brain. An individual's ability to orient themselves in external reality or to manipulate it effectively also depends on the brain: these are the most specific cognitive abilities. The ability to regulate every inter-human relationship also depends on the brain: this is

affectivity. Those experiences that Damasio (1999) calls primitive feelings, which give an individual the sense of existing, of being a perceiving subject, of distinguishing perception from their imagination and from their memory, of being themselves in time, of being the creator of their actions and intentions, also depend on the brain. All these manifestations as a whole come under the current concept of "mind". It therefore does not make sense to distinguish between "mind" and "psyche".

8. Therefore, what we scientifically call mind today does not coincide with the abilities that were labelled as intelligence or cognition, thought or otherwise, nor does it coincide with what the individual feels happening inside himself, or what he believes is happening, and of which he feels convinced, conscious, the owner and originator.

9. The brain works independently of the fact that it is realised or not: the mind is therefore primarily and essentially unconscious. It is estimated that about ninety-five per cent of the brain works over and above what our capacity to be conscious can feel is happening inside us. In addition, what appears to our capacity to be conscious may be totally misleading with respect to what is going on in our minds and depends, as well as on the individual, on the time and interpersonal circumstances. What we are perfectly convinced of in good faith may be completely wrong: we are the worst connoisseurs of ourselves. Elsewhere (Imbasciati, 1978), I have spoken about *Il Bugiardo Sincero* or *The Sincere Liar*. Our mind does not coincide at all with "what we have in mind". This expression is emblematic of our preconceived traditional "consciousnessism".

10. What today we can call emotions does not coincide with what we feel, i.e., with feeling emotions, but rather it refers to what is happening in the mind, beyond any possible awareness we may have. This means that it refers to what our mind is processing. This is why our adjective "emotive" should be distinguished from "emotional". The best measure of our emotions is therefore to be sought at the biochemical level of the brain. Here we have had the surprising discovery that most of the work by the brain can be said to be emotional.

11. The whole of the right hemisphere and much of the left one is "emotional brain" (Schore, 2003a, 2003b) and it is on this basis that part of this processing is transformed, in circuits in the left brain, into operational skills that we can call cognitive, possibly conscious.

We can therefore state that every human being "reasons" on the basis of the emotional work of their brain.

12. In the first eighteen months of life, only the right brain works. The connections that allow the left brain to work are structured gradually and subsequently. The first things learned, which are fundamental for the foundations of the mind, are totally emotional. They are essentially learning of the functional abilities of the brain itself; "function memory" (Imbasciati, 2013b, 2014b), not memory of some "contents" that can possibly be re-evoked.

13. The brain's work does not depend directly on the neurons, but on how these are connected with one another; there are billions and billions of connections and these are constructed by the processing of experience (*cf.* points 2 and 3 above). Each experience can be processed by generating new connections, or reinforcing some that are already structured or weakening or cancelling others. The genome determines the number of neurons: experience generates their connections, which are called "connectome." Our mind depends on the connectome that is active or can be activated at a given time. We are our feelings, as said Damasio (1999); we are our connectome, as says Seung (2012).

14. The memory also depends on the connectome. What we remember is a small part of our memory and may not correspond at all to what had been memorised earlier. The memory is not a warehouse, but a continuing and changing activity. Learning means acquiring memory, in some cases conscious, and every new memory can modify the previous ones, even cancel them, as well as condition the ones that come afterwards. We have to make a distinction between the concept relative to the word "recollection" meaning the thing remembered, and that relative to "memory" as every other memorising ability. Most of our memory is not "remembered" and indeed, can never be remembered, even though it continues to regulate all our abilities, every tiny fraction of our behaviour, and even our body (*cf.* Imbasciati, Margiotta, 2005).

Does the brain decide for us?

From what has been stated so far, it would seem that the mind depends on the brain and that the latter, as it works unbeknown to us (Eagleman, 2012) is what decides, instead of our decision or will, not only about how and what we think but also about our decisions to act. However, we know that everything we learn modifies the brain, especially when

64 MINDBRAIN, PSYCHOANALYTIC INSTITUTIONS, AND PSYCHOANALYSTS

the learning concerns the very functioning of the brain and that this modifies it according to the emotional level of the interpersonal situations (*cf.* Chapter three section 2): the brain learns (*cf.* Chapter three section 5) and everything it learns consists of creating new synapses and new neural networks. The mind therefore depends on the brain, as an expression/performance of its functioning, but experience, as it is processed by the quality of the work of the individual brain, modifies it. We can therefore state that the brain generates the mind and insofar as the latter functions in every new experience, generates or, to put it better, regenerates the brain through continuous feedback. This is what epigenetics studies: how the events of life (and not only of exterior life but even more so of interior life) structure the brain biologically. Some of these structured are transmitted transgenerationally, as they are imprinted in a particular part of the genome, called the promoter (Heard & Martienssen, 2014). In other words, we can state that we are indeed determined by our brain, but also that the processing that takes place in it as a consequence of our life experiences determines the brain itself. To what extent then, can "we" orient our experiences so that they can modify the brain in the direction desired by this "we"?

Underlying this conclusion, we can discern a biological solution to the much-debated problem of the philosophical concept of free will: to what extent, in the continuous brain–mind–brain feedback circuit, is self-determination, in other words the ability to determine, or at least orient, our fate, possible (Merciai & Cannella, 2009; Imbasciati, 2014b)? Abundant experimental literature is developing in this perspective, since it was seen that the time of activating those areas of the brain which control a motor activity is shorter than that in which the subject decides to perform it (Wegner, 2003).[1] There is a lively debate on this subject between the results of different sets of experiments. A majority of scholars today tend to conclude that the freedom of the human being to decide has to be considered as limited to inhibiting what is decided by the brain, but that it is the latter that decides by actual choice (Merciai & Cannella, 2009). The problem, that is waiting for a solution to come from research, concerns consciousness, not simply on questions of milliseconds, but because of its variability and the different levels at which "consciousness" can be discussed (Imbasciati, 2014a).

On this subject we have schematised (Imbasciati & Cena, 2015) a diagram that visually summarises the feedback we have outlined between "the brain that produces the mind" and "the mind that produces the brain".

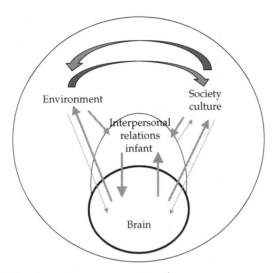

Figure 2. Mindbrain and transgenerationality.

Interpersonal relations, above all the early, intimate, and prolonged ones, and in any case those that entail the adequate emotional level (not necessarily aware), involve reciprocal messages (mainly non-verbal ones): the afferences that convey them are detected and processed by the brain and structure the neural networks. In this way the brain is constructed, and restructures itself continually throughout all its significant relationships: this is how it functions. In turn, the brain, depending on how it functions in relation to the structure acquired, conditions the way by which it assimilates messages coming from the relationships, and therefore its further structuring and conditions the relation itself (and the people it has relationships with), depending on the type of dialogue (syntonic, asyntonic, discordant, invasive, pathogenic, etc.) which can be established, as described in the previous chapter and schematised in the relative diagram.

In the figure shown here, the large circle represents the formation of the mind with the brain in its centre. The mind is the expression of the functioning of the brain which is progressively constructed through the brain's processing of the internal and external sensory afferences. This processing of experience leads to increasing functional capacities, which are acquired as memory by the brain (function memory). The sources of this experience can be divided schematically into three groups: first of all, interpersonal relationships (in the centre), above all intimate prolonged, and early ones, to a lesser extent what comes from

66 MINDBRAIN, PSYCHOANALYTIC INSTITUTIONS, AND PSYCHOANALYSTS

the socio-cultural setting (society-culture, on the right) and from the environment (on the left), in a geographic, economic and work-related sense. The thickness of the arrows indicates the different intensity or incisiveness of these contributions and the relative conditioning in their integration: consider the arrows that go towards and inside the small circle, the brain. This, in turn, not only processes and transforms (depending on how it functions) the components that it takes in, but transforms them and this way integrates them with one another, thus progressively constructing its own functions. The functional structure of the brain conditions and transforms the interpersonal relationships, depending on how it functions throughout its evolution. Over longer periods, it also conditions and can transform the culture of a given society and the environment itself. See the arrows in the opposite direction. The brain thus generates the mind and is generated by it. In turn, the "environment" and "society-culture" are reciprocally conditioned by one another and each transforms the other. The greatest contribution to the construction of the brain comes from interpersonal relations during infancy: on the upper part of the small circle, "infant" is written in smaller characters meaning that in infancy the brain is far more likely to be structured, as early as in the foetal stage, by the type of relationships offered by caregivers. Moving around the large circle and following the arrows, a transgenerational circuit can be identified. Insofar as changes come about in "environment" and "society-culture" and therefore the interpersonal relationships, including and in particular the early ones, change, the brain will differ. Individuals who are structured in this way will produce children with whom they will form different relations and they, with the contribution of the other two sources, will be differently structured people. In turn, they will produce further changes and further different structuring of their children and so on with the children of their children. The mind, or rather the "mentality" perhaps, of groups and peoples change, which in turn changes the circumstances according to which both the minds of individuals and the collective one are formed.

This change may be positive or negative (Imbasciati & Cena, 2015) and so may be the quality of the mind of the future individuals. As will be seen in the next chapter, the quality of the mind of an individual depends on the quality of its foundations, in the dialogue with the caregivers. If this is syntonic and if the caregivers have sufficiently adequate basic structures (= "sensitivity" according to attachment theory), the infant's mind may also have good basic structures. If, on the other hand, the dialogue is dystonic, or intrusive or poor in some way, since the caregivers (in the first place the mother) do not have adequate mental structures, due to external impediments or to obstacles (socioeconomic conditions, abandonment), the infant's mind will not have good foundations. In the first case, the child, when an adult, will have a good probability of becoming a parent with adequate skills to give his children well-structured minds. In the second case, the adult is unlikely to have these skills and in all probability will not be capable of transmitting them to his children: these are "children at risk" or, to put it better, "families at risk" (Imbasciati & Cena, 2010; Cena, Imbasciati, & Baldoni, 2010, 2012; Imbasciati, Dabrassi, & Cena, 2011; Cena & Imbasciati, 2014; Imbasciati & Cena, 2015).

It is obvious that the final outcome of an adult brain does not only depend on the quality of its early foundations: throughout life, other experiences and other interpersonal relationships can contribute to modulating the construction of the brain, for better or for worse. However, the probability that this is for the better is far greater in the first case ("good" bases) than in the second, since—as already emphasised several times—it is not the experience in itself that "is good" or "is bad" for the child, but how it is processed by the brain. This is why we talk of risk. At the collective level, however, as far as the evolution of a human community is concerned, the matter of effects (in a domino effect) from one generation to the next may be of great significance. We can speak of the fate of a culture, or better of a "civilisation". The transgenereational question, which we have reached by degrees, shows the evolution that could happen to our "mindbrains" in the future of humanity. Perhaps for the better, but ... and I leave the conclusion to the reader.

The neuroscientific discoveries we have shown here schematically, especially the latter on the "mindbrain", may still encounter frequent objections. The most frequent is that they would invalidate the concept of the freedom of the human being to self-determination, i.e., it would go against the age-old philosophical question of free will. They actually seem to negate the responsibility of the individual. Yet they are incontrovertible scientific discoveries. Something similar to this happened sex centuries ago with Galileo, when he discovered that the earth revolved around the sun. Then, there was a religious conviction, fuelled by the emotional nucleus of human pride, that humans were at the centre of the universe. Today there is another ideology (as I defined it in the previous chapter), that I have called "consciousnessism" (= nothing but consciousness) which it is painful to give up, and that of omnipotence, which we proudly attribute to what, on the other hand, is a limited power over ourselves. What we have said about the mind and the brain considerably limits our age-old conviction that we are our own masters and in control of our own fates, however it does not eliminate it. Scaling it down, however, is disappointing. And yet ... the transgenerational approach opens up a new horizon, extending responsibility to the whole human community.

Construction of the mindbrain

The development of the human individual, from pregnancy onwards, is governed by the brain, in *"statu costruendi"* we could say, both somatically and, with greater evidence, psychically. The word psyche has to be understood today as synonymous with mind. In order to avoid misleading legacies of philosophical intellectualism of idealistic origin, it is therefore opportune to use, for development as a whole, the adjective "neuromental", to recall that the mind is inseparable from the brain and that the brain depends on the mind and the mind depends on the brain, as shown by epigenetics. The term, still in common use, of "neurological maturing" is therefore misleading. The term "maturing" implies the semantic aura of a process that comes about due to nature, suggesting due to the genome, whereas this misunderstood maturing depends on the experiential activity in which the mind works and is constructed. There is maturing in the true sense of the word for the embryo, in the early months of the pregnancy, and subsequently decreasingly until a few days after birth. From as early as the foetus, however, and increasingly exclusively in the baby, experience, neural work, construction and the connectome are at work.

It has been said that development depends on the emotional level determined by the processing of the experience in interpersonal relations. In (experimental and psychoanalytic) infant psychology, and in particular in our Perinatal Clinical Psychology, the role of the "relationship" and its structuring action has been emphasised for some time now (Imbasciati, Dabrassi, & Cena, 2007, 2011; Imbasciati & Cena, 2010; Cena, Imbasciati, & Baldoni, 2010, 2012), both in a positive sense for an optimal neuromental development of the child and in the negative sense, in an anomalous and pathological development. The quality of the early relationships that the baby and child can enjoy is decisive for his good development, rather than for its pathological future. This "quality" depends on the type, or even better, on the quality of the (unconscious) affective communication (= dialogue) between the child and its caregivers. This quality of dialogue depends in turn on the unconscious affective structure of the caregivers, as well as on the material possibilities that this can take place and the child can benefit from it. Global literature on infant research and, above all, systematic observation (follow-up) of mother–baby relations in psychoanalytic psychotherapy have shown how the quality of the (unconscious) dialogue which can be established is the matrix of the type of neuromental development constructed in the child. The mother–child dialogue, through non-verbal signifiers, transmits meanings to the child, that can be positive or negative for the acquisition of functions (see in this regard the figure on page 73 by Imbasciati, Dabrassi, & Cena, 2011 and relative explanations). What has been summarised here in psychological terms and what, in particular, has been called affectivity and unconscious affective communication makes up the clinical intuition that anticipated the demonstration offered today by neurosciences; the processing by the infant's brain following the dialogue described above constructs its neural connections and the new networks remain as a memory to distinguish the functional acquisitions that form neural development.

The model of "embodied simulation" (Ammanniti & Gallese, 2014) offers more detailed information about what happens at neural level in non-verbal interpersonal dialogues, whereas I have developed and have repeatedly described a model of a psychological type using the term of Protomental Theory (Imbasciati, 2006b, 2014a). This model has its origin in a first extension I made of the psychological and psychoanalytic concept of "representation" (cf. Chapter three section 6), in terms so that it could refer not simply to mental contents, or images of objects, but also and above all to personal modes that are acted out, for example the "manners of being with", the internal working models (IWM) of attachment theory; or experienced, for example subjectivity, the self, as well as any operational acquisition identified (which has been constructed) in the functioning of the mind. It is this "acquisition of functions" which is the result of learning, from the caregivers in early life, subsequently modulated by all the interpersonal contacts throughout one's existence and particularly by those which take place at the adequate emotional level (at neural level), i.e., in an affective climate of intimacy. How many and which of these acquisitions take place in the development of a child in the first year of life, and how many more in the intimate and prolonged relationships of an adult (cohabitation) or in the psychoanalytic relationship has to be considered. These "acquisitions of functions" remain in the brain, in the interneuronal connections and in the new networks, which therefore form the memory of them. They "represent" what has been acquired by the mind in the brain; they are an implicit, therefore completely unconscious, memory, perhaps the most fundamental part of every further development and further memory: the unconscious is memory. I have called the extended concept of representation "engram", reviving and developing an old and neglected neurological term (Imbasciati, 1998):[2] function engrams. I further expanded the development of the Protomental Theory after 2004 into a new metapsychology, congruent with the neurosciences and therefore to replace the Freudian theory (Imbasciati, 2013b, 2014a). Freud, with the knowledge of his time, had formulated his drive theory to try and explain how the mind originated and developed, Today, one hundred years later and with the new knowledge that has been acquired, both psychological (for example, analysis of children with their mothers, observation and experimenting with infants), and neurobiological, on how the brain works, we are able to give a more exhaustive description of neuromental development. The term "metapsychology" has been kept to indicate, as Freud did, that what we know today about how the mind develops and works has nothing to do with what an individual may feel, understand, and be convinced of what is happening in their mind, i.e., with their consciousness.

With many more reasons that Freud had, we can state the unconscious essence of everything that makes up the mind: no longer an "unconscious" to explain with the reasons of the consciousness, but a finding that comes to us from the neuroscience: of how the mind is, in its essence, beyond our ability to be aware of it. Consciousness is an epiphenomenon that is secondary with respect to our present-day knowledge on how we function. Indeed, as it is partial, changeable and misleading, research into why our mind, which is unaware, produces that phenomenon that in homo sapiens turns out to be consciousness, is a subject for future study (Imbasciati, 2014b).

The knowledge we have today on neuromental development and its origins leads to a conception which, in my opinion, marks an epochal turning-point, not only in science but for our future culture and civilisation. It is focused on the fundamental importance of the impact of interpersonal relations on the development of the individual and how this becomes a transgenerational circuit. In this perspective, adequate assistance in the form of Perinatal Clinical Psychology, addressing in various ways and from different points of view all birth professionals, requires maximum and compulsory attention.

CHAPTER FIVE

Transgenerationality and Perinatal Clinical Psychology

Mind and brain

The brain is unlike all the other organs in our body. Strictly speaking, it is not an "organ". All the "organs" perform their specific function, except for minor variations, whereas the brain does not perform its predetermined functions, except the general one of directing, to a better or lesser extent depending on how it is structured in the individual, all the organs of the body, and generating the mind, which is not the same for everyone. The commonly considered "mental functions", usually catalogued as memory, thought, language, affectivity, etc., as well as varying from one individual to another, do not correspond to analogous functions or functional areas of the brain. The stubborn efforts (supported by illusions and ideologies, *cf.* Chapter Four) of over fifty years to localise specific functions in corresponding areas of the brain has proven to be in vain. The brain works since from its billions of neurons connections are formed, which make up neural networks, which in turn have involved and interwoven almost all the areas of the brain. The functions which most properly concern intelligent behaviour, i.e., the whole that people most easily think is connected with the brain, cannot be reduced to that of the common idea, nor are they produced by

74 MINDBRAIN, PSYCHOANALYTIC INSTITUTIONS, AND PSYCHOANALYSTS

analogous functional areas of the brain, as is the case for individual functions of other organs, but combinations of some, often very many, neural networks, which are continually in action. Some nuclei of the brain are indispensable for there to be certain effects, but they are not capable of producing these by their own. The neural networks, on the other hand, are not preformed: they are made up by synapses following experience. This is what produces their connections. In other words, the brain has to learn; each learning consists of the construction of new neural networks. What it is capable of doing—its actual functions, not the effect that appears to the common idea—are performed to the extent and in the ways with which that brain has learned them, depending on the structures that have been constructed there.

The development of the brain, i.e., of the neural networks, is not regulated by the genome: a "normal" brain by nature therefore does not exist. The brain is constructed on the basis of experience. It is by experience, or, to put it better, certain types of experience, that the synaptic connections are formed. The brain receives a continuous large and highly varied amount of information from the body: from all the external (retina, cochlea, vestibule, tactile, pressure, thermal, pain, gustative, and olfactory receptors) and internal sensory systems: osteo tendineousmuscular proprioception, enteroception from the viscera, haematic chemioreceptors and others. All this information is "processed": the brain is like a computer (which is actually called *"elaborateur"* in French), which continuously and in different ways assembles, transforms, and organises all these "afferences". Each type of organisation involves new synaptic connections which give rise to new neural networks, forming "memories".

"Memories" are not to be understood, as in the common sense, as images, objects or perceptive configurations of something as it is perceived by an adult. The latter have to be considered memories of contents, but the essence of the memory is given by memories of functions: *memories of functions* of the brain. The brain has to learn, it has to learn the functions it will perform, and what it learns is memory, which is stored in the neural networks which are formed on each learning occasion. The brain is not a recorder of "images": the neural networks which are formed represent learning and memory of what the brain has learned to do and what it can therefore "do" when necessary. Of particular importance are the first functional networks which are formed in

TRANSGENERATIONALITY AND PERINATAL CLINICAL PSYCHOLOGY   75

the baby: they will allow and modulate all future learning by the child and then by the adult, in a chain in which each learning conditions the following one.

"Memory" therefore does not mean "a recollection": there are two different words in Italian which are often commonly confused. Remembering is only the effect of what moment by moment some neural networks show in the subjectivity of the consciousness; both in the individual who is having an external experience—the afferences are organised in perceptive recognition—and in the person who is trying to "think", which means selecting, recognising and using other memories, which are often translated into words (= memory of a learned language). The brain is not a video and sound recorder: when we remember, i.e., recognise a certain object or place or a context, a mental "content" (of which a memory has remained) it is not about any image but only what is formed in the subjectivity of the consciousness following the functioning of some neural networks. Memory is always the memory of brain functions.

A primary memory is important but often not mentioned because it is so unconscious as to appear obvious. So an individual has learned to feel being himself, having a body, indeed being a body, being in a real situation rather than an imaginary or dreamed one, in which he is, with his past; he feels he lives and is the author of his actions and his thoughts. This memory cannot be remembered, but without it a person would feel every experience, external or of memory, as in a dream; or in a hallucination of delirium or as an external and extraneous event. This memory has been conceptualised as a progressive formation and with various levels, described in different ways depending on the authors (Damasio, 1999; Panksepp & Biven, 2012), of the "self". There is a whole *implicit memory*, constructed in the neural networks, which are continually constructed and reconstructed, also by the interior experience of reprocessing, as functions in new networks, sometimes deconstructing the previous ones. Another memory which cannot be remembered, called "procedural" is the one which concerns having learned how to move, walk, pick up an object, measure every movement of every segment of the body in the right way, calibrate the relative muscular tone, ride a bicycle and so on. Even before that bodily memory (which is addressed the exterior), there is a visceral memory, inside the body, which is changing and continuous: this is, important in the baby and it is mediated by the vagal system (Porges, 2011). Even there is an implicit and individual memory of how to behave according to the people with whom one is in relation (the memory of "being with" described by Beebe & Lachmann, 2003; the internal working models (IWM) identified by the school of Bowlby): all these are memories which cannot be recalled or described in words, but which make us act. Otherwise we would be as awkward as a new born.

Therefore neural connections quite represent functional abilities and continually produce new networks with every experience. This is the continuous "mapping" (Damasio, 1999) of what the body recognises and transmits, including through the whole of the interior of the body, due to the state of the innards, the haematic situation, the state of the mood and so on. This the continuous processing activity that a brain does: that brain of that person. Each brain learns and in its own way. Learning is concretely made up of the new connections, which are memory; the brain progressively learns increasingly new processing abilities, i.e., functional skills; it learns to develop. Each new neural network which is constructed following the processing of new combinations of afferences, forms memory: memory of functions.

It follows that, as the afferences which reach the brain of an individual are never the same as those that reach the brain of another person (each subject is immersed in an environment which is his source of information and is never the same), each brain is made in its own, highly individual way. Each brain has learned to function in its own way. Nobody has a brain that is the same as that of someone else. Nobody can have a mind that is the same as someone else's.

The debated question of whether the mind is produced by the brain can be seen here: the question has been answered today by epigenetics. The brain produces the mind and at the same time the mind, i.e., the functional whole that processes information, generates in its continuous experience new neural networks and therefore new abilities of the brain (*cf.* Figure 2, Chapter Four). The brain is thus constructed on the basis of the experience of the mind. There is a continuous and circular feedback between the mind and the brain (Imbasciati, 2014c; Imbasciati & Longhin, 2014, Chapter Twenty One).

The Western philosophical-theological tradition has accustomed us to thinking that the affects are something different from the "mental" processes, i.e., cognition, intentionality, consciousness: many terms have been coined, such as "psyche", "character", "temperament", "mood",

TRANSGENERATIONALITY AND PERINATAL CLINICAL PSYCHOLOGY 77

motivations, drives and others, to differentiate what we see of human behaviour. All these differentiations are apparent, or better, merely descriptive of what appears to the abilities of consciousness of a common observer.

The neurosciences have shown how everything that could be differentiated by the common observer, however it has been labelled, is a product of the "mindbrain", but does not correspond to areas of the brain, but to the combined function of many neural networks, which always, each in a different way, concern all or almost all the various areas of the brain. One notable example of how many distinctions of little use have been coined was the term "psyche", which does not actually correspond to anything different from what can be called "mind", except the artificial differentiations from the prejudices of our tradition (Damasio, 1999).

From the concepts schematised above, it is clear that "mind" does not correspond at all to what the individual realises, feels and knows about himself, to what he thinks, understands or does: these subjective events concern his abilities of consciousness, but not his mind as a whole. One hundred years ago, psychoanalysis discovered the unconscious: in the past thirty years, cognitive sciences and neurosciences have shown how almost all the mind's activity is performed beyond any consciousness of the individual. The consciousness or better, the capacity for consciousness of every single individual at a given moment (Liotti, 1994, 2001), is only a subjective epiphenomenon, always partial and sometimes misleading, operated by some neural networks, from amongst the millions of these that are continually functioning in that individual unknown to him (Imbasciati, 2013b; Damasio, 1999). We could paradoxically say that the mind is not at all what we think we "have in mind".

From the above, it can be understood why, for the psychic (and for the brain), it is wrong to think of a pathology provoked by some cause that has altered an otherwise natural development. Development by nature does not exist, it is by experience and depending on the experience. We cannot think of a psychopathology based on the usual model in medicine. The human genome only produces the macromorphology of the brain of all humans, but it is experience, starting from the foetal one, through all the various afferences that reach it as the active sensory systems are formed (and which are indeed formed by the genome), which makes up the functioning of that brain, and therefore the mind of a certain person.

78   MINDBRAIN, PSYCHOANALYTIC INSTITUTIONS, AND PSYCHOANALYSTS

When talking about psychic pathology, in order to avoid slipping into very simple and old prejudices, "how it originates" always has to be borne in mind, i.e., not for a cause that altered nature, but because that mind and that brain were constructed that way. This means always bearing in mind the origin of the mind in the progressive construction of the brain throughout individual experience.

The experience of the brain

Let us now go on to specify better what this "experience" involves, in order to understand better why each of us has a brain of our own, even though we have lived in the same environment as another person, even in the same family. What psychology means by "experience" does not refer to the external environment of an individual, or even to all the information that the active sensory systems send to the brain: it is the result of its transformation by the brain into a functional memory; this is what the mind learns from the experience. This does not consist of external events which are passively imprinted on the brain: the mind is not a video-sound player that stores the recordings of what it receives, but a far more complex active and selective apparatus, functioning continuously (and also continuously transforming its structure and therefore its very functioning) which makes thousands of transformations of very different assemblages and very different organisations of the information which it continually receives, mixing it and integrating it with all the previous mnestic traces (Imbasciati, 2006b, 2013b); these traces are also not to be understood as images (or even as codes of images) of some objects or events, but traces of functions that have been acquired (and are being acquired).

At this stage, we can better understand what determines what the mind learns. Referring to more specific texts (Ammanniti & Gallese, 2014; Imbasciati & Cena, 2015), I can summarise here the two main factors responsible for what the mind, and the brain, learn. The first is the structure that is already operative at the time when a given mind starts learning; the second is the relationship that at that time it has with the environment, essentially interhuman, present at that moment and above all interacting with that structure of that subject. The "type of relation" depends on the neuromental structure of the people interacting at that moment and how those structures are functioning at that contingent moment (Schore, 2003a, 2003b; Siegel, 1999). This second factor is decisive for effective learning, as shown at epigenetic level: the emotional level, as recorded biochemically, determines the quality of the modification of some neural networks (Alberini, 2012, 2013). This means that learning depends on the affective quality of the relations with other individuals: learning is therefore primarily a relational learning. This is of the greatest importance for the infant in its early relations; these form the foundation of his neuromental development.

Infant psychoanalysis in its most recent developments (baby-with-parents), attachment theory in its psychotherapeutic evolution, epigenetics, and the neuroscience have allowed observing increasingly meticulously, in the baby and in the child, the progressive acquisition of his abilities: perceptive, of comprehension of the environment, of recognition, of interpersonal contact and gradually of what was approximately called *affective communication*, recognised as the first ability of some *cognition* of the world; and of others and of the self. In these studies, both observational and experimental, the different sciences mentioned above converge in showing us the fundamental importance of the first months of life, both foetal and neonatal, in determining which functional structure is constructed in the brain, and in the mind, as well as in conditioning all the further development of that individual.

We noted above the first of the two factors that determine the neuromental development of the individual: we emphasise that it is the structure that is learning, that determines what the subject learns *from* the experience he is encountering and *in* the experience he is going through. This concept prompts a question: if experience is made up of a processing functional device, what operates at the beginning? What can start an experience that constructs the functional structure that will work? We know nothing or hardly anything about the construction of the first nucleus of the functional structure that will start the possibility of "having experience" and therefore constructing the relative structures capable of further processing. At what period in foetal life? Elsewhere (Imbasciati, 2006a, 2006b) I have hypothesised on this "point zero" of mental development. We do not know to what extent this is due to genetics rather than to epigenetics, i.e., to the biology inscribed in the genome of homo sapiens and in all mammals (as Panksepp states) or to an environmental contact (even in the foetus) which has modified the genetic expressivity, and not only for the individual but also for his descendants, as inscribers in the genome. In other words, does the genome only give the macromorphology of the brain and the number

80   MINDBRAIN, PSYCHOANALYTIC INSTITUTIONS, AND PSYCHOANALYSTS

of neurons, or some neural (functional) networks capable of processing a first experience?

What determines the aforementioned importance of the first periods of life in that the structure that is formed here conditions the following ones, with a domino effect. To the extent that the basic structure is not optimal, it will negatively condition all subsequent learning and therefore all subsequent construction of functionality; we thus have children at a risk of psychopathology. All this is through a dual way, biological and interpersonal psychic.

The second factor that we mentioned in determining the quality of the mind and the brain "to come" is represented by the neuromental structure of those adults who can come into contact with the foetus or the child, therefore the pregnant woman, the mother, the birth operators and all the caregivers. To the extent that these will have a structure of a good quality and obviously the physical and social possibility of looking after the child, they will have the possibility of establishing with him that type of good relation which will qualitatively determine good learning for all the future development of that individual. On the other hand, if the structures of the caregivers have minor and very minor or major defects, there will not be the possibility of a relation with the child of which the quality promises a good development of his basic neuromental structure, which in turn can allow a further good development.

Having said this, it should be easy to see how wrong and damaging is the entrenched idea, by which the development of children is determined by nature (or by the genome), or that it has to be understood as automatic. Neurological or brain maturing are commonly talked of: the verb "mature" is misleading, the brain does not mature, in the meaning that this verb has in our language. The brain is constructed from relational experience and is constructed well or poorly depending on the quality of its relations.

The neurosciences have shown that the quality of the relation, in the continuous communication which there always is beyond words and intentions, produces synaptic connections and new neural networks, which are the memory of what has been learned and even more of learning abilities: a good relation produces neural connections and networks that are more operatively efficient for the purpose of learning of performing functions close to reality: dystonic relations, on the other hand, or intrusive ones also produce new connections and relative memories, but they are dysfunctional and unsuitable for generating a mental development that ensures an optimal mind; they may produce what is indicated as a psychopathology. These effects are regulated by different biochemistries: this means that it is proven, including biochemically, how the quality of relations produces different functional "qualities" of a brain.

What has been stated so far can be found in greater detail in our previous texts (Imbasciati, Dabrassi, & Cena, 2007; Imbasciati & Cena, 2010; Cena, Imbasciati, & Baldoni, 2010, 2012; Imbasciati, Dabrassi, & Cena, 2011; Imbasciati, 2014a; Cena & Imbasciati, 2014; Imbasciati & Cena, 2015), where many illustrative diagrams have been constructed. We show two of them here, from which it can be seen how a Perinatal Clinical Psychology has to be formed. The first illustrates how the neuromental structure of the child is the final result that is processed benefiting from various order of experiences (therefore "composing" different orders of information) including those of the neuromental structure of the parents (or caregivers). Parents structure in turn has inside the processing of the experiences that they have gone through (and are going through in having a child), as well as elements which in their childhood their respective parents, i.e., the grandparents, have transmitted to them.

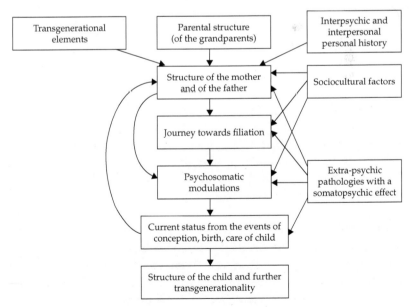

Figure 3. Transgenerationality: from grandfathers to grandchildren.

82 MINDBRAIN, PSYCHOANALYTIC INSTITUTIONS, AND PSYCHOANALYSTS

The second diagram shows (see fig.1, page 55) the interweaving of the various sources of messages which are received and processed (for a more detailed legend see Chapter Three) from which the parental ability (double circled ellipsis), given by the structure of the parents, stands out. It is here that action has to be taken. Perinatal Clinical Psychology has to operate essentially on the couple of the parents, if we want to remedy a negative transgenerational circuit, or if we want to improve it.

As can be seen from the diagrams presented, the communication that delivers the information which from the neuromental structure of the caregivers goes to structure the nascent mind of the child, is essentially non-verbal: in the first few months of life, what the baby's brain learns reaches him essentially from the caregivers and is certainly not via words. Feelings are said to pass, but this is a vague way to indicate the elements from which the brain really learns, which depends on the fact that the messages are emitted outside awareness, nor can they be translated into words; they are "ineffable" (see the ethimon) and yet it is precisely for this reason that they have a structuring effect on the child's brain. The elements that are conveyed and have a structuring effect are the direct expression of the emitting structures: the child one, which is absolutely without awareness, and the caregiver's one, which should be based on that of the child. Psychoanalysis is right when it speaks about the reciprocal communication between two inconsciouses. Schore (2003a, 2003b) describes the experiments of mother/child brain neuroimaging when they are attuned, i.e., in communication, rather than dystonic, in potentially pathogenic communication.

What has been labelled as character is an aspect of the mental activity that is based on implicit memories which also derive from the learning relationships in infancy and childhood. What is labelled this way depends on the functioning of the neural networks that have been formed in relationships and essentially concern the ways of relating with others and the self. The self is as we really are and not as we think or feel we are. The above functions modulate behaviour beyond any conscious intention, let alone beyond what is known as will: often even beyond the consciousness as a whole. It is a sub-symbolic and asymbolic implicit memory. Character can be modified by following other relational experiences in the course of life, but certainly not deliberately by the subject. It a question of unconscious events: we are not the masters of our character just as we are not the masters of our mind. What is known as will, currently the subject of great discussion by neuroscientists, seems

TRANSGENERATIONALITY AND PERINATAL CLINICAL PSYCHOLOGY   83

to concern only a very small part of mental activity: most scientists consider that it can only inhibit what the mind has decided, but not decide (Merciai & Cannella, 2009). Consciousness—what we believe we think, do or are—is a mirror of illusions that we believe is real. The various illusions include the stubbornly entrenched idea, despite the denials of science, that psychic disorders can be remedied when they appear and that it is not worth seeking them out at an earlier stage.

These last considerations make us reflect once again on the importance of preventing the risk of any possible defect, pathology or psychic anomaly, including, if we like, a "nasty character": this prevention, considering the remote roots on which the mind is structured, has to address the perinatal period and the parents.

We have emphasised how it is precisely in the perinatal period that the positive or negative effect of the relationship of the caregivers with the child depends on their mental structure, which was structured when they, in turn, were children with their parents. Everything that happened before the child's birth, in the mother (when she was a child, when as an adult she constructed her relationship with the father of the child) and in the origins of father mind has a great impact on the effects of the quality of the relationship that the parents can establish with their child. A domino effect appears, in a transgenerational chain. The opportunity arises from here to organise perinatal clinical psychology to prevent any progressive negative effects, towards psychopathology.

Perinatal Clinical Psychology and transgenerationality

The majority of "healthcare operators" and also most ordinary people, think of the adjective "clinical" as equivalent to "curative". "Clinical psychology" is thus understood as the application of psychological knowledge to treat those who are psychically or, at any rate, physically ill. In my now long experience, I have always come up against this conception, which reduces the different psychological sciences to a single "psychology in general", different from the General Psychology as officially and scientifically coded, and which reduces the clinical method to artisanal treatment techniques (Imbasciati, 1993, 1994, 2008a, 2008b; Imbasciati & Margiotta, 2005, 2008).

Despite my work in Italian Psychology, as well as that of other scholars (Salvini, 2005) and the very Statute of the "Collegio dei Professori e Ricercatori Italiani di Psicologia Clinica" (Board of Italian

84 MINDBRAIN, PSYCHOANALYTIC INSTITUTIONS, AND PSYCHOANALYSTS

teachers and researchers of Clinical Psychology), which I co-founded, as well as according to the Ministry of Education's official category of Scientific Subjects, the medical meaning of the adjective "clinical" still seems to pervade general culture and dominate the psychological one.

Clinical psychology is not the work of a psychologist who is specialised to a greater or lesser extent to "treat" a possible distress and/or psychic and physical suffering, i.e., to obviate an anomaly that has appeared—this is possibly one of the applications of this discipline—but primarily a science that investigates with its specific methods what the human psyche or, better, the mind, consists of: how it originates, how it functions optimally or within forms and levels of a statistic norm, rather than as an anomaly, in its most widely varying subdued or prominent manifestations. This primary goal, if pursued, is not only to treat, but to prevent. Prevention always ought to take priority over treatment: all the more since when all the psychological sciences and the neurosciences have shown that any psychic suffering, when it appears, has remote reasons in the origin of the mental structure of that individual. Clinical Psychology is therefore identified by its longitudinal study: it is only by working throughout the development of the single individual that an adequate psychotherapy should be considered; otherwise it is only a palliative as a stopgap measure.

This conception of Clinical Psychology, or better the meaning to be given to the adjective "clinical" (Imbasciati, 1993), is still mystified in quite a few healthcare departments, becoming the psychological intervention of the moment. A medicalist ideology applies the principles that are valid for organic pathologies, which have been known as due to external agents, to any intervention to which the name of therapy is given (Turchi & Perno, 1999) and therefore to what can equally be presumed to define as psychic "pathology" which as a consequence is deemed to be treated as though it were an "illness" (Imbasciati, 1993). The result is an intervention which ends up by being symptomatic only, rather than etiopathogenetic. This is far more prominent for mild psychic distress and even more so when it is severe: here, not only it is indispensable to proceed with knowledge about the whole past of that person, but also to consider him in a relational function; and not only relational in his past, but relational of the present, i.e., studying and "treating" his present relationships and therefore the other people with whom the so-called patient is in contact; as well as considering the future of all these relationships. This becomes essential for any individual in the developmental age and is maximum for children. Proceeding this way, the "treatment" can become effective therapy and at the same time prevention.

Contrary to the above indications which today are scientifically proven, there continues in almost all care environments a misunderstood idea that work has to be done on each single individual, who thus becomes the "identified patient", as identified by the Systemic School. Colluding in this ideology are economic reasons, which force bureaucracy to organise the services so that it "appears" efficient, but above all appreciated by users. People continue to have the idea that it is the individual that has to be treated. This is stupid when children are involved: yet precisely here "people", when there is a disturbed child, want him to be treated and only him. The parents withdraw if an expert operator addresses his treatment not to the child but to the parents. Subterranean guilt feelings act here, fuelled sometimes by rash "explanations" of the operator: the parent feels guilty, sometimes accused, if the fact that the child's distress is structured throughout the relational journey with them is outlined.

This is why perinatal clinical psychology, even more than clinical psychology in general, is finding it hard to get off the ground, even though a slow work of scientific penetration is changing the organisation of the services in this field; in many countries but very little in Italy.

I believe that it is fundamental in this laborious process of application to consider transgenerationality. As already illustrated in the previous chapters and schematised in Figure 1 in Chapter Three with the relative explanations, perinatal clinical psychology (addressed obviously to the parents), is not only to prevent psychic risk in some children, nor only to improve parents mind quality, but above all to prevent the domino effects in future generations (Figures 3 and 4 in this chapter). In my opinion, it is the future of our civilisation that is at stake.

To build up a care system based on scientific Perinatal Clinical Psychology, a slow work of penetrating health milieus will be required, at least in Italy. This may be fostered if the awareness of birth operators and the public opinion will be raised on the transgenerational effect in psychic health, rather than on pathology. Parents pathogenicity in relation to their children is highlighted in this transgenerational effect: on children and grandchildren and great-grandchildren (Imbasciati, 2014c). Here the sensitivity of the operator, both clinical and social, in not blaming the parent, who already and unconsciously feels guilty, is put to the test. The parent should have to be able to assimilate the fact that it is a question of causality, not guilt, as nobody can modify their past which has built up their mind: this cannot change, except minimally, and with psychotherapeutic help. This is where the training of the operators is put to the test, in being able to arouse the humility of the user, the parent who has given the best of himself, but is still the child of his past.

Perinatal Clinical Psychological care obviously becomes compulsory and is understandable by everyone when complications arise in the pregnancy, birth and postpartum period or in the case of serious social conditions of the parents. However, in my opinion, necessary should be an insisting, in the training of birth operators, on the need for preventive assistance for all couples. This assistance would include a specialised screening by competent psychologists, to identify "couples at risk": couples at risk of a child at risk. There may be parents who in their family and social existence and as a couple may appear and even be perfectly normal, i.e., appear good parents, but who, when put to the test, do not possess those qualities of inner structure that let them form a good relationship with their child. We remember that it is the non-verbal dialogue that develops in the child's brain a sufficiently good structure for his future life. It will be also necessary to insist on the fact that very often a child's disorder is silent: it will appear later, often at pre-school age, or in adolescence, when it will be too late for therapy or when it will have to be much longer, laborious, difficult, and expensive to be effective. There may be couples who have apparently "normal" children, with parents who are equally "normal" but who do not possess the unconscious endowment of good parenting and they will not be able to structure the "mindbrain" of their children well. The deficit of their children structure may be revealed after some years, in maladjustment at school or in serious adolescent crises which may be perpetuated in youth and adulthood, and which will also mean that these people, when they become parents, will not be able to construct good neuromental structures in their children.

If a parent has good parenting capacities or if he can be helped—this is the work of the hoped-for perinatal clinical psychology for all—to improve his own inner structure, he can germinate in his children the abilities so that they in turn will be good parents. On the contrary, a deficit of "parenting skills", including in parents who are completely normal as people, produces not only children at the risk of psychopathologies, but also and more often children who as adults will not have, in turn, sufficient parenting skills for their children. A pathogenic transgenerational circuit can be triggered off, to be borne in our mind to insist on the need for care by perinatal clinical psychology with a preventive function. Similar assistance services can also be of support for "fair"

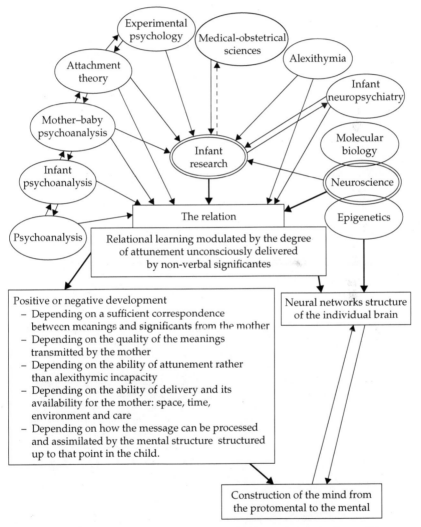

Figure 4. Multidisciplinarity: for Perinatal Clinical Psychology. Diagram by Imbasciati & Cena, 2014.

or "good" parents, therefore increasing their parenting skills, so that they can raise children who in their turn will be better and then they will raise better individuals. This could trigger off a transgenerational circuit that improves rather than worsens.

In order for the above principles of prevention-treatment dictated by the scientific discoveries on the origin of the mind and the structuring of the brain of children, and therefore on their fate as adults and future parents, to penetrate the Italian healthcare milieu, in the first place, all birth operators will have to be involved in training initiatives which give them the elementary principles of psychology concerning birth which are applicable to their health and social profession.

I started to work in this direction, together with many colleagues, to organise training courses in the Faculty (no longer called that today!) of Medicine of the University of Brescia, involving in an ad hoc educational channel (Perinatal Clinical Psychology) not only psychologists who work with children, but also midwives, gynaecologists, paediatricians, nurses, healthcare advisors, infant neuropsychiatrists, neonatologists, social workers, educators, crèche operators, and psychiatrists and anyone else who was interested in finding out about this subject, parents included. These courses were held annually, on many full days of work, reports, discussions and debates.

Deeming it desirable that similar initiatives can be multiplied in Italy, a schematic figure (Figure 4) is presented here, illustrating the integration of multiple and different subjects in their convergence to promote and study "relationality" which features in "our" Perinatal Clinical Psychology.

CHAPTER SIX

A new metapsychology congruent with neuroscience*

The icon of "Freudian theory"

I have outlined in the previous chapters how, at the current state of the art of the different sciences of the mind, neurosciences in the first place, it is possible to define what is to be understood by the term "mind", in its inseparable unity with what we know about the human brain: this is beyond the entrenched prejudicial convictions derived from Western philosophy and theology and from last century's psychiatry, with their concepts and terms, used to try to understand it. A complete or at least adequate comprehension of what appears to us as the extreme complexity of homo sapiens and even more of the human being as he has currently evolved (*cf.* epigenetics) is anything but easy, even in the light of current sciences; it is anything but easy with respect to the scientific instruments available to study what we could define "the marvellous hardware that builds up its billions of software programs

---

*Some of the topics in this chapter, matured in many of my previous works, were dealt with in a more limited way in the chapter of the same name in a previous book (Cena & Imbasciati, 2014), Here I present a more extensive and updated presentation in the specific situation of this book: the psychoanalytic Institution in the face of innovations from neurosciences.

on its own"; it is anything but easy with respect to the conceptualising inference of our conscious reflection on what, within the limits of consciousness, we can reflect on what we feel happening in ourselves.

We have emphasised the limits, differences of forms and degrees, and the misleading nature of our consciousness, with the consequent illusions and tenacious convictions which our emotional structure so often makes falsely lucid as to deem them unequivocally "true". Freud was the first to venture into this intricate and obscure world, discovering that the mind was not the obvious truth that his contemporaries believed. He discovered something important and called it the unconscious and tried to explore it by conceptualising it with the means that his intelligence, knowledge, experience and prudence allowed him to connect and interpret. Today we know much more, but by no means enough. Perhaps it is the anguish of knowing too little that makes us think that what Freud explained to us is still everything we can know about the mind today: this completeness is at present unsustainable, although fascinating in its harmony. This completeness has given rise to a veneration, not so much of the genius of the master but of everything that he wrote, although what he could write is now a century old.

Psychoanalysts maintain that psychoanalysis is a science: as a science psychoanalysis ought to evolve in time. Psychoanalysis has effectively evolved, but only on the clinical side, i.e., in the method and technique, whilst for the theory—theory in the proper sense, i.e., explaining the functioning of the mind (*cf.* below and Chapter Seven)—it seems to keep Freud's old Energy-drive Theory, even though this goes against current clinical and other theories that may have been clarified from the progress of clinical practice. Many authors argue that the Freudian theory has to be understood today in a metaphorical sense, but this removes the explicative meaning that it had in Freud and reduces it to a clinical model, depriving it of the very meaning of theory. The vocabulary of psychoanalysts continues to use terms which helped Freud's attempt to explain the human mind with the means available in that time. Today we consider this attempt superseded and to be abandoned, in the face of other discoveries and other hypotheses. Words such as drive, repression, libido, investment (= catexis) and also the way of understanding "consciousness", "making conscious" and others are still used: the words indicate concepts which date back to one hundred years ago. They are concepts conceived (precisely!) by Freud with the means and the knowledge which he had at that time, to explain the functioning of the mind. It can be said that these terms are used now with a different meaning compared to the original one, as a metaphor, but why are these terms still used? Don't we have today other terms that are more effective to indicate the different and new understanding of mental life that clinical psychoanalysis has offered us in the course of its progress?

Words always underpin an emotional semantic halo, whether we want to use them or not in that meaning, and the semantic halo speaks of their unconscious meaning in the mind of those using them, where there are the roots of the thought. All psychoanalysts know this, at clinical level, very well today, but it is hard to apply them to oneself, especially if this opens up questions that are in some way prohibited by an institutional spirit of the community. The community of the psychoanalytic Organisations[1] seems to obey the cult of the icons that were outlined by the master. The words are kept as though they were still suitable to indicate something that still "has to be" deemed valid; even though the relative concept has been so expanded as to appear transformed, or even different with respect to the meaning that it had had in his time. This is also the case for the term "unconscious", kept today even though it is known that it no longer indicates that part of the mind that Freud thought he could make conscious, but that it is the essence of the mind as a whole. The specific object of study of psychoanalysis can no longer be said to be the unconscious but the capacities for consciousness of those who investigate it (Imbasciati, 2014b), as we will continue to explain later on.

In Freud's time, having discovered that a part of the mind made man act and regulated his body, beyond his conscious introspections, was fundamental and revolutionary; this is the unconscious, inconceivable at that time, so that Freud had to immediately do his utmost to explain it. He wrote his *On Metapsychology* (Freud, 1915), the first two essays of which hypothesised an explanation and justification for the existence of this "unconscious": this hypothesis, thanks to the wisdom of the master, revealed a sort of witch (Imbasciati, 2013b), but which the psychoanalysts started to worship as a goddess and which is still venerated as a metaphorical icon, perhaps to protect ourselves from our "not knowing".

My studies concentrated for a long time on the work that Freud entitled *On Metapsychology* (1915) and its fate in the Institutions of psychoanalysis. I believe that a serene criticism of some explanatory concepts, which Freud, in his time, opportunely wanted to show, is

92   MINDBRAIN, PSYCHOANALYTIC INSTITUTIONS, AND PSYCHOANALYSTS

the fundamental assumption to open up our knowledge on the human mind, to understanding what we know today about its origin, development and functions.

Beyond Freud

Most of the works of psychoanalysis tend to trace back to Freud what psychoanalysis tells us today. This is a praiseworthy hagiographic intention, but perhaps we should on the contrary travel down the roads that start from Freud to go as far away as possible.

Freud formulated his metapsychology (1915): it was his intention to explain what the psychoanalytic method allowed him to observe in patients. The theoretical conception that he developed was called the Energy-drive Theory. Its cardinal concepts (drive, repression, libido, energy, dynamic, economy) were useful for almost a century for all psychoanalysts. This theoretical structure has been criticised for a few decades now. We have to ask what it was for and if it is still necessary today and whether we have to continue following and developing this path, or whether we should mark out other similar ones but in different directions. We also have to ask what Freud intended then, what he proposed for the future and how the theoretical conception that he offered can be considered today.

At first, the criticisms of metapsychology were subdued, but then they gradually became more explicit, and often another theorisation was implied but without daring to state an alternative: the shadow of the great master seems to have prevented this. A common denominator underpinning these criticisms emphasises the biologistic structure of Freud, in line with the sciences of the period, but contrasting with the subsequent developments of neurophysiology and, today, in the neuroscience. Another common denominator is the observation of a certain detachment between the theory and the clinical practice of Freud himself. Here I will point out some stages, fundamental in my opinion, of that path of the science of psychoanalysis. This path could be summarised as the progressive passage from an endogenist theory and focused on the individual, to the various developments of the theories of relationships, focused on experience.

Fairbairn was perhaps the first to clearly state his conviction that it is not libido that gives shape ("invests") the objects of reality, which in that way become psychic objects, but the objects encountered ("real parents") give shape to the libido, and that it is the search of the object and the encountered object which condition psychic development, and not the original endogenous source of the drives (Fairbairn, 1952; Guntrip, 1961). As early as 1965, Holt produced a substantial work with the significant title, "A review of Freud's biological assumptions and their influence on his theories" (Holt, 1965). Here, precisely because we are talking about the neuroscience, i.e., neurobiology, I believe it is fundamental here, to recall that the biological assumptions of Freudian metapsychology have been considered both of little coherence with its clinical practice and no longer justifiable by current neurobiology.

Freud took nineteenth century neurophysiology, dominated by electrophysiological studies, as his model: electrophysiology, by implying the importance of electric charges, suggested a conception of a flow of energy at the basis of the functioning of the brain; it was therefore logical to transpose this conception to an explanation of the mental processes, Other principles of the sciences of the period, such as those of thermodynamics, homeostasis, and communicating vases, contributed to the Freudian formulation of the concept of drive and therefore of a more general dynamic of energy quanta, with a consequent economy, which would have explained the origin and the development of the mental "system".

This theory had the merit of offering Freud a political strategy of establishing psychoanalysis as a science, with a "strong" theory in tune with that of the other contemporary sciences. Time passed, however, and sciences progressed. Holt again produced other works with significant titles: "Freud's mechanistic and humanistic image of man" (1972) and "Drive or wish? A reconsideration of the psychoanalytic theory of motivation", and the volumes he edited with Peterfreund, in the series Psychoanalysis and Contemporary Sciences (Holt & Peterfreund, 1972, 1976). They comment on the divergence, if not the contrast, between Freud the clinician, who investigated the psychology of man, and Freud the theoretician who wanted to explain it with a biological model which inevitably becomes mechanistic. Another work by Holt (1981) has the significant title of "The death and transfiguration of metapsychology" and appeared in the official journal of the IPA. The inadequacy of the Freudian metapsychology was thus recognised, unless it is "transfigured".

This is, in my opinion, an attempt to discreetly tell the audience that venerated Freud, that his metapsychology had to be changed, or at least

94 MINDBRAIN, PSYCHOANALYTIC INSTITUTIONS, AND PSYCHOANALYSTS

its way of being understood had to be changed. In the community of psychoanalysts, we come across a subterranean current of reticence, almost shame, to openly "repudiate" some parts of the Freudian work: Freud is "the master" and his theory is a doctrine, and as such, cloaked in sacredness. Sometimes, the sacredness prevents clarifying the object of knowledge.

In the meantime, Peterfreund (1971) proposed a new explanatory system of mental functioning, based on the principles of computer science: a new metapsychology, not stated as such, which was more in line with what was being discovered by the neurosciences. In the 1970s there was a proliferation of critical literature on metapsychology, but this mass of studies was followed by silence and even today Freudian metapsychology forms part of the training for trainee psychoanalysts. Pulver, in 1971, published in the *International Journal* an article which in my opinion went unnoticed, but was important: "Can affects be unconscious?" The author, examining a thread running through Freud's work, shows that Freud presumed that affects "had to be" conscious and therefore used his wits to consider the various reasons why analysis found unconscious affects. How can affects be unconscious? This is what the title says. This article actually contains the embryo of a problem which we can explain much better today. What is found in analysis as "affect" is made up of what the analyst infers and/or from what the patient can realise and express in the setting: both these events are mediated by the consciousness, the analyst's "equipped" one and that of the patient made more conscious by the analysis. We can therefore conclude that what is called affect is psychoanalysis is a mental event, or a product of the mind, which reaches us as it is filtered by some consciousness; or better, by some capacity for consciousness.[2] The affect, when observed, is conscious—to the person who observes it. So, what is the unconscious affect? It is what is inferred that there must have been before the analyst or the patient realise it. However, this raises the problem of what it is made up of, beyond, or before the description, that the expression of the patient—the possible verbalisation—as well as the capacity for consciousness of the analyst allow.

An explanation is necessary. We have to go from the clinical level to the theoretical level: the former is what is experienced, albeit always experienced through some capacity for consciousness; the second is made up of hypotheses that explain to us what may happen beyond every experience and description, i.e., beyond every form of consciousness that can indicate it to the person investigating it. In this hypothesis we can use the contribution of other sciences. The explanation was the intention of metapsychology (Imbasciati, 2005b): Freud used his intelligence to explain what could happen in the mind beyond what he had been able to describe with the psychoanalytic method. This is equivalent to saying beyond what we can describe with our capacities for consciousness.

It is worthwhile recalling the distinction between description and explanation, underlined by the epistemologists, but in my opinion not very clear in psychoanalytic debates on theories and the very concept of "theory". Any informative exposure of an observed event has a descriptive level which is useful for understanding the "how" of the phenomenon observed and an explanatory level which attempts to infer its "why". This would be better underlined by using "explicate" rather than "explain". The description is in relation to discoveries, made possible by observatory methods and instruments, whilst explanation has to do with the invention of some theory, of which confirmation is sought in experience, experimental or in any case practical, clinical in our case. Many epistemologists maintain that the real why is never reached, but it is precisely for this reason that a science progresses: the invention of theories is believed to drive new observational methods and instruments, which in turn allow new discoveries and this would lead to new theories. This way we would reach the ultimate why; in philosophy this journey is defined as the passage from the *post hoc* to the *propter hoc*. In this perspective, if a science progresses, the theories change: they would thus never be true or false, but only useful at a given moment in the development of a science.

This clarifies the concept of what can be understood by "theory". As far as psychoanalysis is concerned, the term and the concept, in my opinion, are to be reserved for a general theory on the origins, development and functioning of the mind, reserving the term of theoretical model to descriptive-interpretative hypotheses which are only metaphorically explanatory, and concerning partial and mainly clinical aspects of the mind (Imbasciati, 2004, 1998b, 2005a, 2005b, 2006a, 2006b). It would be pointless for me to discuss this subject at length, and I refer readers to my previous works (Imbasciati, 2013b). Nor is it possible to dwell at length on the very substantial literature by others, even vaster and richer, to be quoted here exhaustively. I will therefore limit myself to the quotations that may be of use to those who want further clarifications

96   MINDBRAIN, PSYCHOANALYTIC INSTITUTIONS, AND PSYCHOANALYSTS

on the leitmotiv I will follow, and in parallel quote only those authors who can be usefully linked to this leitmotiv.

Schafer (1975) wrote, again in the official journal of the IPA, "Psychoanalysis without Psychodynamics", presenting a psychoanalysis which does not have recourse to the dynamic concepts (force, energy) of Freud, i.e., a psychoanalysis without the Freudian metapsychology, A year later, Gill entitled a chapter in a book (Gill, 1976), "Metapsychology is not psychology". Freudian metapsychology is considered as having little coherence with the clinical corpus of that psychological science which is developing as psychoanalysis. This theory is confirmed and perfected in the book, unfortunately never completed, by George Klein (1976). It presents a psychoanalysis without all the dynamic concepts and terms proper to metapsychology, which is considered a confused biologistic legacy and no longer biological, of the nineteenth century.

In one of my books, on the basis of an exegesis of Freud's work, I maintain that metapsychology is a theory constructed by progressive and undue generalisations from the conscious sexual experience of the male (Imbasciati, 2005a). It is therefore a methodologically "wrong" theory from the explanatory point of view (regardless of any coherence with neurosciences) as it starts from a hypostasis, or reification of conscious feelings and pasts. It was constructed from the tenacious explanatory intention of Freud and was very useful. If it is no longer so, as well as considering why and how it was useful, we have to ask whether we can reformulate the explanatory intention of Freud otherwise: a new metapsychology?

Freud's intention

The term "meta", which Freud, after some hesitation, wanted to use in his 1915 essays (there should have been nine, we only have five of them: goodness knows what he was thinking for the others!) aimed to mean a psychology beyond (= meta) what until then "psychology" was thought to be. At the time, mental coincided with what the individual could consciously feel and report: psychology essentially meant psychology of the consciousness. A psychology in a scientific sense which disregarded the consciousness of the individual was not conceivable: introspection, considered innate with the consciousness and with the natural endowment equally possessed by all human beings, was an indispensable condition for an experimental psychology. Only the words of writers and some philosophers intuitively put forward an unconscious, but at scientific level, "psychology" was psychology of the consciousness. We can recall the School of Wurzburg, founded by Külpe (1883), whose contributions were certainly known to Freud.

The inference of unconscious psychic processes, made possible by the psychoanalytic method, was a revolutionary discovery: "metapsychology" therefore means a psychology beyond the consciousness. Freud's discovery, as it was revolutionary, demanded an explanation in the face of the conception of psychology which at the time, as an *"a-priori"*, dominated. Freud sought this explanation, constructing a series of hypotheses that he arranged in a theory that explained the origins and the functioning of the mind in relation to the discovery of the unconscious. The theory, like all theories, was a conceptual invention that had to be in tune with the sciences of the time and at the same time with psychoanalytic clinical practice. *"Trieb"* corresponds exactly to what is found at clinical level: the impelling nature of a tendency, the "drive". This would be the English term that most corresponds to what the subject can "feel", i.e., what he can become aware of. The German term was in ordinary use and lent itself well to multiple and comprehensible meanings: translated into other languages, especially with neo-Latin terms (*pulsione, pulsion, pulçao*), but also with instinct, it took on an esoteric flavour, with a semantic halo that lends itself to consecrate as ascertained what Freud only wanted to wish for; that in the future a biochemical substratum of the drives would be discovered, concretely conforming his theory: a flow of energy that can be identified in the flow of the "libido" Freud, (1895, p. 200; 1905a [1901], p. 113f; 1905b, p. 168f, 214f, 218f; 1906, p. 277f; 1914, p. 78; 1915, p. 125; 1915–1917, p. 320; 1931, p. 240; 1933a, p. 96). "Libido" however, is a concept which refers to a psychological hypothesis and not to a physical reality. If on the other hand, we keep the term drive in the general sense of a "force" (= *trieb*) and we remain on the descriptive clinical level, the concept lends itself well to describe what we can feel and observe in ourselves as well as in the patients: we keep the sense of a metaphor for the term to better contextualise what is observed at clinical level. The Americans are right to use "drive" rather than instinct, as in British English.

Trieb is therefore a relatively simple clinical observation, of the descriptive type, and as such expressed by a word used in ordinary German; today we would say motivation (Lichtenberg, 1989). Its being unconscious (with everything that this entails, for example repression), does not lie in the observation in itself, but in the explanation that Freud tried to give of it; an attempt to pass from the clinical observation to a biological kind of explanation.

The Energy-drive Theory and its concepts are hypotheses, put forward by Freud with the cognitions of the time: as these hypotheses, desired, were not ascertained and indeed today we have many elements that contradict them, the theory can remain as a framework which lends itself to collecting what we observe in the patients, but this framework is only metaphorical. We can use it metaphorically, i.e., at clinical level, but it is a quite different matter if we think that under aspects, which appear to contextualise and orient our clinical practice, there are analogous biological processes that explain how the drives originate; how they are distributed, how they condition the individual or how there is a repression of the contents of consciousness and so on. Making the clinical observation equal to its explanation means giving credit to the hopes of Freud as though it had been ascertained: as though the biochemical substratum of the drives, as well as of repression, had been discovered. This was not the case, however: psychoanalysts (and with this term I am not limiting myself to the IPA) continue to use concepts and terms as though they referred to events that explain (in the proper sense: "to explicate") what happens in the patients. In other words, there has been a reification of abstract hypotheses. Freud had, in my opinion, felt there was such a risk when he called his metapsychology "witch" (Freud, 1937; Fabrozzi & Ortu, 1996; Vassalli, 2006). At present, many declare his concepts metaphorical, however in their clinical work they use them as scientifically proven explications: it is easy to slip emotively into reification.

Freud wanted to find an explanation in the terms of what after him was identified as a specific discipline called Psychophysiology: to explicate psychic events by physiological processes. Freud's explanation, obviously, drew on the neurophysiology of the time and the models of other sciences of the period. In the light of current psychoanalytic knowledge, the metapsychological level requires a new and different explication (psychophysiological) in line with current neurosciences.

In current psychoanalytic language often we hear "becoming conscious", or the act of keeping consciousness and so on,[3] as they were the basis of psychoanalytic process. But consciousness is not an on/off process. Psychoanalytic process is the work of two abilities of consciousness, in the relational moment of the setting, which try to describe to the proper self (and in a comprehensible way to others) what happens in their subjectivities: the psychoanalyst's one and the patient's one. Unfortunately, sometimes the psychoanalyst thinks his own description may happen also in the patient. We can then also wonder, about this "thing" or these somethings, not only how what is felt in clinical practice takes place but also why: what happens in the mind beyond what our instruments of consciousness try to describe? How does the mind work? Why does it work like that? These questions have to be asked not only for that moment, when some consciousness is reached, but "before" in the massive submerged part of the iceberg of non-aware processes. Such an explanation can only come about by equating an explanation of the mental processes with what neurosciences explain to us about the brain. The answer to "Why the unconscious?" is taken for granted today but it lies in the work by our brain which never stops.

These considerations however, are still waiting for a scientific status coherent from the point of view of a psychological theorisation and one that is new at the same time. A new scientific status has to be given to unconscious processes, as a work by Westen says, before asking "Is Freud really dead?" (Westen, 1999). Above all, it has to be clarified whether and to what extent and how these processes can be made conscious in some way, and not only for the patient but in the analyst's mind as well. This means that it has to be investigated how consciousness is formed in the analyst who feels that he has understood something of a patient at a given moment, and whether this something corresponds to another "something" that can be recognised by the patient. Today we know that much of the unconscious work of our mind is averbal, i.e., purely emotional processes: can these be translated into "some" language? "Language" or *langue*? Today, presuming as obvious that this has to be a verbal language, as if it was the only innate form in the "consciousness", appears a legacy of the consciousnessism of the past centuries. The accent on the efficacy of verbal interpretation by the analyst appears fairly naïve. Today, communication between the analyst and patient is said to take place from unconscious to unconscious: how then can it be better described? But above all how can it be explained and how and what does it "get across"? (*cf.* Chapter Three).

An explanatory intention as was Freud's is to be pursued, for the progress of psychoanalysis: just as Freud did then with the help of other sciences of the period, we should do the same today with present-day sciences, thus pursuing explicative hypotheses.

100 MINDBRAIN, PSYCHOANALYTIC INSTITUTIONS, AND PSYCHOANALYSTS

Let's look at what drove Freud to "pursue" the explanation. Much has been said about his political intention: to give psychoanalysis a status so that it could be accepted as a "science"; this could be obtained by showing a theory that explained its discoveries in a way similar to that required of the sciences of the time, as an explication of the phenomena observed. Therefore, metapsychology represented Freud's political strategy. In my opinion, the master's truly scientific curiosity was driven by other motives. Here I will consider two of these: the discovery of the enormous variability between individuals in the psychic and the correlated one of the *Nachträglichkeit*.

In the panorama of medical sciences, the assumption that the psychic functions depended essentially on the functioning of the brain and that this was the same for all humans (for genetic reasons, unless it had been compromised by some cause: *cf*. Chapter Four), was dominating. The concept of illness and the dichotomy normality/pathology was understood in terms of linear causality, depending on a cause that had altered the natural norm: this was taken for granted both for the physical and for the psychic. The consequence of such an assumption was that, except for cases of pathology (which would all have to be explained), the psychic functioning had to be the same for everyone. On the other hand, how was the psychic functioning catalogued? In large categories: affectivity, cognition, conation (will?), orientation in time and space, and so on. Today these categories appear to us all-inclusive, because with the observational instruments (including the psychoanalytic one) we have today, we know how many different functions there are under each of those labels. To the psychiatric observation of the time and the psychological one (cosciousnessistic and introspective one, let's remember the School of Külpe, 1883), the aforementioned categories appeared simple and unitary, so they were observed as though they were the same for all subjects: except for those, as stated, which were declared "pathological" and which were considered as damaged in their "normal" functioning by some "cause" acting on the brain. If, in people considered "normal" any inter-individual variability was found, it was attributed to their bringing up, considered extraneous to the "brain" or to genetics, or "temperaments" were invoked, with their genetic-endocrinal presupposition.

Freud, on the other hand, with his instrument, could observe "the psychic" in more detail, and came up against a new fact: how different one individual could be from another "because affects" and therefore in

A NEW METAPSYCHOLOGY CONGRUENT WITH NEUROSCIENCE   101

the behaviour, in conducts and in life's destinies, without it being justified to speak of "pathology". In the face of the acknowledgement of this enormous (infinite) possibility of variations in the inter-individual psychic functioning (Imbasciati, 2005b), the Energy-drive Theory, with the concept of "investment" was presented as an excellent explanatory key: nature (the "source") of drives and their economics dynamics (investment of objects, counterinvestments, repression) could explain in terms analogous with those of the neurology of the time (bioelectric charges as a biochemical support of drives) the inter-individual variability discovered through the psychoanalytic method.

The other reason, which I choose to recall here, is the discovery, disconcerting at the time, that the memory, with the passing of time, cannot simply cancel itself out, but continuously changes: the present modifies the past, this is *Nachträglichkeit*.

Freud and memory

In Freud's time, the memory was considered more or less still as Ebbinghaus (1885) and many other pioneers of psychology had studied it: an engraved trace, i.e., faithful to the reality that had been perceived and as such remembered: if it was not faithful, it was not considered memory, but deficit of memory. The memory was conceived as "all or nothing": either one remembered or forgot. The principle of constancy, as defined by Katz (1944) for perception, was extended to the whole of memory. The concept and the use of the term "engraved" recalls what can be engraved on a tombstone. This is also how the experimentalists of the time considered learning: either something was learned correctly or it was not learned. These conceptions still remain in popular culture; "If you remember well, lucidly with conviction, what you remember is what truly happened in the reality which you witnessed." Memory is made to coincide with recollection and people are amazed that it is not so. A psychology of testimony, as was experimentally cultivated by the School of Gestalt,[4] is still not assimilated in the common mind: resistance, we can say as psychoanalysts. In Freud's time, however, in the framework of the scientific psychology straddling the two centuries, a memory beyond consciousness, or other than the reality perceived, and changeable in time and above all to be distinguished with respect to the recollection, was not conceivable. On the other hand, the brain and the sensory systems were considered faithful sound-image recorders of

102 MINDBRAIN, PSYCHOANALYTIC INSTITUTIONS, AND PSYCHOANALYSTS

reality. The discovery of *Nachträglichkeit* was disconcerting and Freud, in order to explain it, had recourse to supposing that events were "transcribed" and "retranscribed" in the memory (Imbasciati, 2002b, 2005b). Although in "Remembering, repeating and working through" Freud (1914) gave the greatest importance to the work of working through (*Durcharbeiten*) of the recollection and therefore suggests his intuition on the characteristics of memory known today (Riolo, 2005), the conception of memory which he uses more often elsewhere is that in line with the concept of memory in the general culture of the time. When he speaks of transcription and retranscription, the concept that emerges is that any retranscription is not the continuous changing physiological transforming of every memory, but a "special" event, of which the causes had to be investigated; for instance, an important event (like the concept of "trauma") and that could have caused the retranscription or at any rate invoking the "affects", considered events other than the "mental", as responsible for the changes (alterations?!) of the memory.[5]

Today we know that the memory does not change for particular causes, but that it is in continuous physiological mutation, and above all that the affects are to be considered in exactly the same way as other mental functions, and above all those elementary psychic functionalities that regulate the type of working through of each cognition, therefore of every acquisition (learning) and of every memory. The memory is *"per se"* changeable in that it does part of the global and continuous work of the central nervous system.

Underlying the consideration of a static and faithful memory, there was in Freud's time the assumption of a brain that was the same for everyone, on condition that it worked in a "norm" deemed laid down exclusively by nature. A "normal" brain was believed to have a "normal" memory and cognition. As for learning, the base of every recollection, it was considered (and perhaps still is today) a natural and simple "carrying inside" the brain (and inside the memory) what the sensory systems recept. Recollection was considered, as a consequence, a carrying outside what was learned. On the scientific horizon of the time, there still was not (and there still is not in the common feeling) the idea of the complex work implied in all learning, nor of the complex processing inside the memory, as a continuous integration of what has been processed with what the brain is continuously processing, including regarding what it itself becomes capable of producing (Imbasciati & Margiotta, 2005; Imbasciati, 2005b).

A NEW METAPSYCHOLOGY CONGRUENT WITH NEUROSCIENCE 103

As for the affects, the psychology that was contemporary with Freud considered them completely crudely and consciousnessial: the merit goes to our master for having discovered their complexity, importance and unawareness and their integration with the memory: today we can say with cognition. This would open up the difficult matter of how the entrenched historical Western distinction between affect and cognition has distorted psychology and psychoanalysis (Imbasciati, 1989b, 1998b, 2005b, 2006a, 2006b; also *cf.* Chapter Two). Perhaps this is why the word learning was banned from the psychoanalytic lexicon for decades (we had to wait for Bion, to find it again) as well as the word memory. This memory, however, precisely starting from Freud, marked the opening of the road which today has led to experimental psychology and the neuroscience considering how it escapes every consciousnessial cataloguing: today we have the discoveries of the implicit memory.

No longer memory of objects, no longer representational memory, but *memory of functions*, from the most elementary ones, for example motor, to the most complex ones, like the way of functioning of what we have called so far affects, or defences or conflicts or motivations, or even "internal working models", relative to styles of attachment, or the obscure psychosomatic connections: not simply of the brain to the soma, but from what happens in that brain, i.e., in the mind that has been constructed in the brain, to that soma, and from this to the mind and in the soma itself: see Pert's theory (Pert, 1997; Amadei, 2005) on the possibility of neuromodulators in the whole organism, i.e., that the mind is in the whole body. More in general, we consider a memory which concerns all those acquisitions which are observed in the infant in the early months of life (*cf.* Chapter Four).

It is a memory which is absolutely unconscious, indeed which cannot be made conscious, as it is without any "form", we could say ineffable: an unconscious that has not been repressed, some say. Beyond the terminologies we may choose, the neurosciences have highlighted two systems of memory, one focused on the amygdala, already in function at birth and another focused on the hippocampal formations, which start functioning after a few months of life. At the time of these first discoveries, an unconscious that had not been repressed was attributed to the former system (Mancia, 1998, 2004a, 2004b; Mancia & Longhin, 1998): this unconscious is believed to be connected with the areas that oversee the implicit memory and which would concern the most primitive functions. The repressed unconscious, as explained by Freud, also called the "dynamic unconscious" was attributed to the latter system. The "dynamic unconscious" was attributed with the specific quality that would have made it interpretable with words. These distinctions today appear arbitrarily identified; today it is proven that the first system (amygdale) has to do with the implicit memory, but as in the early times of life everything is constructed as an implicit memory; other systems have not yet been formed.

The implicit memory concerns the functioning of the neural networks of almost all the memory. As for the second system, although true throughout the development of the baby's memory, in the adult it is also connected indissolubly with the whole memory, i.e., to the implicit one. The fact that something unconscious is translated into the possibility of some consciousness also belongs to work by the whole brain; hippocampus included, but it is not the hippocampus that produces it. The hippocampus is essential for almost all the functions, just as it is a general rule (*cf.* Chapter Three) whereby a certain area of the brain may be indispensable for certain functions but not sufficient, as these functions are always produced by a much wider system of connections. Lastly, connecting the concept of unconscious to that of memory, shows no neurological reason for the concept of repression. We could, at the most, think that the continuous work of the memory, i.e., the work of *all* the neural connections, can originate different degrees and forms of consciousness and that this sometimes involves the possibility of *some* verbalisation, perhaps in a continuum,[6] but this is not to do with a pushing back (repression = *Verdrängung*). It is one thing that there is the possibility of *some* verbalisation of *some* form of memory, it is another matter to connect it with the neurologised concept, i.e., reified, of repression; this concept was and remains purely speculative, for the explanation that Freud could suppose. The distinction between repressed unconscious/non-repressed unconscious is due to the old concept of an unconscious-memory as a store: there is no store, the memory is continuous work, changing in its effects on the result that may appear to the consciousness.

Distinguishing two kinds of unconscious is a stratagem to save a Freudian icon. If we assume that there is some force that represses or better removes something that otherwise would have been conscious, we presuppose that the psychic has to be conscious, unless something intervenes that removes it. This is an assumption from before the old consciousnessist psychology, according to which everything should have been conscious.

On the contrary, today we know that everything is unconscious, except the cases in which those functions which originate some consciousness enter into action (Edelman, 1989, 1992; Dennet, 1991; Imbasciati, 2005b; Siegel, 1999; Schore, 2003a, 2003b). What we observe at clinical level is that the patient cannot "understand" what the psychoanalyst tells him with the interpretation and is unable to assimilate it; this is what Freud called resistance (= *Viederstand*) and not repression (= *Verdrangung*). We also observe that something that was clear (seemed?), subsequently no longer is clear: forgotten? Do we say that it has been repressed? In both cases we make an illegal leap from the descriptive clinical level to an unproven explanatory level. Is this due to a reification of concepts?

The concept of unconscious therefore needs to be reformulated. Freud, discovering something that existed before any consciousness, of the patient and the analyst, felt the need, in the cultural climate of his time, to explain its existence, and he started off from the question "Why the unconscious?" This question has dominated psychoanalytic research. Today however, the question can be different. The unconscious, indeed the unconscious-implicit memory, is the substance of the memory and memory is the most substance of mind. On the other hand, we do not really know what we have hastily called consciousness is.

The difference and contamination between theory and clinical practice: what image for psychoanalysis?

During the course of my professional experience, especially as a supervisor, I have experienced how metapsychology can be misleading with respect to the mutative (therapeutic) intention pursued by analysis. Referring to metapsychology whilst performing clinical practice, i.e., with the patient, is, I believe, unanimously recognised as a handicap, and indeed some colleagues (Ferro, 2011) openly maintain that while we are with the patient we must not keep any theory in mind. In the clinical descriptions comparing psychoanalysts, it may be opportune to refer the clinical finding to the theory, but which one? In addition. what is meant by the term "theory"? In clinical reports, there is frequent reference to the Energy-drive Theory stated by Freud in his metapsychology (1915): repression, drive, investment, libido, ego, es, and superego are recurring terms. This also happens however when the pure and simple description of the session does not seem to imply a conceptualisation corresponding to the drive theory (obsequiousness to the icon?), even when, for instance, highlighting the analyst/patient relationship, reference is made to the concept of projective identification, which belongs, if anything, to another theory. Or perhaps is this a concept that is not properly theoretical but clinical? It refers effectively to something observed clinically. Not to a hypothesis of biological functioning, as in the Freudian explanatory concepts. Freudian concepts must be understood as metaphors, people will say, but did Freud mean them this way when he hoped that the drive would have biological support? (1895, p. 200; 1905a [1901], p. 113f; 1905b, p. 168f, 214f, 218f; 1906, p. 277f; 1914, p. 78; 1915, p. 125; 1915–1917, p. 320; 1931, p. 240; 1933a, p. 96).

More than metaphors, as today many understand them, they were "explicative hypotheses", with respect to the events "described" in the clinical finding. A distinction is therefore necessary between "description" and "explanation", or better "explication", to define what theory is and what clinics, or method, or technique are. In the descriptions of cases, concepts may also be mixed without defining them whether they are theories or names of clinical findings. Besides concepts by one author (for instance Freud) are mixed with those by another author (for example Klein, or others) without any concern over checking whether they are contradictory. Sometimes different theories are opposed, for example "relational" theories against "drive" ones, but without specifying their effective contradictory nature. The tendency is thus found to want to make everything get along, which means "putting everything together", old and new, clinical and theoretical, discoveries and inventions-explanatory hypotheses. This way you can hear that Freud discovered drives: are they discoveries? Or hypotheses that Freud himself defined "our mythology" (Freud, 1937), "the Witch" (Imbasciati, 2013b).

I have noticed, for example, how colleagues, whose clinical practice (illustrated in their reports) has seemed excellent to me and in line with the progress that has changed psychoanalysis in many past decades (which presupposes clinical and theoretical concepts of recent acquisition), use words that refer, on the other hand, to the old metapsychological explanation—repression, investment, drives, libido, Ego-Es-Superego—without the relative concepts showing correspondence with what, from their description, appears to have taken place in the patient's mind (as well as in that of the analyst): almost as though the use of terms was approximate, or even casual, or merely conventional, or ritual, in deference to venerated tradition. In these cases too, of optimal clinical practice, I have observed the obstacle of an implicit and submerged reference to old metapsychology (Imbasciati, 2013a). This has led me to think that, in the mind of many psychoanalysts, what is meant by "theory" is not sufficiently precise from the epistemological point of view. They talk of the usefulness of several theories simultaneously: this could be fully justified, if they were not in contradiction with one another; however, what "theory" means remains vague, without distinguishing this concept from that indicated by "model", without distinction between "theory" (in a word) and theoretical concept, and how these terms are not distinguished from what, on the other hand, should refer to the clinical observation of psychic and interpsychic events; such as the emotions felt to varying extents or which have occurred between the patient and the analyst; and the relative reciprocal changes in the progress in the short or long term in the relationship. Feeling, observing, understanding, describing, and explaining are verbs which each imply a concept of their own (like all the abstract words in our vocabulary). But which of these can be implied in what is called theory? In my opinion, only the last one, whilst the others more correctly should apply to clinical practice. For this distinction, what is meant by the term "theory" should preliminarily be defined.

A certain level of confusion therefore reigns in psychoanalysis, which authoritative colleagues have called the "Babel of languages" (Wallerstein, 1988, 2005), in my opinion euphemistically: if there is a Babel of words, there is a conceptual Babel, at the level of theory or better, at the level of what we want to distinguish as theory with respect to other conceptual terms coined to "understand" the situation found in clinical practice and described. There is a confusion between what is explanation and what is description of observed clinical events, above all those which constitute "discoveries", or methodological and technical suggestions for further investigation. If these confusions do not prevent analysts from understanding one another, between colleagues of the same work, it must not be forgotten that theory is useful to make a science progress and also, not to be underestimated, to present a science to scientists of different sciences, who, obviously, cannot be familiar with clinical practice and the relative ambiguity of description.

The term "theory" seems to be used by psychoanalysts in a polysemous way, as shown by the meanings of the term in Italian (and

108 MINDBRAIN, PSYCHOANALYTIC INSTITUTIONS, AND PSYCHOANALYSTS

English): "theory" can be understood in a strong sense, as a systematic set of general principles, hypotheses, and deductions which characterise a given science, or an event or a phenomenon contextualised by it, and which are used to explain and predict (e.g., theory of relativity, theory of the constitution of the atom, Copernican theory, theory of the evolution of the human species, etc.), but it can also indicate a set of rules or techniques to obtain a certain result; or even any abstract, speculative, or conjectural reasoning, to frame, if not explain, a certain phenomenon, up to meaning simply a point of view, or even imagine a hypothetical situation with respect to practical reality (e.g., in theory it ought to …).

Psychoanalysts talk of the Energy-drive Theory to refer to Freud's metapsychology, thus using the term in its strongest meaning. Similarly, in everyday language we hear "theory of psychoanalysis" as equivalent to "Freud's theory", almost always meaning by this expression the Energy-drive Theory of metapsychology. However, psychoanalysts speak of several theories, within psychoanalysis, distinguishing each time, "relational theories", in the plural, therefore assuming their differentiated plurality, opposed to the drive theory, just as they speak of object relations theory, theory of the Ego, theory of the self. In all these expressions, the term "theory" seems to be understood in the strong sense, as though framing, in different ways, the global functioning of the mind. This strong meaning is however, gradually diluted when saying, for instance, "theory of the projective identification" or "theory of the container/contained" or even "theory of listening" and "of listening to listening", framing in this way a particular clinically observed and recorded phenomenon, and not a general theory, up to using the term and concept of "theory" to indicate the particular vision (albeit always clinical) of an author: "Bion's theory", "Baranger's theory" and so on, indicating the point of view of a particular author, almost always in reference to particular clinical facts they have described.

In other words, alongside the first—strong—meaning of the term "theory", this word is used in another meaning, i.e., to indicate and "understand"—much more than to "explain" in a causal sense— particular and limited events, or the point of view of an author, i.e., in a completely different meaning of the term. In the first case, it is a way of enriching a particular description offering a key of comprehension rather than an effective explanation. A real "explication" is to be understood in a causal sense. I can recall here the fundamental distinction expressed by German scientific literature with *"erklaren"* compared

A NEW METAPSYCHOLOGY CONGRUENT WITH NEUROSCIENCE 109

to *"verstehen"*, used originally by Dilthey to frame the *"Geisteswissenschaft"* or science of the mind with respect to the sciences of nature. In the language of psychoanalysis, there is an unclear meaning of the term "theory": in particular, there is an epistemological shift between the level of the description and that of the explanation. This shift overshadows the difference between hypothesis of explanation and the way of describing a certain event, i.e., between an effective explicative theory—a historical example in the first essays of *On Metapsychology*—and clinical practice, as Freud already begins to do in the fifth essay. This, in my opinion, generates confusion, especially with those who are not sufficiently familiar with what psychoanalysis really is.

Elsewhere (Imbasciati, 1994, 1997, 1998a, 1998b, 1998c, 1998d, 2001a, 2001c, 2002a, 2002b, 2002c, 2004, 2005a, 2005b, 2006a, 2005b), I have noted how important it is to distinguish different epistemological levels in the language of psychoanalysts; one thing is the description (how, how well or the Latin *post hoc*) another is the explanation: why (*propter hoc*). I consider it fundamental that this distinction has to be clear, for two reasons: the first is that of stimulating in scholars of psychoanalysis the scientific investigation of the—causal—explanations of psychic events (Imbasciati, 2011b) and not only noting the sequences of clinical events observed, the second is to allow non-specialists to understand how psychoanalysis explicates human behaviour: and how it explicates it today, not how Freud was able to do so one hundred years ago. This last reason for the aforementioned distinction, overlooked by psychoanalysts, leads to discerning the possibility of distinguishing what the explanation one hundred years ago was with respect to the current progress of clinical practice. In this way how, as I will explain in detail below, there is the possibility of offering to those who, not being inside this science, may not have the ability to understand the fine distinctions between description and explanation and between clinical and theory but only the possibility of understanding a simple general theory, a public image: updated today, as it was for Freudian metapsychology which in its time became "the theory of psychoanalysis" (Imbasciati, 2013c).

The idea of an explanation of mental facts (however hypothetical and provisional it may be) can be better considered by those who are not inside psychoanalysis. This phenomenon is anything but unimportant for the public image[7] of psychoanalysis and for the prestige that psychoanalysis can enjoy, or not, with other scientists.

In order to be able to formulate such a theory in an updated way, there has to be a clear distinctiveness between description and explanation, which may be translated between clinical and theory; the former concerns the descriptive level, i.e., what is observed in the clinical setting and what is described in the most comprehensive ways possible to colleagues who have not yet been able to observe it, whilst the latter concerns the explanatory level, through abstractions from clinical observations, to formulate general hypotheses for their effective explication. In my opinion, this has to be clear for psychoanalysts themselves.

I can observe (= realise) that the patient induces something in me (or vice versa, I in him as well) and describe it, in the various ways I can; coining concepts, such as countertransference, projective identification, passage from unconscious to conscious, or other, or using the Bionian terms of beta element of alpha function, or referring to the "unthought known" of Ogden, or to the concept of the memory of the body, or others. I need terms and concepts to identify different nuances of what I have observed and sequences of psychic events identified in order to be better able to describe everything to colleagues. However, this is not yet an ultimate "explication". English-speakers talk of how and how well, but suggest a why, the ultimate explication, although they feel that it cannot necessarily be given; this is where we recur to hypotheses. Here we can formulate, or rather it would be better to say invent, a theory, in the strictest sense. This is therefore the invention, often reified and confused with a discovery. This is what Freud wanted to do with his Energy-drive Theory shown in his *On Metapsychology*. This theory is a general abstraction from all his previous clinical work to formulate a hypothesis of global explanation of the origin, development and functioning of the mind, conducted in terms of hard sciences.

After Freud the distinction was not so easy, because, while the clinical descriptions as well as being multiplied were diversified by their different viewpoints, the unity of the original Freudian explanation was missing; different "theories" were talked about, but without formulating them, let alone with the clarity and the intention of Freud, nor comparing or opposing them to the metapsychology of the master; and also using the term theory polyhedrically, including for simple clinical descriptions and observations in psychological terms, instead of for an explanation, effective even though "invented" and provisional, in terms of hard science.

It is true that when any phenomenon whatsoever is identified and observed, we try to connect it with other ones we know, and in the case of an observed sequence, we try immediately to connect the two or more events observed with one another; it is also true that this implies the implicit application of some theoretical pattern that makes the events observed more "intelligible", however, speaking in this case of "theory", extending the meaning of the term does not help the need to distinguish a particular fact from a coherent whole of connections, which in our case may help to frame mental functioning as a whole; not does it help, as said and as will be developed further on, the image of psychoanalysis.

For a definition of "theory" in psychoanalysis

The above distinction—describing/explicating—was, I believe, present in Freud's spirit; in writing his *On Metapsychology* he had the intention of giving a theoretical unity, a One Theory, to psychoanalysis and he also had a strategic intention: to make the other scientists, in other disciplines of the time understand that psychoanalysis was a science, since, as Freud deemed opportune to show, its psychological foundations were similar to events known in other ways to these other scientists. The strategic intention of metapsychology is confirmed by the fact that its concepts rapidly spread, making psychoanalysis known—in these terms—to the whole world, and from the fact that they have still stubbornly remained in current culture, even though psychoanalytic clinical practice has changed enormously and the references to the other sciences even more. This last event is due, in my opinion, to the fact that psychoanalysts, after the strategic promotional explanatory attempt by the master, no longer dared to formulate another one that was more up to date, which today I believe would be more effective and, I think, more popular.

The persistence of the old Freudian pattern has been fostered, on the other hand, by the fact that the current scholar of other sciences (who about psychoanalysis may only know a few theoretical notions) who wanted to approach the other "theories" that today psychoanalysts propose, would be in great difficulty, both due to their great complexity, and above all as these theories, lacking a formulation in the strictest sense of what is meant by "theory", are not formulated with ad hoc accuracy, nor are they even compared with the original "Freudian theory", as well as being confused with clinical practice.

With so much talk for many decades in psychoanalysis on the clinical importance of relationality, gradually describing its complexity (from

112   MINDBRAIN, PSYCHOANALYTIC INSTITUTIONS, AND PSYCHOANALYSTS

the discovery of countertransference to projective identification, up to speaking of non-verbal communication from unconscious to unconscious and all the transformations of the unconscious structures of the analysand and of the analyst's one, following the reciprocal dialogue of the two unconsciouses), up to speaking of theories, first "objectual" then "relational" or something else, these "theories" (note the plural) have not, in my opinion, been formulated accurately, without a clear comparison been made with the Freudian drive theory; if somebody have ventured into this question, their work has remained in the shadow of the Institution.[8] The dating of the works I mention in the section "Beyond Freud" above is paradigmatic: they are works which are fifty years old. The comparison, in my opinion, should today hesitate in an opposition or at least make clear a contradiction. In this latter case, the comparison all the more so should involve, both a finalisation of a new theory and making explicit that the previous one has been superseded and can have value only as a heuristic historical example.

For example, stating, consequentially to the above, that every psychic process in analysis is relational, seems to contradict the endogenous instinct theory on the origin of drives, unless we want to stretch out infinitely the concept of object investment on the analyst. In this case too, the origin of the drives remains linked, if we follow Freud, to the instinctuality of the body—erogenous zones understood biologically as the primary source of energy[9]— in contradiction with what we know, from infant psychoanalysis and psychoanalytic clinical practice derived from the applicative development of attachment theory, that it is the primary foetus/mother caregiver/child (need for protection) relationship, and not a genetic inscription (erogenous zones sources of libido); which structures a "corporal mind" (implicit memory, "incarnate" mind, biological processes too); and it is the subsequent significant relations (the analysis itself) that continues in this structuring, by structuring the relative neural networks (Imbasciati, Dabrassi, & Cena, 2011). It is because of this neural structuring, if anything, that a different significance is given to the afferences coming from different areas and parts of the body (Imbasciati, 2010c; Imbasciati & Buizza, 2011), but not because meanings primarily come from them; let alone delivered by supposed incretions determined by the genome. The relative behaviour depends on the meaning attributed by the neural system to that area, not by the area itself. The body is the vehicle of a highly individual relational learning, rather then an expression of an instinct.

A NEW METAPSYCHOLOGY CONGRUENT WITH NEUROSCIENCE 113

The scholar of other disciplines, to be able to get a correct idea of current psychoanalysis, by defining what is meant by theory needs the multiple quotations of different "theories" talked about in psychoanalysis should be formulated in a clear form: general principles which explain globally the origin and functioning of the mind. This will probably not be possible for some so-called theories, as they are improperly called theories. The idea has remained in the common feeling that psychoanalysis has only one theory, that of Freud. The fact that the Rules of the IPA still defines (article 3) psychoanalysis as the theory of Freud has perhaps corroborated this misunderstanding.[10] The misunderstanding lies in the fact that the various theories which have developed have been identified with their name in reference to clinical practice, but they have not been accurately formulated as properly theories. Such a phenomenon is, in my opinion, due to understanding the term theory as too elastic, or inaccurate a way, and indistinctly similar to the different meanings that it has in the dictionary.

The fact is that the conception deriving from the great progress that clinical psychoanalysis has made in the seventy years since Freud's death is not known at popular level, and not even at the level of general culture. This lack of knowledge, from which today's ignorance of what psychoanalysis originates, is due, in my opinion, to the fact that no general theories on the mind, comparable to those formulated by Freud one hundred years ago, have been extracted from the progress of clinical practice; together with the fact that those who are not "insiders" of a science can only know a few and clear theoretical formulations.

All this produces, in my opinion, an "image" of psychoanalysis, not only at popular level, but also in the opinion of all scholars of other sciences—scientists—, that is distorted, obsolete and even criticisable. This is where the opinion that psychoanalysis is not a science comes from (Imbasciati, 2011a, 2011b, 2012a, 2012b, 2012d). In this picture psychoanalysts should officially formulate[11] a general theory of the origins of the development and functioning of the human mind, comparable to that formulated by Freud, but updated, according to the process of psychoanalytic clinical practice and the other sciences of the mind. Upstream of this, however, a correct epistemology has to be followed to specify what is meant by theory. The term has to be understood in the strong sense, as Freud, besides, outlined it.

Is a new metapsychology necessary? I have outlined a theory in this direction (Imbasciati, 2013b).

114 MINDBRAIN, PSYCHOANALYTIC INSTITUTIONS, AND PSYCHOANALYSTS

Freud had the ambition of giving "the world" a strong and unitary image of psychoanalysis. Do we have to sacrifice that ambition as today it is more complex? Many psychoanalysts do not seem to see this opportunity and any attempt in this direction is considered an inopportune discussion, a hindrance to the real progress of psychoanalysis which would [only] consist of clinical practice; or even an obsessive rationalisation. This is in my opinion due to an institutional climate (institutional in the sense of Jacques: 1955) of many Societies so that psychoanalysts study and write "amongst themselves", clinging to a "faith" which I believe is too optimistic on the destiny of psychoanalysis (Bornstein, 2001; Merciai & Cannella, 2009). "Faith" often covers up ignorance.

In actual fact, psychoanalysts do well to dedicate themselves almost exclusively to clinical practice: this is the field from which progress starts and in this setting they do not need too many theoretical clarifications, especially if referred to how "theory" has to be understood in a distinctive sense. Psychoanalysts can understand one another, in their professional work, using the word "theory" in the polyhedric and extensive sense as shown above. For professional work to call itself scientific, however, we have to be "scientists", which means, apart from the due epistemological correctness, not forgetting the scholars of other sciences, who cannot have all the knowledge of psychoanalysis that psychoanalysts have, but may have only fairly simple and general ideas about it: these must however be up to date, as it is from these "other" scientists that these ideas are transmitted into general culture. In an isolationist spirit, there is a tendency to forget the "others" and how these thousands of others can produce an image that may mark the destiny of psychoanalysis itself.[12] The doubt arises in these "others" that psychoanalysis is not a science, as what is offered to them and used today is still the old metapsychology, which from their knowledge of current sciences appears clearly criticisable and obsolete. All this makes analysts look like writers, philosophers, artists or craftsmen, in the best of hypotheses, or even the bearers of a religion.

What is the image, in a market of patients in a media society, that the people have about the psychoanalyst?

Repression

One paradigmatic example of how the recurring use of terms relative to Freudian metapsychology in the language of psychoanalysts suggests

A NEW METAPSYCHOLOGY CONGRUENT WITH NEUROSCIENCE 115

that the psychoanalyst who uses it is at that time making an inevitable unconscious reference to theoretical elements which have nothing to do with his current and advanced clinical practice: it is the continued persistent recurrence of the term "repression". Although qualified experts, such as Fonagy (Fonagy & Target, 2001) have stated that this term should be banned (Merciai & Cannella, 2009), it is still used, heedless that this concept entails an implicit semantic halo, i.e., of comprehension (in this case false), in the framework of a theory which nevertheless is considered superseded; heedless that the concept means to be unaware of how much this concept derives from the thought of the Western philosophical tradition, or that the "substance" of the mind is, indeed has to be, consciousness. With this implicit idea, Freud discovers the unconscious: he must explain it, and he did it by supposing a mechanism of obstacle to becoming conscious: repression meant the hypothesis of an obstacle to becoming conscious of something that should "naturally" be driven (= *trieb* = drive) towards the consciousness. Without some countercathexis (Rapaport, 1951), i.e., without a strong repressing force (repression), psychic contents, which today we would call emotional events, could have—should have—been conscious.

Elsewhere (Imbasciati, 2001a, 2001d, 2006a, 2006b, 2007c, 2010a, 2010b, 2010c, 2011a) I have emphasised that Freud, at the time, could not have failed to be a consciousnessist, at least in part; he had discovered the unconscious, but he still believed that the fulcrum, the centre, the sun so to speak, of the mind, in practice the substance, was made up of the consciousness. Consciousness with a capital "c",[13] has always been understood as a natural "quality", specific and the same for all human beings, which could be expressed, almost identified, with language.[14] Having discovered consciousness, Freud, thanks to his brilliant methodological invention, also discovered the difficulty of the patient in realising what to the master seemed clear and clearly comprehensible as logically verbalised: the event was called resistance (*Widerstand*). Starting from the implicit *a priori* of a natural flow of the unconscious towards the consciousness, and that this could be expressed with words, and on the other hand acknowledging resistance in clinical practice, Freud could only suppose that there was an obstacle which "pushed back" (= *Verdrang*) the natural "drive" (= *trieb*).

Some neuroscientists (Alberini, 2013b) have recently wanted to justify the Freudian concept of repression by stating that Freud conceived it not in terms of "hydraulics" (Meltzer,1981) but of memory. Quoting a

116   MINDBRAIN, PSYCHOANALYTIC INSTITUTIONS, AND PSYCHOANALYSTS

passage from "Remembering, repeating and working-through" (Freud, 1914b), in which the master speaks of how repression can be removed using transference, the author maintains that the master had guessed how repression was to be understood as a disconnection between the neural networks due to subsequent changes of the mnestic traces. By carefully examining the passage, this attribution to the Freudian text appears arbitrary, and moreover Freud never repeated it anywhere else. In my opinion, there is a desire to ennoble the Freudian concepts at all costs with those of the neurosciences. Furthermore, if the attribution were true, we can only think that the master, although he had this intuition, let those who came after him believe in repression with the easier and more fascinating hydraulic model, as an obstacle to the drive: a promotional aim for psychoanalysis. This is not surprising, if we think of how he himself ironically referred to all his metapsychology as "witch" and "mythology".

The later generations nevertheless confused *Widerstand* with *Verdrängung*. This tells us how much human beings are fond of the idea that the mind has to do with the consciousness. If the need is felt to explain resistance by hypothesising an obstacle to consciousisation means that *a priori* it is accepted as certain that the unconscious otherwise has to become conscious, in the face of the verbal clarification by the analyst. Today there is no reason for the aforementioned initial *a priori*: we know that the mind is, in the first place, unconscious and independent of language; the observation of infants shows it. We should instead explain why sometimes this unconscious is translated into some form of verbal consciousness. The Freudian idea of *trieb* also implies that the presumed flow from the unconscious towards consciousness, as if it were "natural", could be identified in something biologically very concrete and not in a functional effect, as we know today. In these assumptions, Freud posited the activation of a mechanism of pushing back (counterthrust: *Verdrängung*).

The *trieb* implicitly contains the hypostasis of the idea of a natural thrust towards consciousness. Freud hoped that with psychoanalysis, humankind could free itself from the uncomfortable "backwards thrust" and reach a greater, truer, consciousness; psychoanalysis could represent an endeavour of worldwide importance, comparable to that (at the time in course) of draining the Zuider Zee (Freud, 1933a on p. 190 ff.).

Repression is therefore not a discovery at all, as is still said ("Freud discovered drives and repression"), but a conceptual invention made

A NEW METAPSYCHOLOGY CONGRUENT WITH NEUROSCIENCE 117

compulsory by the *a priori* of a natural *trieb* towards consciousness. At that time, it was thought that consciousness was a natural and constant quality in all human beings: neurosciences had not yet proposed that "the mystery of the consciousness" had to be studied. It was thought of as a dichotomy, of the unconscious opposed to consciousness, as if this were a constant and not a capacity that was variable from one individual to another and variable in time in the same individual and according to the relational situation, A panel of the American Psychoanalytical Association, as early as 2006, studying consciousness, suggested considering a continuum between what is considered more unconscious and what can come to awareness, but this reflection seems to have been without any results in official psychoanalytic literature. This idea could have been developed to see better how consciousness is an inconstant and variable epiphenomenon of all the continuous mental work, or of what the mind continuously in its substantial unconscious globality, produces.

Today we have to invert the drive model that Meltzer (1981) defined of the hydraulic or indeed hydrostatic type (Imbasciati, 1994): no longer a flow from the unconscious to consciousness, except to find the block of repression which verbalisation of the interpretation ought to remove, but to consider the unconscious work, on the quality of which what the consciousness at a given time is able to process and give the subject to perceive depends. The relational situation, understood as a transit of unconscious emotions (analysis) may favour some understanding of this "something" that is happening in the mind: we then have to study how and when (and possibly why and how much) a certain work takes on some form of awareness; in other words we have to study the capacity for consciousness. This can be done by investigating how in the analytic relationship, both the analyst and the analysand reach *some* experience felt in some form of awareness, well beyond the claim of formulating it in the classic verbal interpretation. The mind—and this has to be repeated—is in its unconscious substance (Colombo, 2008; Imbasciati, 2012a): on what bases are the various and varyingly clear capacities of awareness activated? Today we can say: how is it possible to increase our capacities of feeling emotions?[15] On which we will claim to construct a verbalisation.

The allusion, indeed the implicit, that an unconscious content or psychic event becomes conscious if repression is removed (or if there is none) is hard to die in the mind of humans, including that of

118 MINDBRAIN, PSYCHOANALYTIC INSTITUTIONS, AND PSYCHOANALYSTS

psychoanalysts: the feeling, as entrenched as it is unconscious, of being our own masters and masters of our thoughts and feelings, in the face of the discovery of the unconscious has nevertheless remained. We have not become resigned, at the cost of believing that with analysis the inconvenience could be obviated. Here is the idea that there is a barrier towards awareness, but that it can be removed reconquering the unconscious; here is the idea that repression, on which we can put the blame of not being totally our own masters; and the idea that with analysis "repression can be removed".

This idea, that the unconscious is linked to repression, and that otherwise everything could become conscious, was perfectly justified in Freud's conception, at the time, in the face of the discovery, then astonishing, of the existence of an unconscious mind. Today we are aware that the substance of almost all our mind is unconscious and that the most unconscious part can never be verbalised. Repression is a concept that was structured by the primal wonder in the face of the discovery of the resistance of patients to interpretation. The difficulty of realising—resistance—can today be explained otherwise as due to repression. Repression is a concept that derives from the reification of the experience of the analytic couple before the difficulties of "thinking together".

This reification can certainly not be attributed to Freud: his use of two differentiated terms, *Widerstand* and *Verdrangung*, prove it, nor can an implicit consciousnessism be attributed to him to any great extent. This can be felt by examining his metapsychology, but we have to remember that the matter was for other scientists who at the time were all consciousnessists. The first section of *On Metapsychology* is entitled "Justification of the unconscious": Freud wanted to validate his discoveries before the others who were consciousnessists and therefore explain—metapsychology is a hypothesis of "explanation"—whilst the rest of the Freudian work is "description" (Imbasciati, 2011a, 2011b) of the discoveries. He wanted explicate to "them", with their conceptions: a "why" of an unconscious mind. In Freud's time the School of Würzburg, with Külpe (1883) dominated and everyone, in conformity with traditional Western philosophy, thought that "mind" meant "consciousness". Freud had to fight this conception and strategically invented metapsychology. I think that Freud himself did not believe in his invention as though it were the "truth": it was the "witch", "our mythology" (Freud, 1932a, 1932b).

Reification may then, if anything, be attributed to those who after Freud, now inured to the idea that "an unconscious exists", continues to

A NEW METAPSYCHOLOGY CONGRUENT WITH NEUROSCIENCE   119

identify resistance and repression, mixing a concept concerning clinical practice with another concerning a theoretical invention. Underlying this, there is another idea, that the conscious mind can, except for problems and hindrances, assimilate and transform the work of the unconscious mind. There was not the idea, as we may have today, that the mind is essentially unconscious and that only sometimes something already transformed and altered with respect to its origin, can reach some awareness. Consciousness is not a natural quality that is the same for everyone, nor should it be conceived in a dichotomy with respect to the unconscious: it is a function which sometimes, in a completely individual way and to varying degrees in time and depending on the relational moment, transforms (and misinterprets) what, already transformed, the unconscious mind has transmitted to it: exaggerating, we could say, "what it gives it to drink"!

The fact is that the illusion, that the mind "ought" to be conscious resists implacably in our culture. Many colleagues, including those who say that Freudian metapsychology is an out-of-date metaphor, let slip the words "repression", "has repressed" and so on. Pure coincidence or a lapsus? I think that the concept of repression has remained stuck in the brain of many psychoanalysts, as though it were an unquestionable discovery, and not a theoretical concept with which Freud thought he could explain resistance. Besides, all metapsychology, for its metaphors which reify passions, is too easily fascinating to be really abandoned. It remains a legacy that is almost fixed in our implicit memory. If anything, the problem is the fact that the Institution (Jacques, 1955; Schoeck, 1966) ideologised it: ideology always arises from the affects of a community.

Could we say ironically that psychoanalysts have repressed their resistance? Or that repression is the materialisation carried out in the face of their difficulties with the patients. These difficulties of the analyst have to do with what Freud called resistance: so we have to clarify further why and how resistance appears in the analytic couple, but not taking the shortcut of the concept of repression attributed to the patient. We have to investigate where, how and to what extent, the patient becomes conscious of what the consciousness of the analyst wanted to transmit to him and whether, how and to what extent, the analyst's mind is capable of understanding and perceiving and then communicating with the patient. If we assume as valid the concept of repression, the idea that everything ought to be able to become conscious is also implicitly assumed: in other words, we are in the consciousnessism which Freud himself could not escape, with the implicit idea that the mind could and

120 MINDBRAIN, PSYCHOANALYTIC INSTITUTIONS, AND PSYCHOANALYSTS

had to be made conscious. Hence the emphasis on the power of verbal interpretation. Today, with the progress of psychoanalytic clinical practice, we are very far from all this: we have experienced how difficult it is, in patients, that what is verbalised to them through an interpretation truly entails a profound restructuring; how difficult it is to make conscious the unconscious by this way; or perhaps even how greatly this is not necessary for the mutative effects; and how the unconscious has a whole part that can never be made conscious: the pre-verbal, sub-symbolic, non-symbolic unconscious, the implicit memory.

We continue to speak of repression today and, in correlation, of drives. Thrust and counterthrust. Here too the comprehension of the complex unconscious emotive work which leads to an action or an intention is avoided and this work is reified in an endogenous thrust of instinctive origin. Lichtemberg (1989) quite rightly maintained that we have to speak of motivation, instead of drive. The use of certain terms translates the undergrowth of ideas that are as latent as they are tenacious, in the mind of many analysts. An elastic use of terms covers them.

Confusion and the vague use of terms could be avoided and latent ideas clarified, if a clearer epistemological competence could be acquired: I am referring once again to the fundamental epistemolo gical distinction between description and explanation, which reflects the one between clinical practice and theory. I can observe ("realise") that the patient induces something in me (and vice versa as well) and describe it, in its various ways just as I can, with the "instruments" available, coining and using suitable and specific concepts and terms, which are used to identify difference nuances of the experience which I have had and which I have "observed", as well as the sequence of similar experiential events, of which I am trying to understand the reason. All this helps to be able to describe adequately to myself and to colleagues, but all this is not "explanation": causal, effective, the "ultimate" explication, which perhaps as "true" will never be given. We therefore use hypotheses, we invent, by formulating a theory, in the strictest sense. The explanation is always hypothetical. Freud wanted to explain, with his *On Metapsychology*: he was aware that his explanation was hypothetical and provisional, but perhaps he trusted that "the others" would not assume it as such: a strategy?

Freud attempted to explain with the hard sciences of the time and he did so for other scientists. "Justification of the unconscious" is the title of the first section of *On Metapsychology*. Why "justify"? because the others presumed that the mind as such had to be conscious, but perhaps because Freud himself finally thought that everything could (had to) be conscious (or made such): unless … here is the obstacle, the *countertrieb*: *Verdrangung*, repression!

The method invented by Freud had allowed him to discover the unconscious: in the background of the picture that the community, including Freud, had of the mind, an explanation was necessary: "strong". And Freud used his brilliance to give it to us, his witch (Freud, 1932a). Today, however, we no longer wonder why there is the unconscious. If need be, we study how, when, to what extent, at what time and degree of the relationship we—patient and analyst—can in some way be conscious; and beyond the ability to verbalise. The neurosciences are studying the network that connects the work of the right hemisphere with that part of the left in which a supposed "consciousness" may originate (Schore, 2003a, 2003b).

Can the neurosciences today give us an explanation of how the brain is born, develops and functions, in terms similar to what the progress and the expansion of the psychoanalytic method has allowed us to identify? I mean in the emotions that circulate between patient and analyst, and which mutually re-orient the mental functioning of both.

This last subject leads us to consider how much the growth of clinical practice is due to progress of the psychoanalytic method. Today we no longer operate as in the time of Freud. In this evolution, the progressive interior formation, given by the equally gradual application of the personal analysis of the analyst has entered increasingly forcefully. This has allowed identifying the interior instruments with which today the analyst operates: they have been called in general psychoanalytic function of the mind, and partially "listening" (and "listening to listening"), or negative abilities, tolerance of the unknown, capacity of recognising the so-called emotive turbulences and so on. All this is, epistemologically, "method" which has joined the setting made explicit by Freud (external setting, dreams, free associations and similar) and which, condensed in the intuition of the importance of the fluctuating attention of the third ear, has made it evolve to the point of revolutionising it.

The object of psychoanalysis has changed

Epistemologists assert that it is the method that forms a specific science, as with its "predicates" it defines ("cuts out") the object. We can therefore assert that in psychoanalysis, once the method has changed, the way with which the object (the predicates with which it is cut out) is presented also varies.

Tables 1 and 2 offer a general view of the first psychoanalytic science and the gradual evolution of the discipline after Freud.

The elementary epistemological principles applicable to knowledge such as the psychoanalytic one, which can characterise it as a science, are (Agazzi, 1976, 2004): 1) that the object is defined and that 2) the protocolarity (= method) that cuts it out (every object is cut out from its predicates) is coherent and defined.

The object of Psychoanalysis called unconscious has changed, in that the method for identifying it has been updated, no longer

Table 1. Freud and early psychoanalytic science.

1. A method (the way Freud operated) is discovered which allows understanding that in the individual's mind there is *something* beyond his consciousness and that that method allows it to be formulated in words, just as we are used to formulating conscious events with words.
2. It is discovered that this *something* is in some relation with the behaviour (conduct), with the somatic functionality and with what the subject thinks and says about himself.
3. It is called unconscious, and that method is perfected as it is discovered that, using it to formulate in words what is intuited (= interpretation), something in what the subject shows (in behaviour, in the body, in his introspection) may change.
4. It is thought that in this way the unconscious can be made conscious: with words. The talking cure comes into being.
5. Generalising the above point, it is thought that more or less the whole unconscious can be translated into consciousness by verbalising it. "Where Id was, there Ego shall be", "Draining the Zuiderzee" (Freud, 1932a, p. 190).
6. The illusion of the Western tradition on the mind is implicitly grasped: the ideal state and the principle of the mind is that of the verbalised consciousness; and everything *ought to be like that to be able to be made conscious*. Here however, resistance is encountered; an obstacle is then thought of and it is called *repression*.
7. With a reification of the endocrinological type (Imbasciati, 2005a) of what is felt consciously in sexuality, Freud puts forward the concept of drive and extends it to all mental functioning: hypostasis of the experienced feelings (Imbasciati, 1994).
8. A general explanatory theory of the origins, development and functioning of the mind is formulated based on the above: Freud outlines his metapsychology.

Table 2. Evolution and change of psychoanalysis after Freud (from the 1970s onwards).

1. It is progressively discovered that that *something* which makes people act and acts in the body, depends on the relationality (intersubjectivity) and goes beyond that something identified earlier, as it eludes the method as conceived and applied (= interpreted) earlier and seems to have a greater, absolute degree of unawareness. It is discovered at clinical level as the psychoanalytic method is extended (projective identification, listening, consideration of the metaverbal and then non-verbal communication, transmission from unconscious to unconscious, including inside the soma, and in the analytic couple, psychoanalytic function of the mind etc.). Psychoanalysts talk of primary unconscious, of unrepressed unconscious then of subsymbolic then non-symbolic unconscious (Bucci, 2009; Moccia & Solano, 2009).

2. It is realised that what was thought made conscious with the first method is *only* what that method identified, wishing to translate it into the verbal language of awareness; and that what in the point above was being discovered is much more decisive of what was highlighted in its translation into words, respect to the effects on mental functioning (behavioural conduct, relational styles, psychosomatic equilibrium). The concept of implicit memory, borrowed from the experimental studies of General Psychology is drawn on; *something* that can *never* be translated into words, but which can be seen in action: behaviour, acting out, enacting, soma, mobility skills, attachment styles, IWM, other events that can be observed with experimental methods.

3. Whilst at psychoanalytic level it is discovered how the ability of assimilation of the interventions (interpretations) of the analyst varies depending on the type of relationship and the analytic moment, experimental studies discover the inter-individual and intra-individual variations of the consciousness (Liotti, 1991, 2001); a consciousness understood as an ability that is variable along a continuum. This overwhelms the separation, if not the dichotomy conscious/unconscious implicit in early psychoanalysis and also the idea that consciousness consists of verbalisation.

4. The neurosciences discover and are still investigating the primary work of the right hemisphere, beyond any possible translation of it or conscious acquisition, as well as its integration with the whole brain's neural work, only a part of which appears to be responsible for what "appears" to consciousness (Schore, 2002a, 2002b; Salvini & Bottino, 2011).

5. The above information is still stimulating a possible psychoanalytic instrument, identifying for the time being in the expression "psychoanalytic function of the mind", that can allow intervening on that ineffable "something"—in the etymon: "that can never be rendered in words"—that determines the relational conduct of human beings. Psychoanalysis is no longer a "Talking Cure" (Imbasciati, 2010d).

through the translation into words, but through an extension of the capacities of consciousness obtained by a training to use non-verbal factors (point 1, Table 2). I believe that the majority of colleagues agree that our conception of the unconscious has changed, therefore our "conception" is none other than a set of predicates with which the extension of our method identifies (= conception) the object.

Reproducing schematically better clarifies chronologically the evolution of psychoanalysis due to the updating of the method: the identification of what was called unconscious has changed and it can therefore be asserted that the object of this science has changed. The "unconscious" of which Freud nevertheless intuited that there was much more still to be revealed, is today seen essentially as depending on the capacity, above all by the analyst, not so much of making it conscious with words, but having "some form of consciousness about it": never complete.

Both in psychoanalysis and with methods of other sciences of the mind (Liotti, 1994, 2001), it is discovered that consciousness is not a natural "quality" of the mind that is the same for every individual at every time, but a continuum (APA, 2006) of different levels of comprehension of the self, variable from one individual to another and in the same individual depending on the time and the relationship he has in that moment. That "something" which in some way the capacity of consciousness of the analyst has grasped at a certain time of the relation, must then in some way be "passed" on to the capacity for consciousness of that patient in that moment of the relation: current psychoanalytical practice has made us aware of how difficult this passage is, how easily it can be false and how it can transit into "something more than interpretation" (Stern & BPCSG, 2005; BPCSG, 2011).

Paradoxically, we could then assert that psychoanalysis is becoming the study of the capacity for consciousness of the single individual, in this case the analyst together with the patient. In this regard let we observe the summary of this passage in the second table which illustrates the chronology of the transformation of our science.

Here is the origin of a further problem of method, which deeply affects the training of the psychoanalyst. Until now, psychoanalysts have been trained to translate into words, with adequate interpretations, what they have understood of what is happening in the patient's mind. However, if the words are not an adequate translation of what moves

A NEW METAPSYCHOLOGY CONGRUENT WITH NEUROSCIENCE 125

and is transmitted between the unconscious of the patient and that of the analyst, on the basis of what does the analyst "understand"? Above all, on the basis of what, with what, can he transmit his understanding to the patient? Stern has told us that "there is something more than interpretation" (Stern & BPCSG, 1998), that is the mutative agent of the unconscious structure of the patent: some authors (Foresti, 2013) have discussed, in my opinion too "prudently", if this should be understood as something more but different from the interpretation or something "about" the interpretation itself, as in the institutional tradition. In my opinion, the thesis outlined by this author could be developed: not only "something more than" or even "something about" but "something than": I would maintain that what acts as an effective mutative agent is not something more than words, but "instead" of the word. Analysts have effectively known for some time that the *denotative* content of the interpretation is not sufficient, but what counts is the *connotative* meaning, i.e., the "affective" halo, the interpersonal context, the feeling's moment of that meeting, which have effect. It is the emotions felt by the analyst which, adequately conveyed by non-verbal physical media which accompany or surround the interpretation (for instance the tone of voice and its correspondence with feelings perceived by the analyst: transference and countertransference) which have a mutative efficacy in the patient. They were called "non-specific factors" of the therapeutic effect, but for many years their fundamental value was emphasised despite the name, and their consideration was extended to all those events, including behavioural, that take place between the analyst and the analysand. In this conception, we will have "something more" alongside the interpretation. For some years, though, quite a few colleagues have been wondering whether it is not these, conveyed inside words but not coinciding with these, that act: therefore "something than" something instead of the word. It is these "somethings" that convey the communication from unconscious to unconscious, moreover as is obvious in caregiver/child communication.

We can then seek how these can be better identified, and how the analyst can be trained in becoming capable of perceiving them and, above all, using them; without them becoming acting which compromises the progress of the analysis. It is then a question of entering into the problematic study of the processes that shift the various types and various forms of the analyst's consciousness in his relation with the patient.

126   MINDBRAIN, PSYCHOANALYTIC INSTITUTIONS, AND PSYCHOANALYSTS

The progress of our knowledge on the unconscious, or better on how our mind—our neuromental system—continually and unexpectedly works, has highlighted the new horizon of psychoanalysis; how, when, to what extent, with which means, from which vertexes, with which methodology and with which limits can we study the possibility of acquiring some consciousness? The capacity for consciousness is therefore presented as the present-day object of psychoanalysis.

To what extent in the future will other sciences of the mind be able to support or be integrated with the progress of the psychoanalytic method?

Unconscious and ability for consciousness

The neurosciences tell us that the brain is constructed in an unrepeatable individual way, by the progressive construction of neural networks (synaptic connections, dendritic proliferation, perhaps cell proliferation, selection of certain neuronal populations, etc.) specific to each individual, which then distinguish the functionality of that single individual. This unrepeatable construction has taken place through the progressive acquisitions that the events in the life of that individual have produced through the mediation of the caregivers, with particular attention to the relational events in the prenatal and perinatal periods and in the first few months of life (Vallino & Macciò, 2004; Imbasciati, Dabrassi, & Cena, 2007; Imbasciati & Cena, 2015), as well as the continuous interaction between what is processed and acquired and what the incipient mental structures start to produce (*cf.* external inputs/internal inputs: Imbasciati, 2006a, 2006b) along the whole life. In this context, the neurosciences show us that each single and singular neural-mental system works without interruption, beyond and much earlier than any glimmer of consciousness. What sense is there in asking "why the unconscious?" The mind is essentially and in the first place absolutely not aware.

We then have to ask—and we have a great deal to investigate—"why the consciousness?" How is that set of neural-mental functions within which we can observe the capacity of consciousness of an individual (including oneself) in his various existential and relational moments formed and constructed? The ability of a patient, at the various times of the analysis, and that of the analyst. This ability, as we know today (Liotti, 1994, 2001; Gilbert, 1989) is variable from one individual to another and for the same individual variable in time and in his relations. This last detail should be well known by analysts in the setting. The variations of the abilities for consciousness are not casual: psychoanalysts attribute them to the affects, which flow in the analytic relation, but what are the affects? Beyond the clinical observations? As mental events, they have to be able to be homologated with what happens in the central nervous system, in the same way as the so-called cognitive processes.

As they are generated by relationships and in the relationship, the affects, if we want to go from the clinical level to the psycho-physiological explanatory level, have to be explained by involving non-verbal communication (NVC), with all the host of experimental studies, above all on the coding and decoding of messages at the level of the emitter and receiver, and the relative processing at central level of the two communicants. We cannot, therefore, talk of consciousness in an absolute or universal sense, but only of that ability which, to a greater or lesser extent, changeably comes into function in the life and relational contexts of a certain individual. In this context, it is my opinion that psychoanalysis can further study "why the consciousness?" Why that individual consciousness?

Is it useful and valid to speak about repression in this context as well? That something that we are used to calling repression refers only to something that we experience in subjectivity: a difficulty. It is therefore about a clinical level. Freud called it resistance because he thought that the psychic ought to reach the consciousness: if it did not reach it, there had to be an obstacle that stopped it. This was his hypothesis. If the assumption from which we start, i.e., to reach the consciousness, fails, another explanation is necessary. At a psychophysiological level, the transformations (Bion's intuition?) whereby some mental processes take on and lose the conditions that make them appear along the continuum that goes from the unconscious to the consciousness will have to be clarified; and the factors that modulate this "coming and going" which appears in subjectivity will also have to be clarified. Into which forms perceived by the individual this is translated will also have to be studied (Panksepp & Biven, 2012).

Psychologists and neuroscientists have helped us a great deal in recent decades: by way merely of example, we can mention Dennet (1991), Edelman (1989, 1992); Damasio (1994, 1999); Kaplan and Solms (2000); Solms and Turnbull (2002); Kandel (1998, 1999); Siegel (1999), also in integration with psychoanalysts (Fonagy, 2001; Fonagy & Target, 2001) but there is still a great deal ahead of us to investigate. In the past few decades the concept of subjectivity has recurred in the area of psychological sciences. The term appears perfectly suitable for those psychologists and neuroscientists who have rejected a crudely understood dichotomy of consciousness/unconscious, but today it is also used by psychoanalysts and it is essential to indicate the experience that the subject makes of himself, or that he expresses externally so that others grasp it. The use of the term is, in my opinion, indicative of an insufficiency of the previous concepts of consciousness, unconscious and even of preconscious: "Consciousness" and "unconscious" lend themselves to being understood as a dichotomy and on the other hand, "preconscious" is a concept that has not been greatly developed. The use of the term "subjectivity" is therefore useful; however, we have to distinguish it from that expressed by psychoanalysts with the term "intersubjectivity".

In parallel with the concept of subjectivity, that of "experience" has become established. Subjectivity and experiences better conceptualise the continuum between what is unconscious and what could acquire some characteristics of consciousness, but they also emphasise that their distinction is not essential for psychoanalysis as the consciousness is anything but natural and constant: it is not about "restoring" the consciousness, in psychoanalysis, nor "making conscious", but increasing, with the relation and in the relation, any abilities for consciousness. In my opinion, the use of the Italian term *"vissuto"* (= something that is lived) is indicative of a changed conception of consciousness amongst psychoanalysts; and therefore of a changed conception of the unconscious as well. Our current clinical perception says that the mind is primarily unaware (impenetrable?) and that in the continuous work it does, sometimes something rises, which gradually can be "expressed (ex-press)": recepted by others (amongst these the analyst is particularly well equipped) and also sometimes acknowledged by the subject himself. Nobody guarantees that this last perception may be adequate: it nevertheless concerns what, or perhaps it would be better to say "something of what", was taking place in the mind (*cf.* anti-alexithymic dimension", Imbasciati, 2006a, 2006b).

What I am trying to outline on clinical observation appears in line with what the neuroscience tells us about the continuous work of the brain, the right hemisphere in the first place, the connections of the formations of the paleoencephalon with the limbic cortex and from here to the frontal lobe. This confirms the importance of what were called "affects" for the global functioning of the mind, the continuous change of the memory, the prime importance of the unconscious and that interindividual variability that Freud tried to explain with his drive theory. The neurosciences thus give us an "explication" of what present-day psychoanalytic clinical practice acknowledges. This explanation is however in terms of vertexes and methodologies of investigation other than the psychological one: biochemistry and neuroimaging techniques (and molecular genetics) which "explicates". Can we make do with this type of explanation? Freud wanted to give a psychophysiological explication: while hypothesising possible future discoveries of brain biochemistry (physiology) he intended to explain what takes place beyond the consciousness (meta) in psychological terms; useful to psychoanalysts. The construction or "invention" (Vassalli, 2001) of his metapsychology was truly useful. Is another metapsychology possible today for psychoanalysis, i.e., an explanation which, while coherent with the neurosciences, is of a psychological nature and method?

Considering the enormous evolution—revolution—of psychoanalysis, that "notconscious" something, which today we deem decisive for the human individual in his different and multiple relationships, is very different from what Freud called the unconscious, and so was called for decades after him. We could continue to call it unconscious,[16] but, transforming the recurrent saying that "our conception of the unconscious has changed" into an epistemologically more correct language, we can state that the object of psychoanalytic science is not the same as in the past, as it is no longer the same method that determines it. All this has to be borne in mind if we want, in my opinion, to defend the image of our science in the face of the anthropological change which, on the wave of the technological race of the media society, pursues and locks up man in the *hic et nunc* of a consciousness of the moment, or even in action without consciousness (can we recall Jaynes? 1976) and which in this race is producing a distorted image of psychoanalysis (Imbasciati, 2012a).

In this last context and in this intention, we will have to bear in mind, not only a theoretical and epistemological clarification amongst analysts, although always useful and opportune, what the "others" may know about psychoanalysis. Amongst those competent in our science, i.e., analysts, we can always understand one another: despite the theoretical inaccuracies and in the plurality of theories we still understand the common term "theory". But other scientists, of different sciences and even of sciences of the mind other than psychoanalysis, what they do know about psychoanalysis? In my opinion, only a general theory. On the basis of Freudian metapsychology, an image (understood in the precise meaning given to the term in Social Psychology) has been formed, that from "other" scientists has flowed into the current public image. It is with metapsychology that an image of psychoanalysis has been formed: it actually portrays what psychoanalyses used to be like, even though it still remains accredited as though it were the current one.

The problem is that today many people and other scientists have the means both to criticise it, and to take the statement that psychoanalysis is not a science to an extreme level.

In conclusion, it is worth repeating that a new metapsychology is needed, formulated with precision and a correct epistemology and offered to those who cannot have access to a greater comprehension of psychoanalysis. I have gone in this direction several times and I have tried to outline a different metapsychology (Imbasciati, 1998b, 2001a, 2002a, 2002b, 2006a, 2006b, 2007b, 2007c, 2010a, 2010b, 2010c). My intention, which would need the development of a collective thought, turned out, however, to be "solitary": can the veneration of psychoanalysts for the master and the religiosity of the institution shape (unconsciously) my position as a heresy? It would be useful for psychoanalysts to work in the same direction as a whole.[17] Today the endeavour outlined by Freud as "making the unconscious conscious" is to be understood in a very limited way. In 1949, Bateson (Bateson, 1972; Casadio, 2010, p. 47) had stated that the above proposition was to be considered an epistemological absurdity. Today we could clarify the statement by considering that most of the unconscious work is "ineffable", i.e., beyond words, in the continuous reprocessing of the implicit memories, non-symbolic and therefore difficult to explore with the talking cure, possibly deducible with the current preparation of the analytic mind, but in its effective substance or better in its effective "why?" which can be explored with other means, perhaps by the neurosciences.

With regard to point 4 in table 2 above, it should be noted how quite a few colleagues maintain that neurosciences and psychoanalysis are two different sciences that are not comparable, not even the latter should depend in some way on the former. Four reasons can be opposed to this

A NEW METAPSYCHOLOGY CONGRUENT WITH NEUROSCIENCE   131

objection. The first is that considering uncomparable two sciences dealing with the same area (although from different vertexes or methods) is a simplistic, or even an aprioristic prejudice (emotional? Ideological?). Their objects can be compared, even though different, if they obey to a general principle according to which it is indispensable to check where they may contradict one another. This is Wilson's principle of "consilience" (1998). The second reason, for the comparison of sciences, can come from the example of Freud: his metapsychology was formulated precisely by bearing in mind the hard sciences of his time. The third reason: having recourse as is done today to the concept of implicit memory implies a necessary connection to experimental psychology, and from this to psychophysiology, and from here again to the neuroscience more in general.

As the fourth reason, I can emphasise how the progressive discovery of the relationship, in its interpersonal complexity, especially with its references to the importance of non-verbal aspects, nevertheless still refers to how the subject organises the sensory nature that comes from the "other". This "how", i.e., how the relationship with its effects develops at inter-subjective level, can be described in psychological terms: this is what psychoanalytic clinical practice does. The "why" has to be sought in the experimental sciences; in this case in the psychophysiology of perception and in the neurosciences more in general. What is described in psychological terms is described by the concepts concerning inter-subjectivity and unconscious communication, between unconsciouses, always refers to perception: this is to be understood in its complexity, as described, and also explained by experimental psychology (Imbasciati, 1986, vol. 2, Chapter Two). The perception which nevertheless is incurred in some communication, cannot be "explained", by circumscribing it with the concept of inter-subjectivity, nor even labelling it as unconscious communication, but it always has to contemplate physical vehicles that convey that something sensory which makes up the communication between two or more human beings. Nor can it be explained by simplistically calling on the mechanism of the mirror neurons: the "mirroring" is in actual fact the final event of neural work on the afferences confronted with memories. At psychophysiological level, perception implies physical vehicles. These vehicles, in their composition and assembling of multi-sensory natures (to a great extent subliminal), which characterise how two or more people code and recode them (incoming and outgoing, in the reciprocal answers of the "dialogue" which they receive and then perceive) convey, precisely, communication (Imbasciati, 1986). In this regard, we have to draw on the semiology of communication, nor can we ignore the literature of perceptology. We are therefore in the area and in the vertex of psychoneurophysiology.

That "something" that flows between human beings, influencing their development and behaviour, cannot therefore be described in terms of therapeutic effects, and in the impressions that the consciousness—quite it!—of the analyst succeeds in grasping. This "something" requires, in my opinion, a comparison and perhaps an "explanation" between the different sciences that study it. Exemplary in this regard is what we know today about the osmosis that is taking place between infant psychoanalysis, with babies and mothers, and infant research (Imbasciati, Dabrassi, & Cena, 2007; Cena, Imbasciati, & Baldoni, 2010, 2011). The mother–caregivers/foetus–baby–child interactions lay the foundations for the latter's mental structure: how? With the formation in reciprocal dialogue through coding and decoding the flow of information reciprocally received. And why? The information of the reciprocal dialogue, which is individual and completely non-verbal, structures the neural networks, in optimality rather than in the pathology, depending on the "quality" of the interactions. We have to bear in mind that what structures the neural networks is not the information in itself, but the code, in emission and in reception, which makes up the meaning. This meaning is vehiculated by physical vehicles of this communication: this the "why" in the nascent neural networks. What happens with babies and small children also takes place in any intimate relationship between adults, in the first place in the psychoanalytic relationship. It is therefore necessary to consider the non-verbal, in its physical vehicles and in the codes with which their configurations assume meaning: the "something more" of Stern (Stern & BCPSG, 1998, 2005) or the "vital forms" (Stern, 2010) structure mind and brain; and the "something that".

The psychoanalysts still have a very long way to go.

Psychoanalysis of the cognitive processes

The study of cognitive processes remained for a long time, in the panorama of the psychological sciences, as pertinent to experimental

A NEW METAPSYCHOLOGY CONGRUENT WITH NEUROSCIENCE   133

psychology, in particular to behaviourism, cognitivism (precisely), and neuropsychology, whilst the pertinence of psychoanalysis was considered in the area of affects. The cultural stereotype of a dichotomy between affect and cognition (*cf.* Chapter Two) is clear in this division of fields of study. And yet psychoanalysis has always dealt with how human beings perceive the reality of the world, regulating their conduct; if with analysis the patient changes, it means that he has "learnt". Yet psychoanalysis is not considered a theory of learning (Imbasciati, 1989b) and the term learning does not in fact recur in psychoanalytic literature: it was almost banned from it, until Bion published his famous *Learning from Experience* (1962).

Experimental psychology is based on the behavioural results rather than on the individuals' accounts: its research has almost always been set up by disregarding introspection and therefore the awareness of the subject on his thoughts and feelings. This disregard of the conscious accounts of the subjects seems to presuppose that what the subject can say about himself is negligible or even misleading and deceptive. This is shared by psychoanalysis, in favour however of the study of what is unconscious in the subject. A concept of the unconscious recurs in experimental literature, but remains a mere and moreover nebulous hypothesis, to be attributed only to the neurological and therefore to be excluded from the area of psychological investigation. The term "unconscious" is essentially despised, relegated to a doubtful discipline called psychoanalysis. In essence, it appears that both parties have considered a mind outside the consciousness, but one ignored the part studied by the other; psychoanalysis has ignored the complexity of learning and the experimentalists have studied learning, ignoring the study of the unconscious work (*cf.* Chapter Two). Why have the two sides not tackled one another?

One reason, in my opinion, can be identified in the fact that in Freud's times, perhaps in the wake of Köhler's theory of isomorphism (1929), moreover consolidated at length before and afterwards in tradition (Kaufman, 1974, called it "The picture in the head Theory"), it was thought that learning meant making a faithful representation of an external event enter the mind: it was learned, to be precise. If a discrepancy was found, it was not considered learning, but wrong or lack of learning. Insignificant discrepancies were not recorded, considering the instrumentation used. At the time, there was not the consideration that learning means transforming, nor were Freud's pupils very familiar with what in the 1930s the American new deal of perceptologists and then cognitivists were studying. It was only with Bion, with his "from" (Bion, 1962) that psychoanalysis rehabilitated learning, in the framework of the consideration of how experience, given by the senses, is transformed by the apparatus (= that individual, with his unconscious, or better with work that was completely outside any consciousness) that transforms it.

Another reason for the incomprehension between experimentalist psychologists and psychoanalysts on the unaware work of the mind when it learns can be found in the fact that the former only infer this work by logic (the declaration of behaviourism about the black box was exemplary), whereas in psychoanalysis it was thought that it could be translated into terms of language, as though it were, or had been or could be conscious: this is the work of psychoanalytic interpretation, which translates the unaware into terns of conscious subjectivity that can be verbalised (Imbasciati, 1989a, 1989b, 1991). What the experimentalists deduce from the results has been criticised by psychoanalysts as extremely general: the experimentalists declared that the mind does work, but they referred it to the brain without trying (until recently) to investigate it here. What the psychoanalysts interpret was, on the other hand, also criticised by the former, as the translation of the unconscious work of the brain into terms of verbal language as though it were conscious, would be a claim invalidated by subjectivity, especially the analyst's one.

In reality, in the light of current psychoanalysis which deals with the archaic layers of the mind, the unconscious is considered prevalently ineffable: so, the translation of ineffable into verbal terms should be a non-sense, for psychoanalysts too. At the time we are referring to, the criticism by the experimentalists was based on the fact that they doubted whether the training of a psychoanalyst could disregard the inconvenience of the black box. On the other hand, the psychoanalysts supported their conviction—that the work by the mind could be translated with interpretation, i.e., the verbality of the consciousness—on their theory of repression: by removing repression the mind could be conceived as similar or at least comparable to the consciousness and thus to verbalisation.

I have already raised the problem of how Freud, who discovered the unconscious, had essentially remained a consciousnessist: therefore, what was not conscious, "should" have been, if there had not been the

A NEW METAPSYCHOLOGY CONGRUENT WITH NEUROSCIENCE   135

work of repression started by the affects. This, however, conceived in terms of drive, made the psychoanalytic conception of the unconscious appear as unacceptable in the eyes of the experimentalists: the theory of the affects as derived from drives could not explain the fact that the transformative work of the mind could be rendered in words. For them, the unaware work had to remain a black box. On the other hand, psychoanalytic culture had remained anchored to the conception of learning as simple transfer, almost automatic recording, of the "outside" on the "inside", except when the drives intervened. Similarly, perception was conceived as a simple automatic impression in the mind of what was conveyed by the sensory organs.

Bion's work not only produced a revolution in the exquisitely psychoanalytic general panorama, but introduced a principle on learning, which in my opinion has played a fundamental role in bringing psychoanalysts closer to a consideration of the cognitive processes, regardless of the drive theory and abandoning the implied axiom that cognition was an automatic and natural "bringing inside" the image of the outside world; except to consider, in this framework, the modelling action of the drives. Bion brings attention to learning as an active process of the mind, which does not "bring inside" any image of reality but uses the sensory information to produce an internal reality, different from the external one: an active process which is intrinsic to the mind, which tells about the activity of the unconscious in producing cognition, without invoking the work of drives for this explanation. That is not making the affect-cognition distinction that had acted as a weighty legacy (of Western culture) in the explanatory conception of Freud. Bion gives an effective explanation, although in abstract terms of a mathematical type, of how the mind functions; precisely by using his "learning *from*" experience (1962), where the "from" is fundamental. Experience is not learned, in other words, external reality does not enter the mind, but the mind constructs its cognition of reality. The senses are not an automatic video and sound recorder which stores memory, but the mind carries out laborious work from the sensory information—this is experience—to construct cognition. This is the work, totally unaware, of the brain that "learns" (Chapter Five).

The perceptologists already knew the matter, thirty years before the Bionian contribution: the merit of Bion is having said, in a psychoanalytic language and to a more mature psychoanalytic audience, that what was first conceived as affect and drive was none other than unaware work of the mind in producing cognition. Sensoriality did not mean perception: learning is needed. With Bion's work, there was a turn, in psychoanalytic culture, from a drive-unconscious to an unconscious that can be defined representational, extending the meaning of "representation" no longer as an image that can in some way refer to external objects, but as a sign—in codes, I would say—that the mind builds up, to be able to represent in progression its cognition of reality; which, in the first place is unconscious: an internal reality to have cognition (the word is extended here too and disregards a lucid conscious ideal) of the external world through the internal one.

Bion's work focuses on how the mind is formed by transforming sensoriality from the beta elements to the alpha elements and from these to other progressively more articulated elements, according to the well-known grid (Bion, 1970). Beyond the abstract-mathematical language he used, Bion presented a model that opened up the way to an explanation of how from external reality something was extracted that allowed the subject to "learn it". In other words, the ways the "outside" external reality could enter "inside", were considered, but deeply transformed in a transformation by the subject's mind; while on the other hand, until then the psychoanalyst had considered how the "inside" of the mind (= drives) modelled the "outside", taking for granted that this outside should have been imprinted inside by nature, if drives had not intervened to shape it. This way, with Bion, a conception, that was similar to the one intrinsic in the study of the mind by the experimentalists and now by neurosciences, was opened up. The endogenist conception of Freud, having put forward the Energy-drive Theory, "had to" observe the opposite direction—from inside to outside—and deal with this. It is true that early psychoanalysis was not unaware of how it was formed inside: see the literature around the various terms used by Freud, *Darstellung, Vorstellung, Sachvorstellung, Dingvorstellung, Representanz* (Imbasciati, 1991). Freud's attention, however, was polarised on explaining "the forces of the inside", in the spirit defined "hydraulic" by Meltzer (1981). The epigones followed him. The essentially dynamic conception of the unconscious prevented developing an adequate study of a representational unconscious.

When Klein's work shifted the emphasis, from what pushed outside from inside to what was inside, we spoke of internal objects. Freud considered (external) objects which, depending on the drive investment, took on particular and individual value and meaning, but did not linger on a description of them and how they may be formed: he wanted to explain how the subject regulated himself in his interior and exterior life depending on the possibility of releasing the drive. We can recall "the source, the object, the aim" of drives (Freud, 1915). Klein described the internal object more: she did not describe it in detail, in the representational sense, as, a prisoner of her reverence to Freud (Imbasciati, 1983), she could only define it as an object of affects which were referred to drives (psychic representations of drives); however, she gave a sort of description of the "good" and "bad" "Breast" object, and then of the "phantasies".

A subsequent opinion current amongst psychoanalysts emphasised that the internal object was not a representation, as it did not represent any real object.[18] We observe how negating a representational status to the internal object depends on conceiving it in terms of affects considered of a nature other than the cognitive processes.

In actual fact, we have to agree on what representation means: if it is assumed as a true, almost photographic correspondence of reality (Köhler's isomorphism?) the aforementioned statement can be agreed with; if, on the other hand, small children are considered, an internal representation that corresponds to real objects is impossible. However, for the child the internal object still represents something. What does it represent then? It was said to represent affects, but what are these? If we no longer refer to the drive conception of affects as of a nature other than cognition, we still have to consider a trace; the trace of some mental functionality that indicates that affect, and those sets of affects, all the more so. If we refer, as we are doing at the moment, to what is being structured in a baby's brain, it is cogently logic to assume that in the neuronal network a set of connections has been formed which "represent" the functionality that has been acquired by that child; and that it can be activated when what has been called affect is deployed in this. This is memory: function memory.

By observing babies, what the baby is inferred to feel or "think" can be described, or meanings of its behaviour and expressions or somatic events can be inferred: these are nevertheless still inferences made in analogy with what an adult feels, does and expresses. What do these descriptions grasp of what really takes place in the mind and in the brain of the baby? As long as we talk of constellations of affects, a certain

138 MINDBRAIN, PSYCHOANALYTIC INSTITUTIONS, AND PSYCHOANALYSTS

type of comprehension by analogy with the adult is obtained, but if we talk of a something that we call object, and we think that this something is worth identifying, how can we describe it better? If we had to describe this something as an object, in terms of some picture or another, it is very difficult to succeed. Does another way of identifying a representative description of what happens when we talk about internal objects exist? Or would it perhaps be better to use a term other than that of representation? Such as that of "engram" of which I have spoken and will speak of, which seems to lend itself to name the mnestic trace of some elements, even without a form, even untranslatable into words, such as what we can infer in babies, and that can represent some acquisition of the nascent mind, and that above all has to have a neural equivalent. In this perspective, any "information that reaches the brain has to have a representation" (Siegel, 1999, p. 205, Italian edition). Below we will specify better the concept of "representation of function".

The fact is that insufficient consideration has been given to how the external world, with its objects, is transformed "internally": how from the afferences provided by the senses we go to "something" that we can define as mental but which cannot be illustrated. We then have to wonder which physical media are collected by the sensory systems, how these transmit information to neural systems and how an organisation takes place here (which we could call processing), which is translated into something mental; and lastly how the nascent mental system of the baby organises it into some significance for its operativity and further development.

Perception and affect

In the past (Imbasciati, 1978) I have already tried to describe the internal object as shown above, in the light of the developments, both psychoanalytic and experimental, on the observation of the baby and child. In the foetal period as the sensory receptor systems and the relative nervous pathways mature, and neural impulses, specific for each type of receptor, reach the brain; this does not yet mean "perception". Neural networks and populations have to be organised in the brain and their activities, by collecting from the specific nervous pathways the relative neural impulses, have to be able to process a specific response; the most elementary one is the recognition of the quality of the afferent impulse

A NEW METAPSYCHOLOGY CONGRUENT WITH NEUROSCIENCE 139

(for example hearing or sight). We thus know that between the fourth and the fifth month of pregnancy, the foetus recognises sound stimuli: they therefore have a specific "meaning" and therefore we can say that the foetus "perceives" them. Even though this perception has an extremely limited discriminative nature (we could say without an object with respect to what will progressively be organised in the following months and after birth, up to the ability to distinguish sounds from words and therefore understanding a language), we can consider it as a first form of perceptive organisation. Similar maturing takes place with respect to what is sent by other receptors: we specify here that "maturing" does not mean at all that it has to take place by genetic prescription. It takes place by experience; the experience, in this case simply receiving neural impulses from the peripheral receptors, produces an organisation in the neural structure which receives them, so that it organises the afferent which receives in some rudimentary perception.

What has been exemplified for the sensoriality coming from the cochlear system also takes place for the other receptor systems: vestibular for movement and the position in space, pressor for the relative receptors of the dermis and epidermis, thermal, chemical (endogenous and gustative-olfactory), luminous (which will have the greatest development after birth). A capacity for perception will be organised on the experience of this reception and a progressive type of perception will gradually take over. The organisation of the perception of pain, which appears to enjoy a major innate component, called nociception, is questionable and obscure regarding maturing by experience. This perception shows reflex characteristics, therefore it would be innate by genetic prescription, rather than by response by a perceptive organisation; perception will be built up subsequently. The construction of visceral perception is similarly uncertain.

The afference coming from all the receptors, distributed in the inner viscera and in every other organ (including blood) of the body, mediated by the vagus nerve and already partially processed in the paravertebral ganglia (the first processing centre of what has been called the sympathetic system and the parasympathetic system), deserves special attention. All these afferences are organised at a subperceptual level, which in the baby represents a sixth sense (the polyvagal theory of Porges, 2011), which is almost conscious insofar as we can speak of consciousness in a baby. Unlike the other "senses", this type of

140 MINDBRAIN, PSYCHOANALYTIC INSTITUTIONS, AND PSYCHOANALYSTS

neonatal perception does not reach a more properly aware discrimination in the adult.

Alongside the neural organisation that processes the reception of the afferences in perception, neural networks that can regulate the efferent are organised: in the perceptive experience which is organised for almost all the types of afferences (especially proprioception which in turn is organised from the tactile one, pressor, and tendon-osteomuscular afferences) the motor skills mature or better the psycho-motor coordination is organised. The above does not yet mean however that the baby and then the child perceive defined objectives from the receptive-perceptive organisation, as an older child or adult perceives them. A baby a few weeks old begins to distinguish an auditory perception from a visual one, or tactile-pressor or vestibular, or proprioceptive, or visceral and so on, but cannot yet perceive defined objects. On the basis of his progressive capacity to distinguish the different sensory orders and then perceptive ones, and at the same time integrate them with respect to their sources, the child will become able to identify "forms" of the different sensorialities (= different impingements) that mean objects of the world surrounding him: perception of visual, auditory, tactile-proprioceptive objects, etc., which are increasingly closer to real objects, with which he will learn to interact. At the beginning, however, in the foetus and in the baby of a few days, nothing authorises us to think that he can perceive defined objects. A baby cannot see, in the sense that a baby of a few months can see. It is the same for the other perceptive capacities. In a baby, the afferences of various orders are mixed, for example thermal and sound, in a single perception: the same applied to visceral, pain and visual afferences, or gustative or tactile ones and so on. The "objects" which are thus perceived are therefore absurd compositions which do not correspond to any real object. This is the psychophysiological explanation of an "internal object".

And the affects? We can start to talk about what we call affect when the different neural organisations matured by the various experiences from the exterior and from the body become capable of producing something more complex, and internal: for example, an absence of perception of pain and heterothermal perception (= cold/hot), with the presence of a tactile, proprioceptive and gustative perception together with the disappearance of biochemical sensorialities of haematic origin (hunger/ satiety) could be combined in a single trace, which remains active for a possible recognition of similar experience, in a sort of protomemory,

A NEW METAPSYCHOLOGY CONGRUENT WITH NEUROSCIENCE   141

in this case being breastfed. This trace could in turn be compared with mnestic constellations of other experiences in which there is some nociception, not only the classic ones, by injuries caused by external agents, but also visceral and metabolic ones. One trace that we can say is positive can be compared with a negative one and they could be combined in unique recognition of an external event: the result may have a valence of aversion as of rapprochement, towards the event that has arisen again. What I call "valence" here is a functional capacity; a "trace of function". We can consider this trace of neuromnestic-perceptive processing a prototype of affect (Imbasciati, 1991).

We could align this activity (or ability?) with the unpleasure principle (Fairbairn, 1952; Guntrip, 1961) and schematise it as the protomental operation "pain yes/pain no", the starting point for a series of subsequent acquisitions of various levels of "protomental operations" (Imbasciati & Calorio, 1981).

Insofar as the traces remain active even in the absence of new perceptions of afferences combinations, their relative stabilisation constitutes an ability of the nascent system to produce and reproduce that something which forms the prototype of the affect: the "product" of the incipient operating capacity of the mind, which will gradually be integrated in articulations with further experiences.

The formation of a first rudimentary affect can thus be explained, which will then increasingly be articulated and differentiated and will allow, for example by being integrated with the visual perception that has developed, identifying "objects of affect" (objects with promote the activation of the internal process just described) in external reality; we could say the mother, or even the Breast. We know that this Breast is not a breast or a bottle: it is an absurd set of various perceptions together with that internal product just described, which can be called protoaffect.

In addition, we cannot think (as adults do) that the baby can feel this object as if it is placed in external reality, rather than in the internal one. An experiential primal trace has to be formed, to recognise what "the exterior" may be, respect to something that will be identified as interior and corporal. The baby cannot know if that something he has learned to recognise, and which adults identify as a nipple, comes to him from outside or whether it is part of his body, or better, of the same experience that he is having at that moment. Even the idea of the body as such, or more simply of the mouth, are conquests that the baby will

142   MINDBRAIN, PSYCHOANALYTIC INSTITUTIONS, AND PSYCHOANALYSTS

access. A first idea of outside/inside of the body must be articulated, to which a different exterior/interior will then be attributed, in order to be able to reach the idea of an object that is different from his own body. All this has to organise a sort of rudimentary "space", on which the mental product that we can call identification of a self, first only corporal and then again a differentiated self/other (Imbasciati & Calorio, 1981, Imbasciati, 2006a, 2006b) which is also corporal has to be implanted, and only much later as a psychic experience of continuity.

The mental aggregates that we are progressively describing—here the name of "engram" can be recalled—will be increasingly articulated by every subsequent experience, enriching the ability of the neuromental system to "produce" new internal functions, therefore considered "products" to use in the encounter with every subsequent perceptive-experiential configuration. In this process, what we can call "product" or "ability" to produce new internal functions therefore also considered internal "products", which will be used for every new experiential-perceptual configuration. What we can call internal product, or ability to produce new internal functions (they also are internal products), will be increasingly articulated with the experience of external derivation, and will be differentiated to resemble the affects that flow in adults. All this is similar to what the neurosciences tell us about the formation of new neural networks on each new "experience" which is organised, both for what arrives from "outside", often interpersonal, and what is integrated (flanked?) into all the pre-existing memory networks, but above all for what is produced, as a final functional outcome, by the new and pre-existing neural networks.

It is worth recalling here how the conscious experience of affects felt by an adult does not coincide at all with the affects that flow in him without him realising it. This is one of the discoveries of psychoanalysis. Nor can we consider what happens in an adult as equivalent to what happens in a baby, nor vice versa, with a simplistic inferential analogy.

In an adult the affect can be described by analogy with the conscious affect, but in the child, who does not yet have consciousness, we cannot describe it or even identify it. We therefore have to have an idea of what it consists of. In other words, we need a psychophysiological "explanation" of what happens; afterwards on these grounds we can attempt a "description" of what he could feel. In the frame just described, the affect finds its explanation. In the baby and in the small child this is a first internal functional product (by his incipient neural processing activity),

A NEW METAPSYCHOLOGY CONGRUENT WITH NEUROSCIENCE 143

which is connected to perceptions, in the random way described. This first internal product, or construction of functionality, is the result of a neural organisation which has been built up and which is the trace of it; it "represents" this internal product.

We can then speak of representation of the affect, by extending the term representation and not imagining it like an image, or a picture, as the consciousness of an adult may suppose it.

In this "internal product", represented by a trace of functions (neural networks), we also have to consider what in an adult we will call memory, or rather mnestic trace of some previous integration of various sensorialities. This trace, which we can call memory (but not recollection) due to its varied and for us absurd composition, cannot be distinguished from what can be assembled internally with other traces at psychic level: we call it (Imbasciati & Calorio, 1981) proto-imagination.

It can often be evoked, in the mind of a baby by some sudden perception: the external object from which it comes in this case, together with previous traces, is thus "hallucinated"; it is a sort of imagination, but very different from that of an adult. Hallucination for babies is talked of, but in actual fact this is not exact, as the child has not yet learned to integrate the various orders[19] between one another (nor separate them from his internal products) with what the activity of other neural networks are continuously producing, whether we call it memory or affects (memories in feelings of Kleinian intuition?). There is a real hallucination when in an adult the acquired ability of assembling, efficiently with respect to reality, the various orders of perception and separating them from what is produced by the internal activity no longer functions. The child does not hallucinate, or "split" the real object as Klein said: he is not yet capable of correctly integrating the various orders of perception and the concomitant continuous internal activity in order to perceive the real external object as adults perceive it, and to distinguish it from the recollection or the imagination, as we adults distinctly do.

The strange internal objects that inhabit the baby's mind, and the perception of the world, intrigue what we called affect and what we could call perception, and mix them with its own corporal (preperceptive), especially visceral, afferences. This is the "bad" breast, when a physical pain, a biochemical deficiency signalled by the body's chemioreceptors, a contraction of the viscera or a misplaced position of the mother's arm, or a proto-recollection, enter into the composition of some first engram of the situation of breastfeeding-caring. The Kleinian statement that the internal object is completely dissimilar from external objects as "invested" by affects, could then be recovered, but in a psychophysiological frame of representations and not recalling the drive that would split the external object. This latter proposition is extremely reductive as it infers a natural automatism (not acquired) of perception: "The Picture in the Head"; this does not even take place in the adult (Imbasciati & Purghè, 1981).

The protomental system

From the psychophysiological explanation of the internal object as a set of mixed afferent traces, outlined in my work of 1978, I gradually developed (1981, 1994, 1998, 2006a, 2006b) the protomental theory, to explicate the origin and the entire development of the mind: the basic point is that the internal objects are multiple and progressive. Their differentiation means the equally progressively ability, acquired by the system, of "making" sets (aggregating, assembling), which can be considered as internal "products", functions of the same system, which in turn will be mixed and then integrated with other mnestic-perceptive constellations. At this stage we can speak of affects.

The progressive protomental acquisitions, which lead to the capacity of perceiving a reality external to the self, distinguishing it from one's own necessary mental products, appears very laborious. Klein described the paranoid–schizoid situation as marked by aggressive affects directed at the object and turned against the subject in a persecutory mechanism. This description, consequential to her agreement with the Freudian theory, has been the subject of an explanatory hypothesis which can be categorised in the neuropsychological theory of the protomental processes that I am summarising here (Imbasciati, 2006b): it would be a question of the laborious difficulty of proceeding with the distinction between one's own products (function's constructions) to be attributed to an as yet unformed self, rather than to an external origin of which a perception is being constructed. In particular, this would generate a product, a protoaffect, derived from a sort of frustration (the analogy is adultistic) in the attempts to eliminate (= remove) something that contains negative elements, elements of "pain". This laboriousness of the protomental system as it is being organised could be considered the precursor of that in more adult states we would call "anger". This precursor, perhaps due to its counter-satisfactory content, cannot be attributed to the self, which moreover is still completely uncertain, but it is attributed to an "object", even though nebulous. The latter, due to this process (we could say projection) is formed as even more obscure, unpleasant, painful and indeed pain-giving, "angry" and persecutory.

The "unpleasantness" I defined here as a sort of anger, can be inferred considering the innateness in the child, as in all small animals, for exploring the world, we could say for knowledge: the confused engrams have to be eliminated, something that has been produced has to be removed, denied, and erased. In this process, the beginning ability of an efficiently organising the various afferences, is compromised: in order to remove "something" which has happened and which is painful. There is a sort of erasure, almost self-mutilation, of the nascent system of organising the "mental". The neo-Kleinian schools have spoken about mental pain intrinsic in thought: Bion postulated a negative thought as an anti-cognitive process, which he called—K function. In my theorisation, I have called this process autotomy (*tomos* = to cut): something that could have become knowledge, a "piece of thought" or better a nascent rudimentary protothought, is excised. This "protomental operation" is the equivalent in cognitive terms of the process described clinically in affective terms as expulsion of pain, or better, expulsion of "bad" internal objects. Autotomy is the equivalent, from a neuropsychological point of view, of the process indicated by Bion with the mathematical symbol f(–K). At neural level, we can think of the deactivation of some neural networks.

The process of organisation of the afferences, aimed at representing a distinction between something internal and an external object: therefore, it appears very laborious, contrasted by the inverse process of destructuring the incipient capacity of distinction; internal products— affects?—can be attributed—projected, or perceived?—to external origins, and vice versa, configurations of external origin can in turn be assimilated with the incipient self or better to an inside which can in this way be found to contain something threatening. From this neuropsychophysiological vertex, I have considered the paranoid-schizoid situation differently from M. Klein. I have used the term paranoid-schizoid "metabolism" to indicate the volatility and the permanence of this

146   MINDBRAIN, PSYCHOANALYTIC INSTITUTIONS, AND PSYCHOANALYSTS

situation (Imbasciati, 2006a, 2006b). In this phase of the organisational neuromental process, the engrams that progressively represent aggregations of afferences and of internal products are multiple, variable and unpredictably interchangeable; the "inside" and the "outside" are confused and so is the incipient self with respect to real external objects. Using psychoanalytic language, we say that there are massive projections and reintrojections. At neurological level, we could presume that the neural networks are formed and taken apart.

From the same psychophysiological point of view, we can again describe the depressive position, or better, the change from the paranoid-schizoid situation to a stabilisation of the neuromental abilities of distinguishing[20] the impact with the external reality with respect to one's internal events. The progressive organisation of the previous engrams is flanked by others, in which the external/internal confusion progressively decreases, and therefore increases the ability to perceive the external reality more correctly. Another "sort of perception",[21] or better, sense of belonging to an "inside" or to an incipient self, is organised with regard to the interior products which we have called affects; their "representation" becomes less mixed with elements of a sensory origin. This corresponds to what, in the classic dynamic-affective language of psychoanalysis, is described as the onset of guilt feelings for having hated loved objects: the "sense" of having inside oneself impulses of anger-hate which the previous paranoid-schizoid situation attributed in a persecutory way to the exterior. The confused engrams of the previous situation are, so to speak, corrected, rectified, "repaired" with respect to their possibility of better serving knowledge. It would be a repair of cognitive value, described in neurophysiological terms instead of affects; which inevitably are assimilated with the adult ones, even though referred to infants, to whom, however, the experimental data does not allow us to attribute them.

The depressive metabolism is organised and then consolidated by the original paranoid-schizoid metabolism. The whole system evolves, as the child grows, up to the differentiation of capacities for consciousness, and with these of an adequate perception of external reality, up to a finer discrimination of one's experiences; that is up to what we can call thoughts like we consider them in the common language, when they appear precise and adequate with respect to the subject's conduct, and therefore they appear lucid in the awareness of a more adult individual. In this evolution, from the confused primary objects to more differentiated experiences, from the whirlwind of emotions, to the affects, to the glimmer of an adequate perception of reality, up to what can appear as organised thought, there is a continuous organisation, destruction, repair and reorganisation of engrams.

The following schematic diagram summarises the evolutions described above (Figure 5—Imbasciati, 1991, 2006a, 2006b).

The figure, with a horizontal tree, shows the progressive ramifications (differentiations) of the sets of traces which, from the primitive internal objects, evolve towards the more developed experiences or from the primary affects, with their protorepresentations, to the representations in a narrower sense. The primary internal object is given by a particular mixing of the various traces, which however tend to be differentiated, into the two orders of "the perceived", i.e., the experience of "outside" (afferences) and that of the imagined-recollection ("inside": internal productions). The vertical arrows indicate the possibility that during the evolutionary process, and in the unconscious of the adult, the two orders of differentiation can still be mixed together. The paranoid-schizoid functioning (on the left) represents the greatest possibility of inter-exchange between the various ramifications which had been differentiated, mixing together again the various sets. As long as the paranoid-schizoid functioning yields to the depressive one, the differentiations are stabilised. The adjustment made by the registration of movement by the differentiation and organisation of the efferences is shown by E (= efferences): the whole development is regulated by the interaction with reality and motor efficacy plays a fundamental role in this interaction. An adequate distinction between external and internal reality, as well as an adequate capacity to clearly distinguish these, and to perceive something in internal reality (intrapsychic permeability) are necessary, although insufficient conditions for the representational system to be felt at some level of consciousness.

I have called the theory outlined above "Protomental Theory" as the clinical description of the observation of the foetus, of the baby and of the infant, or about its "protomental" manifestations, has allowed an explanation of the origins and development of the mind in terms comparable to what the neurosciences tell us about the development and functioning of the brain according to experience (*cf.* Chapters Three and Four). The explanation my theory gives represents a way of translating the affective processes described in the usual terms of psychoanalysis

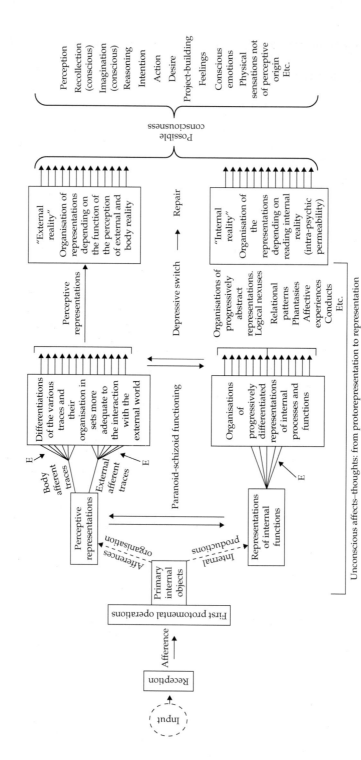

Figure 5. From affect to thought.

A NEW METAPSYCHOLOGY CONGRUENT WITH NEUROSCIENCE   149

in cognitive terms compatible (Wilson, 1998) with the development and functioning of the brain.

A new metapsychology

The Protomental Theory (Imbasciati & Calorio, 1981; Imbasciati, 1994, 1998, 2006a, 2006b), which I have summarised here, has represented the intermediate pathway of my integration of the different psychological sciences, towards the formulation of a new metapsychology. This theory represents a way of organically connecting the concepts in current psychoanalysis, especially in its references to the observation of the baby (Bick, 1964) and to clinical practice with mothers and babies with all the relative literature, to better understand the interior development of the individual up to adulthood. These developments of clinical psychoanalysis can be integrated with the clinical applicative data of attachment theory (infant research) and with the data from experimental psychology (perception, learning, their origin and development). The importance of considering the neuropsychophysiological aspect comes from the latter: this represents the explicative perspective with respect to the descriptiveness of the two other vertexes. I am referring again to the fundamental epistemological distinction between description and explication.[22]

The consideration of a neuropsychophysiological explication cannot fail to recall neuroscience, especially in their current neuropsychoanalytic orientation; unfortunately, this is not reciprocally shared by psychoanalysts (Merciai, 2013). Since the very beginning, my theory has taken into account what neuroscience tells us, at least in not being in contradiction with what we know about the brain. This was Freud's intention one hundred years ago when he wrote his *On Metapsychology* (Freud, 1915; Imbasciati, 2007b, 2007c, 2010a, 2011a). The theoretical structure of his Energy-drive Theory sought "justification" (as the first paragraph of the third essay of his *On Metapsychology* says) of the unconscious: in other words, he attempted to formulate an explanation of the origin and functioning of the mind using the "hard" sciences (which means sciences tending to be explicative), of the time; and in particular what was known then about the brain. Neurophysiology has developed enormously since Freud's time and clinical psychoanalysis has also changed. The Energy-drive Theory, although it has never been declared as superseded by the psychoanalytic institutions which are considered the direct heirs of Freud, appears very remote, or even in contrast with clinical psychoanalysis (Imbasciati, 2011b, 2012a, 2013a, 2013b). Today there is an enormous gap between clinical psychoanalysis and the relative theorisation on mental functioning.

My Protomental Theory, due to its multiple roots, was subsequently developed in particular for its reference to neuropsychophysiology, as a new metapsychology, and I suggested it as such (Cena & Imbasciati, 2013), with the hope that it can be enriched and perfected by the neuroscience (Imbasciati, 2007b, 2010a, 2010b) or even revolutionised, but above all with the hope that psychoanalysts can also enrich it, overcoming their proud mistrust of the other sciences. My theory, as it befits a theory in the proper sense, is a hypothesis (as was Freud's one) which attempts to connect the discoveries and the concepts of the different sciences of the mind in a general explanatory theory of the origins and functioning of the mind, so that, by drawing on a comparison with the various sciences, it can be useful for psychoanalysis: for the clinical practice of psychoanalysts and above all for the public image of psychoanalysis in the general scientific panorama. I therefore expect that others, psychoanalysts like myself, can venture into the other sciences, neuroscience and experimental psychology in particular, to develop, or oppose the hypotheses outlined here. This endeavour however, appears to be difficult for the institution (Brosio, 2015).

Bion, unanimously acknowledged by all psychoanalysts of all "kinds", declared fifty years ago that the psychic structure is organised for "learning from experience" (1962): since then, however, there has been few investigation of how learning means mnestic trace, at neural level, as a representation of what has been learned. Psychoanalysis has always spoken about affects: they are still discussed as though the way of conceiving them were separable, or even completely cut off from cognition and from cognitive processes. This conception starts from not considering the affects are learned and therefore there is their functional mnestic trace, at neural and mental level in the continuous transformation throughout every subsequent experience. Other elementary, and even more primary cognitive processes are learned, starting from learning perceptive skills. Perception is not a simple automatic process by the brain as a record of the sensory afferences, as was believed a century ago, including by Freud (1920g, vol. 9, pp. 210–219): they are the final conscious result in the adult of work by neural structures, which have to be built up in infancy according to experience and which,

A NEW METAPSYCHOLOGY CONGRUENT WITH NEUROSCIENCE   151

once constructed, operate on sensoriality. The baby does not perceive, in the proper sense of the word. Perception must not be confused with sensoriality, nor with a mere compulsory and specific reaction (reflex) to a specific sensory impingement.

Before having the result of perceiving, as in the perceptive consciousness in the adult, in the baby and in the child, myriads of progressive and different assemblages of sensory inputs traces are constructed, which take on "some" meaning; this does not concern representations of any real object, but meanings resulting from the operating possibilities that are used, and that will subsequently be articulated by the nascent system of the mind. As far as a sort of primitive rudimentary cognition is concerned, these assemblages are not organised as in the adult to indicate perceptible objects: i.e., they are not sets of sensorialities solicited by stimuli which come from the external object which we expect to be perceived in the adult (and which people still believe perceived as it is) but by multiple other orders of input, both external (exteroception) and somatic, multisensory and widely varying and confused, and internal, i.e., produced internally by the same incipient mind-system, of an affective order we could say, in their turn relative to other proto-meanings with which the relation with the caregiver is worked out.

When M. Klein said that the external object is split, giving the "internal" objects, she implied the same naïve conception of perception that was known until 1930 (Imbasciati, 1986, vol. 2): the external object is not split at all; for the simple reason that the neuromental structure has not yet learned the ability of assembling the various inputs that come from the physical objects in order to give the perceptive (psychic) result that an adult can have. Speaking of splitting means presupposing a perception of the "picture in the head" type (Kaufmann, 1974), which unfortunately still persists in psychoanalytic culture. The various inputs, on the other hand, between them and between the various sensorialities that the adult learns to separate, are mixed together, and also remixed with the "internal products" that the mind already produces: as if they were considered inputs to be further worked out; we have called them affects and intentionality, perhaps too much from an adult point of view. They are moreover organisations produced by an internal work which are mixed with the various sensorialities. The baby and the child perceive only "precursors" of the perception in the proper sense; configurations which for us are absurd, from the most widely varying inputs, especially internal. In this way, the affects produce the "internal objects".

152 MINDBRAIN, PSYCHOANALYTIC INSTITUTIONS, AND PSYCHOANALYSTS

These configurations, precursors of adult perception, remain potentially active in working out what can be identified as an unconscious affective nucleus in the adult (Imbasciati, 1991).

Each "working out"—or "working through" as a term dear to psychoanalysts—presupposes progressive levels of transformation of the "representations" and therefore of the relative mnestic traces at neural level: this progressive transformation of the neural traces presupposes in its turn that the neural apparatus "learns to do them" and in the most opportune evolutionary way, which means that the brain acquires those functions (new connections in the neural networks and therefore new mnestic traces, i.e., function memories) that allow it. We can then consider that this extremely elementary functional acquisition, represents a trace in the neural system. In this sense in my work I have spoken of "representation" or better still, "function trace", and therefore of engram. This last term can represent the elementary unit of each "function memory". This is implicit memory.

The origin, the development and the functioning of the mind do not take place as Freud had hypothesised in his *On Metapsychology*, due to endogenous psychobiological forces which in their encounter/clash with reality, but has to be thought and described in terms of progressive learning: the foetus, the baby, the infant and then the child and the adult as well, learn progressively and continuously. This learning obviously must not be understood, according to an adultistic habit, as learning of contents, recognition of objects, let alone learning of "notions", but as learning of progressive "functions". These are functions of the mental system which is being formed or progressive ways of operating, in transforming sensory inputs into internal products which in their turn are formed as mental functions, or rather skills; learning of functions from the most elementary ones of a perceptive type, as described above for the baby (and even earlier of protorepresentations of sensory configurations which the foetus shows that it recognises), to other ones which gradually become more complex and allow connecting what he perceives to a self that is being formed, and to distinguish this—first as a body—from what is "understood" as being "outside", and then again from what is produced by the same incipient mind.

The further distinction of a perceiving self, not only somatic, and then a subjectivity as well, will be developed from this incipient ability. Here is the problem: distinguishing a mnestic representation (which can be used to recognise something) from the equivalent perception of the corresponding external event; and from the incipient ability of the

A NEW METAPSYCHOLOGY CONGRUENT WITH NEUROSCIENCE 153

system to "imagine" something. This is the ability, which the child has to acquire, of distinguishing between memory rather than perception or imagination. When this ability of distinction is not yet structured, the distinction between perception/hallucination/memory is not possible (Imbasciati, 2008). The baby does not have hallucinations, as is often said; he has not yet learned to discriminate what he imagines, so to speak, from some "recollection" of previous reality and this from a current perception; as well as from an incipient "affect", to be considered as the first product of an elaborating activity of the mind.

The baby attains these and other discriminatory abilities: "the outside", "the inside", what is experienced as "good" and what is experienced as "bad", the reformulation of the Kleinian concepts of "good breast/bad breast" in terms of internal polysensory objects confused with the psychic products and other ones. He learns a multiplicity of functions and "operations", which are protomental and then more properly mental, progressively evolved. Learning, in a minimal part to be considered accidental (this term to be understood according to the psychology of learning) is for the most part produced by the confirmation/disconfirmation of the mother's response, i.e., by the dialogue, syntonic or not, with the caregiver. In this way the baby learns increasingly articulated ways of learning; each elementary mental function allows learning a more complex one. Similar learning also takes place in all the adult's intimate relationships, including the analytic one. Obviously, the above is learned much earlier than any ability for any consciousness can be constructed in the system.

The engram: neuropsychic mnestic trace

It is now widely confirmed that the origin, development and functioning of the mind come about by learning,[23] but a reference to neurosciences is needed for a real explanation (a "why" = explication) such as that required for a new metapsychology. That there has been learning is acknowledged afterwards, from the effects on the individual's conduct: this is however a description of the observation, conducted with concepts of a psychological type, but not yet an "explication". It is still a "how" and not a "why".

I believe that the key towards discovering a why, in analogy with what Freud did, in his thinking of a psychobiological energy and coining the concept of drive by which hypothesising vicissitudes in analogy with the hard sciences of the time, can be found in the mnestic trace. This key may be found in a trace relative to every progressive learning and ability to learn, above all, in mnestic traces of progressive "functions". Any function whatsoever, even elementary, that the system gradually acquires (= learns), starting from foetal priming, will have its equivalent in some set of neural connections, which by becoming established, forms with its operating potential the trace of those functions; in other words, the ability to function in that way. The functions which are progressively acquired allow further learning, especially of more new functions. In other words, every new ability that is observed developing in the baby and in the child will correspond to some organisation of the neural network, the formation of which is its trace: this organisation will allow further and more complex learning (we could recall the Piagetian concepts of accommodation) of which, and in their turn, a trace will be established. I have called this trace an "engram", using the term in a very general sense, to indicate the neural modification (connections) which forms the mnestic trace necessary for any elementary function whatsoever to be carried out, with this term very far from representing defined, let alone real, objects.

For the formulation of a new metapsychology, a concept is required that summarises the psychological one of representation, the psychophysiological one of mnestic trace and the neurological one of brain structuring: the organisation of neural networks the functioning of which is an expression of an ability, even very elementary, which has been learned; as is experimentally proven today with neuroimaging technology (Schore, 2003a, 2003b), with the greatest evidence in mother/infant relationships.

The concept of "function trace" applies to any ability, including perceptive, even elementary, which is found as acquired in the baby and in the child, first of all that of developing and manifesting what tradition has indicated as affects: a mnestic trace therefore of affects, to the marvel of the reader who has the obsolete content-related—and perhaps consciousnessist—concept of the term trace.

It is worth recalling here again how everything that is described is well beyond any awareness or consciousness. Memory does not mean recollection, nor any similar ability in the conscious subjectivity. Nor does memory mean storage. The memory is essentially plastic, as experimental psychology and then the neurosciences have defined it for some time, as is learning and every trace of it. Not only every moment of new acquisition depends on the previous one, but retroactively, each new ability modifies the previous ones and can actually cancel them. Freud's *nachträglichkeit* can be seen here again, as well as everything that ensued in psychoanalytic literature.[24] In terms of traces, the formation of new neural organisations (= abilities, functions) can retroactively condition the previous ones. This neurophysiological concept also applies to the organising and reorganising of more complex functions, such as those which underpin the progressive development of "thought". The path towards a thought which is increasingly articulated can, due to these reorganisations, not only gradually change but even be inverted: we could speak of the inversion of the function α (alpha) described by Bion, considered in terms of learning which modifies and in some ways cancels what had been learned previously; bearing clearly in mind that this learning with a cancelling retroactive effect is not necessarily learning from the exterior, but could be "learning" some internal work. The term learning therefore does not necessarily have a positive meaning.[25]

Amongst the first functions that are formed in the baby, those which oversee actions and interactions deserve special attention: first of all reactions to stimuli, the specificity of which will depend on a certain way of "recognising" the stimulus in its corresponding specificity, up to the actions in relation to perceptive recognitions; and also, to actions that show intentionality, in which the function is revealed as more complex and implying an internal processing of the protomind, to finally reach—and this is by far the most important processing—effective interactions. In other words, those abilities which are modulated by the interactive dialogue with the caregiver are finally acquired.

The description of this development is underpinned by the recent discoveries on the mirror neurons (Gallese, 2012). The neurosciences have shown how an individual, in the face of a gesture or movement by another individual, activates his motor neurons mirroring the activation of the neural areas that in the other individual perform that specific action. This would mark out the interactive joint participation in the action of the other person, but above all the comprehension of the meaning intrinsic in those actions, in order to be ready to respond adequately. The system of mirror neurons would thus be the base of intersubjectivity (which is of such great interest today to psychoanalysts). This intersubjectivity implies a reciprocal comprehension in a syntonic dialogue which would be evidence that the subjectivity of the two individuals in dialogue has been formed. Subjectivity means the basal sense of having an identity, the feeling of existing and being oneself, acting in the events of one's life and communicating with other "subjects". All this means reciprocal comprehension of a non-verbal communication; this would all take place at motor level and without any awareness.

This system is active in many animal species (Panksepp & Biven, 2012), in primates in particular, and there is discussion about how much is made up of an innate base ad how much is acquired—in interactions. This seems to take place in the first days or weeks of the baby's life, following the interactions with the caregivers. It is also supposed that, just as the system which acts mediated by visual perception has been discovered, there are also corresponding systems mediated by other senses, for example visceral (Porges, 2011).

The system that has been called of the mirror neurons does not mean a mirror-like effect of particular neural cells with respect to a supposed direct influx by cells of another individual, but presupposes major work by the brain, especially considering the receiver, in this case the baby, who participates in the initiative of a dialoguing adult. In the first place neural networks have to be constructed in the baby's brain that can allow perception, i.e., the composition of the afferences in sets that configure perceived "objects"; in the second place, that this first perceptive meaning is further processed as "intention", or a global meaning of the other's action. Only considering this passage, which in actual fact can only presuppose an enormous amount of work of perhaps all the neural networks, can we be right about the activating of the motor areas which in their most precise sequence reproduce what the brain as understood about the motor organisation of the other as it was delivering its meaning.

In other terms, the mirror-system says that the brain becomes equipped, by building specific and adequate neural networks, for an immediate and automatic comprehension of others' intentions; this is the basis of non-verbal communication which can, if adequately syntonic, make the child's mind develop. On these grounds, there is a great deal to reflect on what acts in the immediate and unaware communication between adults and between analyst and patient.

An understanding of the meanings conveyed by non-verbal communication seems to be the essential presupposition for the subsequent learning of language. The progressive acquisition of function traces, as described for the baby, corresponds to meanings which will then be expressed by a language's grammar. The acquisition of perceptive organisations that can configure objects seems to precede the linguistic acquisition of the substantive; the interactive meaning organised with the support of motor skills seems to precede the grammatical meaning of verbs (actions, relation functions, possibly of dialoguing interactions). Later we will be able to speak about adjectives, only when the mind's abilities to produce more articulated affective processing, feelings, affects, pleasure/displeasure and to perceive them "in some way". Then adverbs; the function of processing intensity, duration, temporality, succession. The child has thus acquired the fundamental meanings of language well before language itself: words are only conventional significants of the language of an individual culture.

The problem of acquisition of the trace refers to neurophysiology and the biochemistry of the brain. Freud spoke of investment of the energy drive on objects. Today, we can say that development takes place through the progressive establishment of neural networks; traces of progressive learning functions, "engrams", each of which allows and conditions the subsequent function, the subsequent engram.

Just like Freud, by using the hard sciences of his time invented the concept of drive, with which he built up his general theory of the origin and functioning of the mind, today, by using current cognitions of neurosciences on the brain structure made by the first learning (what was called affects and mother/infant communication), we can formulate the more significant and concrete concept of the engram: a neural trace of any acquisition whatsoever, from the basic ones of the baby (and of the foetus) to all the subsequent ones; all these traces are acquired from relationships, from the mother/baby ones to those, similarly intimate and prolonged, such as relationships of love and living together as well as what is acquired, and structured in the analytic relationship. It is from here that the clinical value of non-verbal communication comes. Freud wanted to "explicate" his psychoanalysis to his contemporaries; today, we can offer another and more updated "explication" to our contemporaries on the basis of the neuroscience; "engram" or mnestic trace instead of "drive".

The key concept at the start of Freud's theoretical construction was drive: a concept defined by the master as "psychobiological". In my theorisation, the starting concept is that of the engram, as I have described it here, which can also be defined as psychobiological, but with the further specification of "psychoneural". It is related to the mnestic trace, which today we know corresponds to neural networks. Molecular biology will further investigate (Alberini, 2013) in which conditions and by which biochemical processes the new synapses are created; which form the neural network which then acts as the mnestic trace of all new learning.

As in the conjectures on the drive investment, relative psychobiological events (in relation to psychic and situational events) were hypothesised, independently of the causal explanation of the biochemistry of the neural connections, we can hypothesise in a new metapsychology how and in which circumstances the trace that marks the acquisition of a function is formed. This is certainly conditioned by the caregiver: this observation should however be clarified. We would have to know how non-verbal dialogue, syntonic or not, between the caregiver and the baby, conveys meanings in the sets of afferent inputs which are coded by both sides: these meanings are constructed, so to speak, on the emanated sets of afferences. We would have to know how a certain trace is conditioned or rather produced, to give functional organisation of neural networks. Neurosciences seem to give us the answer: an optimal (neither too high nor too low) emotional (biochemical) level, is required for the formation of new synapses and neural networks (Alberini, 2013; Cena & Imbasciati, 2014). This assumes the best evidence in the infant/caregiver relationship, but probably occurs in every other intimate and extended contact, such as the analyst/patient one.

At the origin of the mind

A particular problem, but fundamental in the conception summarised here, is constituted in the beginnings of development: how is the first function trace formed? As any ability to process any afferences for the purposes of learning in a given trace that regulates its function (acquisition) depends on some ability of the pre-existing neural organisation, why is the first one formed? We know that the foetus shows the ability to react specifically to a given stimulus; therefore it "recognises" it (Imbasciati, Dabrassi, & Cena, 2007), there it has "some representation" of it: how has this "trace" been formed? Do we have to presume something innate in the neural networks of the brain? Are any engrams, function traces, expressed directly by the genes before there has been learning? The hypothesis is neurologically reasonable; we should therefore be able to identify its psychic aspect.[26]

In Freud's metapsychology, the start of development is hypothesised in the sources of the drives, in the instinctual energy that would come

A NEW METAPSYCHOLOGY CONGRUENT WITH NEUROSCIENCE   159

from the organs, in particular from the "erogenous" areas. In our more updated metapsychology, what should we posit?

I have hypothesised (Imbasciati, 1998b, 2006a, 2006b) that in the baby a primary device has to do with the enteroceptive afferent of hypoglycaemia which could act as a genetically predetermined stimulus for survival: for a first rudimentary psychic event to come into being, characterised by "displeasure". On this first trace, significant of something that we cannot say is psychic, the temporal alternation of appearance and disappearance of the enteroceptive impingement which produces it, would trigger off a complex and progressive path of formation of subsequent protorepresentations concerning a relative progressive and more articulated meaning linked to the afferences of suction. This could lead to the distinction of a first "inside/outside" and then to other afferences, both somatic and exteroceptive, and lastly to the possibility of forming a protorepresentation of the nutritional event as it was independent from its real disappearance of afferences impingement. The possibility would thus be reached of recognising an external object when it appears from reality, in this case the nipple.

From here we would then arrive at the skill of re-evoking it, first of all without distinction compared to perceiving the afferences configuration that had caused its appearance (or disappearance), i.e., not distinguishing perception from re-evocation and therefore producing what has been called hallucination, subsequently experiencing displeasure even in the re-evocation (= hallucinating is to make the displeasure disappear up to a given limit, after which it reappears, and stronger), to the consequent possibility of cancelling its representation as unpleasant (Imbasciati, Calorio, 1981).

I named this operation as an "autotomy" (tomos = to cut off) of what could have become an incipient activity of "thought",[27] which can be considered equivalent to what Bion had intuited from clinical practice and mathematically theorised as negative K function (f—K), but expressed in psychological and neural biology terms; the forming and disassembling of the mnestic trace made up of neural connections and networks following each new learning experience.

I have subsequently hypothesised a further psychophysiological description of the origins of neuromental development, reformulating the clinical Kleinian intuitions on persecutory anguish, the depressive switch and repair: seen no longer in terms of affects, but of representational engrams that can have a corresponding neural biology. The primitive sense

160 MINDBRAIN, PSYCHOANALYTIC INSTITUTIONS, AND PSYCHOANALYSTS

of unpleasantness marked by glycaemic oscillation (and by many other visceral afferents, Porges, 2011; polyvagal theory) would be configured as an "outside" with respect to the primate state of well-being, originated by some agent event which is configured as "enemy". The possibility would be reached of configuring "displeasure" as inflicted by something external (= persecution, paranoid-schizoid metabolism) and the consequent possibility of removing it with a new autotomy (*cf.* also figure 5).

In some subsequent evolution of new afferences which have arrived at times of a correct emotional gradient (affects?), there would be a reorganisation of the engrams that have been produced in what I have indicated as paranoid-schizoid metabolism; that is a different series of neural connections, which would represent what was described in Kleinian clinical psychoanalysis as "depressive switch" is organised. These new engrams (= neural connections) appear as more suitable to mean the external reality as distinct from what the baby "feels": i.e., from an "inside". The further functions suitable for perception (understood in the proper sense, i.e., of the real conveyed by senses), marked by the formation of more suitable functional traces (engrams) than those of the paranoid-schizoid functioning, would be developed from this matrix: I have called these engrams "repaired", compared to the previous ones, recovering in a cognitive interpretation the clinical intuition that M. Klein conceived in affective terms of "repair". These are mnestic traces for the exercise of better functions, that can reach the ability of operating an effective perception. I have reformulated this way the Kleinian concepts of paranoid-schizoid and depressive position through the concept of repair, understood as the ameliorative modification of the engrams that allow perception.[28]

The situation that Klein defined paranoid-schizoid is explained by the fact that the operating whole of a first neuromental structure cannot distinguish what comes from inside the body (for example hunger or stomach ache) from nociception from the exterior, and even a protomemory (in turn confused with imagination and therefore hallucination) of other nocioceptions, and let alone from an accidental origin rather than aggression by some external intentionality. All this means that every unpleasant event is attributed to the exterior, or to put it better, that every unpleasant afferent can be configured pre-perceptively as an evil external presence: persecution. As the acquisition of function traces which allow distinguishing between the various aforementioned orders of afferences progresses, more appropriate engrams are

A NEW METAPSYCHOLOGY CONGRUENT WITH NEUROSCIENCE   161

constructed. They are appropriate to recognise the distinctions of different afference sets, closer to reality than those that an adult would perceive. The previous engrams, unable to recognise realities, are thus "repaired". New progressive engrams are constructed which loosen the persecutory functioning. These include those which concern the possibility of recognising the internal impulse of aversion against persecution—what was called hatred of the object—which involve the destructive tendency which became autotomic. What can be called in the adult's guilt feeling and the depressive functioning can be situated in this recognition of a process, or rather, of an internal product.

The acquisition of engrams that are more suitable for distinguishing different afference sets (we could say the "repair" of the persecutory protorepresentations) distinguishes the progressive acquisition of engrams that allow perceiving external objects, distinct from other somatic or mental events: the birth of perception.[29] This will be the premise that then distinguishes, in the exterior, what is done by the individual (= motor control) or by action of other elements which are extraneous to the individual (*cf.* fig.5).

What I have summarised here, has been developed in my last two books mentioned above, describing in detail eight progressive levels of "protomental operations". They mark the progressive acquisition of an operating logic, made up of functional mnestic traces up to the formation of those functional traces which allow: a) perception, i.e., the ability to distinguish a world outside the self; b) a self but still to be articulated, through the construction of further differentiated neural organisations, implying more complex functional abilities, through the trace of which that self of which psychoanalytic literature speaks can be progressively constructed, and c) what is known as subjectivity, with the possibility of some consciousness. This "some" consciousness still appears, in its formation, development and functioning, somewhat enigmatic, both in in its ability to be described at psychic level in the interactive events that allow its acquisition and even more in a possible explanation of its progressive neural organisation. Both origins of events evoke the anthropological interrogative of when, in the history of the evolution of homo sapiens, progressive capacities for consciousness were acquired (Jaynes, 1976). Even before that, however, what happened in the history of the evolution of animals? Can we draw hypotheses from this on the foetus and baby? The hypothesis presented here is only one of the many that could be drawn.

162   MINDBRAIN, PSYCHOANALYTIC INSTITUTIONS, AND PSYCHOANALYSTS

I realise that what I have said so far, and concisely with respect to the books in which the topic is described in greater detail, may seem difficult to many readers and require close attention: some psychoanalysts, more inclined to interpreting according to the skills acquired rather than others to be acquired, could consider my presentation an obsessive exercise of little usefulness. This usefulness may be little for the "average psychoanalyst", completely useless if all the previous discussion on "theory" and its usefulness rather than impediment to clinical practice has not been assimilated; as well as on being "scientists" instead of only professionals.

The symbolopoiesis of the mindbrain"

The trace which I have called engram, to represent both the neural event that constitutes it and the protomental and then mental meaning of the psychic process, the ability of which has been acquired, will allow constructing further progressive significants as a construction of further organisations of function traces, of as many meanings (operational) made up of further processings of possible external and internal information. These organisations can progressively signify the most complex events; not only those relative to the various assemblages of the most different afferent configurations (let's not forget the somatic ones) but above all the interpersonal processes (significants of functions), which imply the processing of what the mind has learned internally to produce in itself. This is what has been called emotions and affects; what today is indicated as the work by the right brain in generating the emotional base of thought; a part of that thought may possibly transmit, transfigured, to what we call consciousness.

This transmission and even more the construction of what it will form, neurologically but also psychologically, capable of functioning as an ability for consciousness (of "some" consciousness) is still the great question today, on which research could focus: psychoanalytic research in particular. For decades, psychoanalysis was permeated by the question "Why the unconscious?" Today, as the object of this science has changed, as illustrated above, we should focus on "Why consciousness?" (Imbasciati, 2005b, 2014a, 2014b). Why, when, how, and to what extent: the neuroscientists are investigating it, the psychoanalysts will be able to do it in the current analytic setting, in how, when and to what extent the analyst and the patient have some form of consciousness of what is taking place between them.

We can then state that the object of psychoanalysis is no longer what we generally call the unconscious, but more appropriately the path that from the (ineffable) essence of the mind leads to that variable (and misleading) epiphenomenon that we call consciousness: to date how it takes place and why it gives that specific outcome is still anything but clear.

We can then state, paradoxically for somebody, that the object of psychoanalysis is the study of the consciousness, no longer understood as in the past in a phenomenological sense—examination of the states and variations with respect to the average of what the individual is conscious—but in a genetic sense, i.e., how and why what appears conscious is formed. I believe that this study can have little success, if done in reverse with the analysis of what is verbalised. Verbalisation (= interpretation) absolutely does not reveal the unconscious as such, but is simply and only something that the analyst can notice as having appeared in his consciousness, and which he tries to convert into words because he thinks that this way it can be transmitted to the patient. However, he may notice something very different appearing to him at a different level of consciousness and any event that he notices appearing—a feeling? A malaise? A piece of music? A smell?—is still a presence, filtered by the level of his functioning at that time, which signals "something else" to him: often his own emotional events, perhaps stimulated by emotional events that take place in the patient and which nevertheless in their essence are "ineffable". In psychoanalysis, the appearance of and the attention to these events is included in the consideration of the countertransference. However, more appropriate attention and training comes from a conception of the unconscious as fundamentally different from the verbal one that tradition has handed over to us. These are the events that properly move the conducts of man and the knowledge that he has of the world.

What has been said about the functions of consciousness applies both to the analyst and the patient, for the effects of some changes in the unconscious structure: of the patient and of the analyst as well. This attention to these transforming paths from an unconscious to another unconscious and then to consciousness (in the relationship) can be studied in that laboratory represented by the consulting room. This research can be more successful if carried out together with what can be carried out from the vertex and with the methods of experimental psychology and neuroscience ones. These allow us to explore our object in the opposite direction from the one that can be followed in the analysis room. This starts from a consciousness of adults, which appears lucid and precise, to go into the more nebulous, although essential, mental events, whilst the reverse one can show us the formation of the consciousness in a direct way: i.e., how the neuromental system acquires the progressive functions that lead to human conducts in their inescapable communicative relationality, which include and in which[30] we have those functions which lead to the phenomena which we globally call consciousness. We call it this, naively deeming that it is a simple and natural event, that is always the same, and the same for everyone.

I have described this development of acquisition of progressive functioning as a path from a first protorepresentation, which I presume innate, i.e., the displeasure, indefinite and diffused, to other engrams: to those involving the ability of perception and then to those of a progressive further symbolopoiesis (Imbasciati, 2001a, 2001b, 2002b). I have spoken of symbolopoiesis to indicate the production (poiesis) of progressive engrams, for gradual learning. Each engram acts as an operator of more learning, as a significant of further learning of further functions; in neural terms, each system of connections which is built up allows more learning, i.e., constructions of more synapses and neural networks, which, in their turn, will allow more and more highly evolved learning, i.e., further and more sophisticated neural networks. Each function trace acts as a significant to acquire further meanings. Each learning makes further learning possible, and therefore the formation of a new engram and so on and so forth of a further increasingly articulated and evolved engram, which will allow increasingly complex learning functions: "symbolopoietic chains" are thus formed, in which each engram is a symbol but also an operating ability (consider the dual psychic and neural aspect of the concept) to create subsequent new learning, each learning depending on the previous one and conditioning the following ones).

This brings about a vision of the development of the mind as a progressive construction: each moment is generated by the quality of the previous one and conditions the construction of the following ones. The quality of the construction will depend on the quality of the first learnings (relational-neonatal) as well each subsequent psychic, protomental and therefore properly mental structure. However, this progression is not necessarily positive: as already mentioned, some learning can have a negative effect both on the previous learning and on subsequent learning; a destructive effect: pathology is also relational.

A NEW METAPSYCHOLOGY CONGRUENT WITH NEUROSCIENCE   165

In the "chains" of progressive engrams of subsequent signification, I have paid special attention with particular matters that psychoanalysis has identified in the internal processing which leads to the various forms of consciousness relative (above all) to the quality of the relations in which they take place. It is the quality of the relationship that conditions the level and the forms of consciousness. This concerns not only the child, but also the adult, with particular regard for the most intimate relationships, such as the psychoanalytical one for example. Which protomental engrams transit, in that relationship, from unconscious to unconscious, that can increase, or decrease the level of consciousness? Of both, patient and analyst, or even distort it? In the mental metabolism of the adult, all the previous interior symbolisations, up to the most primitive engrams, do not cancel each other out but work and are transformed in contemporary and fluctuating work: this takes place in every relationship, which involves a possible emotional processing. At the apex of the latter there is the ability to transfigure that something which is beyond every consciousness; sometimes up to what may appear as conscious at times and different levels of that consciousness.

The continuum between conscious and unconscious lies in that continuum along the progressive symbolpoiesis (with little success sensed in official propositions; APA, 2006), which eliminates the need to invent some *countertrieb* that represses: in the individual symbolopoietic chains, there may be greater or lesser continuity, rather than hiatuses,[31] discontinuities between symbolisations, non-homogeneities, rather than obstacles in the internal communication between the more primitive mental functions and the more articulated ones, thus allowing more or less communication between processes which are completely unconscious and others which can reach some level, transformed or overwhelmed, of consciousness. I have called this concept "intrapsychic permeability" (Imbasciati, 2006a, 2006b), proposing it to explain the greater or lesser resistance by an individual to be in contact with his self: we can say with his own unconscious. Difficulty, not repression as we can observe in the development of infants. Resistance as a minus, not because of an obstacle.

The start of the mind which I have described takes advantage of what we can know today about the infant: the fulcrum I have chosen is the time of feeding. However, we should start from the foetus. Where can the formation of the first engram be situated here? (Imbasciati,

2008b; Imbasciati, Dabrassi, & Cena, 2007).[32] And, above all, how to seek the why, as well as how, it is formed from the integration of afferent impingements? Does some innate predisposition exist here so that a stimulus meets a proto-representation that "recognises" it? Could this be hypothesised in pain? An innate nociception is found in every lower being on the zoological scale. It is a general principle for survival. How can it be better formulated for homo sapiens? Where, going backwards, is there no longer any learning and the psychic is lost in the rigid biological determinism of the genome? Or in an epigenetic inheritance.

What is a new metapsychology for?

This presentation, summarising the theory stated in the books I wrote between 1981 and 2006, may be complex for the reader, both due to the synthesis of the topics and the concepts on neuropsychophysiological experimental psychology. It is perhaps this difficulty that has distracted psychoanalysts from reading my books. On the other hand, this presentation shows the path I have followed and my writings in my lifetime and I believe that the difficulties that may stud this path are worth it for the progress of psychoanalysis.

Going back to the object of psychoanalysis, today we could say that it could focus on the transformations that move from the real unconscious (as such ineffable and therefore not easily explored by the psychological vertex which nevertheless uses the unreliable instrument of the consciousness and language) towards what appears as ability (also unreliable) for the consciousness. Moreover, Bion intuited this procedure in different terms and concepts in his works (Bion, 1962, 1967, 1970, 1971). It could also be formulated as "from the body to the mind" and traced back to the continuous mappings of all the changeable states of the body, about which Damasio speaks (1999), and to the "polyvagal" sensory challenge Porges speaks of (2011), operated in the continuous activity of the brain, which in its perfection marks the life of homo sapiens. This path, if we do not want to rely on the consciousness as it was idealised, can only be assisted by experimental and neurophysiological research. Its progress could support the analyst at work in his continued impervious commitment to understand what passes beyond what he is tempted to formulate in words.

In the meantime, in view of this integration, both the analyst and the experimental psychologist have to be helped with a theory that can be

A NEW METAPSYCHOLOGY CONGRUENT WITH NEUROSCIENCE   167

adapted by both vertexes. This is the intention of my metapsychology. It certainly leaves many questions open and can arouse perplexity for the unusual juxtaposition of neurological terms, which are moreover imprecise for the time being, with new psychological concepts, which refer to experimental psychology and to semiology.

Amongst the questions that are still open on the origins of the mind, there stands out the one on initial events: is it something that we could trace back to the original "principle of displeasure" first formulated by Fairbairn (1952)? How much of this could be deduced and developed in the light of neural biochemistry? Which anthropological perspective could there be? The questions could continue: on the other hand, they are the essence of science. Theories are built up on them: and if these change, it means that that sciences makes progress. I hope that the theory presented here can also be modified; will some psychoanalysts have to "break away" from the Institution?

Considering the multiple questions which are still open in the new metapsychology summarised here, the reader, and the colleague to whom moreover the arguments adopted appear difficult due to the reference to the many and different psychological sciences, could wonder about the usefulness of such an effort. This metapsychology could appear so nebulous to him as to make him judge it contorted.

As for the open questions, the original metapsychology theorised by Freud also left open as many. Suffice it to think of the ways in which the supposed libido emanated from areas of the body was distributed in the organism, and especially in the brain (Freud, 1895); where it was supposed that, in the encounter with the real experience (which one?) of "objects" it gave rise to all the psychic processes. Suffice to think of the concepts of source, object, destination of the drive and consider the dynamic and economic "explanations" of energy distribution, which so fascinated his contemporaries, as well as the uncertainty between two supposed instincts and between a "sexual" energy and a generically psychic one (Imbasciati, 2005a). And yet all this was useful: for psychoanalysts, who, stimulated, devoted themselves to clinical research, comforted by the base formulated by Freud, making it progress and this is how they made psychoanalysis known to the world. Metapsychology was useful: metapsychology is useful "for the development of psychoanalysis" (Imbasciati, 2011a). Freud's metapsychology, successful in the initial promotion of psychoanalysis, today suffers from the handicap of being venerated to the point of keeping it as a doctrine which, although recognised as obsolete and harmful for clinical psychoanalysis, it has not been "disowned". Thus, it is still what is, outside the professional circle, known about psychoanalysis: with the disparagement of psychoanalysis by other scientists and, perhaps from here, by the general public, and with the consequents of a complementary encouragement for those cognitive and behavioural psychotherapies which can boast of being based on neurosciences and experimental evidence; as well as for those many others, which come from a different matrix, less critical than that of Freudian metapsychology.

"Official" psychoanalysts, making themselves the guardians of orthodoxy and consequently leaving in the shade the indispensable distinction between clinics and theory, have actually shut themselves up in the rite of only (or almost) writing about clinical psychoanalysis, and in their own community, where they are certain no misunderstandings amongst them may exist, even speaking with a multiform language and leaving theorisations to the mere and varied competence of each individual member. They did not take such care in organising the "theory" nor of updating the ingenious attempt by Freud to make known to the public something of psychoanalysis that did not enter into conflict with contemporary knowledge, of other sciences, and on what the public knows about them. What I wrote eight years ago in the presentation of my aforementioned book of 2006b, can still be topical today.

I think that my "repugnance", as I made explicit at the beginning, on the continuing use of the terms derived from Freudian metapsychology comes from an intimate pain in feeling how, in the current general scientific panorama, psychoanalysis in its clinical progress is rejected, and not appreciated enough, or at times despised in the public with respect to other ways with which the mind can be treated. The recent attempt by some colleagues to re-evaluate psychoanalysis through neurosciences— i.e., neuropsychoanalysis—is often judged as contaminating. However, it is still insufficient to re-evaluate its image,[33] if it is sporadic and does not enjoy the support of the Institution.

This is why I believe an effort by all those who are competent in updated clinical psychoanalysis is necessary to emerge from the elite craftsmanship to infer from this a progressive scientific theory, so that today, as one hundred years ago with Freud, psychoanalysis can become known and appreciated: not only for the treatment of so-called pathology but above all for its potential to stem the emotional coarctation that our civilisation today seems to induce. For this reason I hope

A NEW METAPSYCHOLOGY CONGRUENT WITH NEUROSCIENCE   169

that the work I have started can be continued in order to fill in gaps or questions left open by my metapsychology, and overcome the difficulties of understanding that derive from the indispensable necessity, for today's analysts, of a competence that goes into the much wider area of experimental psychological sciences, from which to draw a clinical psychology (Imbasciati, 2012a) which is much wider than clinical psychoanalysis, as well as in the more difficult area of the neuroscience.

The image of psychoanalysis in the comprehension of "other" scientists[34]

For some time now, analysts have acknowledged different languages, depending on the different analysts' associations or "Schools", and terms that at times are different to refer to the same psychic event, or multiplied to indicate all the possible variants of it, often by coining new names, which may overshadow the unambiguity of the previous ones and which at times may give the impression of confusion. Yet analysts, if they speak amongst themselves, almost always understand one another. The transient nature of the main object of psychoanalysis is at the origin of the difficulties of a language that may be immediately clear, with precise and unambiguous terms such as those of other sciences.

The analysts, with the determination of their psychoanalytic background, can also agree to make their science progress, but it may appear nebulous to other scientists. They often reproach psychoanalysts for speaking in a way that is more literary than "scientific", meaning by "scientific" the use of unambiguous terms and concepts that have been defined once and for all, as in the sciences of nature. This is not very practicable in psychoanalysis, if its main object of investigation is only the subjective experience of the affects. Other scientists are not capable of going into this specificity; they can have some idea of it only if they rely on some more precise formulations of a general theoretical nature. In my opinion, what psychoanalysis shows today on this aspect is no longer in line with the progress of its clinical practice. This progress—actually considerable—has not corresponded to theoretical formulations which could be clear in some ways even to "outsiders" of the profession. But psychoanalysts do not seem interested in updating their main theoretical propositions with what their clinical practice can explain today, on the functioning of the human mind. All this gives rise to a bad image, getting worse today, of psychoanalysis with respect to all the other sciences.

170 MINDBRAIN, PSYCHOANALYTIC INSTITUTIONS, AND PSYCHOANALYSTS

In my anything but short experience, outside the professionals and scholars of psychoanalytic orientation, among those competent in sciences other than those concerning the human mind but also among the many who study it from different angles—neuroscientists, psychiatrists, pharmacologists and many psychologists of the multiple Schools of psychotherapy, and almost all Psychology graduates—as well as the contemporary social image, psychoanalysis does not enjoy adequate consideration, nor the progress that this science has made in the past thirty years is known. This poor image is reflected at a more general, even popular, level, in discouraging possible patients, but also and above all in fostering a proliferation of "psychoanalytic psychotherapists" of mediocre and questionable training, who, in the "nebulousness" of a confused image of psychoanalysis can navigate better in competing with the best psychoanalysts. Many of them do not seem to take great account of the existence of negative images of their science, trusting in, I would say with excessive confidence and faith, the value of their profession. There is probably the absence of a more general culture, that would let them grasp what is meant in social psychology by "image" (see note 54) and its effects.

In this framework, many clarifications would be useful, on the concepts which are often taken for granted and unambiguous. This could benefit both the psychoanalysts in the strict sense (IPA) and even more, the many more numerous psychotherapy psychoanalysts. I ask here some questions, which perhaps the professionals take for granted, but uncertain to varying degrees for others.

1. What is meant by "clinical psychoanalysis"?
   The classic, dual psychoanalysis with its setting on the couch and with adult patients? Does this refer to the classic Freudian concepts of the drive theory, such as for example conflict, defence and repression? What is the place in this picture of psychoanalysis applied to groups, in its diversifications? And infant psychoanalysis? And also that for babies with their parents? Is only the psychoanalysis practised by the members of the IPA that may be called psychoanalysis?

   According to what is thought about these questions, for the psychoanalyst and even more for psychotherapists and no less so for the general public, the image of psychoanalysis is different. For example, the very many contributions of all those clinical schools which have hybridised the psychoanalytic approach with experimental research (infant research), above all that on attachment theory

(Riva-Crugnola, 2007) could be excluded from psychoanalysis. All the work-treatments which combine, similarly to what took place for parents–children psychotherapies, the psychoanalytic approach with that deriving from other matrixes, could not be considered clinical psychoanalysis. An integration in this regard appears fairly advanced in world literature, outside obviously that of the IPA. The distinction between psychoanalysis and psychoanalytic oriented psychotherapy and between this and the "application" of psychoanalysis to other contexts, as well as between the technique declared for the object of application and on the other hand what is defined the (interior) psychoanalytic background of the operators (the "psychoanalytic function" of the mind) is played here. These last factors could be applied to any context in which a psychoanalyst operates, consequently qualifying his work as psychoanalysis.

2. The above distinctions appear decisive on a definition about a "general theory on mental functioning that can qualify psychoanalysis". It is frequent to hear things such as "according to psychoanalytic theory" from "outsiders". What are they alluding to with this expression of everyday language? Can we speak of a "psychoanalytic theory"? The above phrase is often equivalent to "according to the Freudian theory", but what is this? All Freud's work? Quite a few psychoanalysts will answer that there are several theories in psychoanalysis: however, this does not eliminate the fact that saying "Freudian theory" is nevertheless reductive compared to the progress of psychoanalysis in the past seventy years. What can we offer for all these uncertainties?

To identify what we could better call the theoretical structure of psychoanalysis, we would first of all have to define what can be called "theory" in the proper sense (*cf.* Chapter Seven). "Theory" is a very elastic term: one obvious meaning can call theory any reasoning that connects observed facts or that categorises clinical events, or that indicates practices to be observed; even a concept, as such, is "theory". Theory of technique and of clinical practice are also talked of, which could sound like a contradiction. We should realise more how psychoanalysis appears to all those who may consider it from the angle of other sciences, who may know about psychoanalysis only through theoretical formulations or who consider a clear theory essential to qualify a science. What do they mean by "psychoanalytic theory"? Which "image" lies behind this expression?

In my opinion, it is possible to formulate a narrower and more precise definition of "theory" that is applicable to psychoanalysis.

172   MINDBRAIN, PSYCHOANALYTIC INSTITUTIONS, AND PSYCHOANALYSTS

The term should be reserved to a coherent set of hypotheses which not only contextualise but give an overall explication of the functioning of the human mind: here we would have a clear example of Freudian metapsychology, even though it is no longer topical. Freud's intention was to offer a global image of his science to other "scientists", as well as a theoretical unity on which all psychoanalysts could recognise themselves (Imbasciati, 2011a, 2011b).

3. Does a "Freudian theory" exist, what does the Statute (article 3) of the IPA say?

Vassalli (2001, 2006, 2007) underlined how Freud was alien to considering psychoanalysis a theory; he considered it a "*tecnè*", according to the Greek meaning, which can correspond to something similar to our "craft". More precisely, Vassalli says that the IPA, i.e., the "Americans" of 1946 revolutionised the spirit of Freud and confused what today can be called "method" with theory and with the discoveries. Article 3 of the IPA Statute effectively speaks of "discoveries" which would form a "theory of personality": the used expression cannot be superimposed, in my opinion, on the original Freudian definition (Freud, 1922).

On the other hand, in Freud's times, the epistemological distinctions between method, discovery and theory were anything but clear: today we can say that the method—a specific method—is exactly what specifically characterises a given science (Agazzi, 1976; Pera, 1980; Antiseri, 1981; Imbasciati, 1994). Psychoanalysis has been characterised by developing the method founded by Freud: let us think of the setting, with its current developments in relation to the analyst's inner equipment (associations, transference/countertransference, psychoanalytic relationship, "listening", ability for reverie, "psychoanalytic function" of the mind, and similar). This is *tecnè*, what Vassalli defines the spirit of Freud. With epistemological correctness we can say that it is the method that allows the "discoveries", but these are not to be confused with the theoretical hypotheses that help to connect them. A "theory" is always an instrument, and as such provisional. Freud had this very clearly in mind, when he hoped that the drive biological support could be discovered (Freud, 1895, p. 200; 1905e [1901], p. 113f; 1905a, p. 168f, 214f, 218f; 1905b, p. 277f; 1914c, p. 78; 1915, p. 125; 1915–1917, p. 320; 1931, p. 240; 1933a, p. 96) and even more so in calling his metapsychology "witch" and "mythology" (Freud, 1937c). The persistence of

A NEW METAPSYCHOLOGY CONGRUENT WITH NEUROSCIENCE   173

an unsuitable epistemological distinction of the above concepts and therefore the ambiguity or interchangeability of the relative terms can explain what happened in 1946, reported by Vassalli, regarding the Statute of the IPA.

A theory, considering the above, is never a discovery, but an "invention". We have to attribute the character of mere conceptual hypotheses to the concepts of the drive theory. As such they are to be considered conceptual instruments which are completely provisional. The many criticisms of *On Metapsychology* (Holt, 1965, 1972, 1981; Holt & Peterfreund, 1972; Holt, 1976; Klein, 1976; Peterfreund, 1971; Schaefer, 1975; Westen, 1999; Imbasciati, 2007c, 2010a) have valid grounds: we should never have recourse to considerations or even to expressions that imply a sort of "existence" of the drives; and repression, as seems to occur at times in the implicit discourse of many psychotherapists; nor can it be said that "Freud discovered drives" as is sometimes heard outside the circle of psychoanalysts. It is not a question of discoveries of "existing" psychic processes, but of concepts put forward as hypotheses to "invent" (= invention) an "explicative" theory. Repression is confused with "resistance" which is truly a clinical fact discovered by Freud. Specifications such as above may be superfluous for psychoanalysts but significant for the public image of psychoanalysis, especially in reference to the other sciences and other scientists.

Freud's intention was not to describe the unconscious as he had discovered (this was a real "discovery") with the method and which moreover and afterwards he outlines extensively, but to formulate a technical hypothesis of explicative value to the other "scientists of the mind". In my opinion this was the intention of his metapsychology, which is confirmed when Freud wanted to present it to the public in "Two Encyclopaedia Articles" (Freud, 1923a). On the other hand, epistemology tells us that a real "explication" (why, not how) is never final, but is always a sort of stratagem or attempt: a theory always has to be confirmed and evaluated continuously in time as a science progresses and in compatibility with other sciences. Quite rightly, Freud considered his metapsychology a "witch".

Non-verbal communication and the future of psychoanalysis

What has taken place at both the popular and cultivated level of image, which here we attribute to the neglect of the psychoanalytic Institutions in offering a clear and comprehensible global theory of psychoanalysis, is due, upstream, to the lack of education of many psychoanalysts—perhaps the majority[35]—to abstract from the fundamental changes of clinical psychoanalysis what concerns the implicit theory underpinning them. The institutionalised and ritualised emotive element of the veneration for the Lost Teacher is entrenched underneath this, which has kept their minds from using the abilities they nevertheless have of abstraction.

A great deal has been written about the change of clinical psychoanalysis, almost always not specifying that it was about the practice but indicating generally "psychoanalysis". But with great efforts we are now starting to sufficiently stress those ideas from which new theories on the general functioning of the mind can be formulated, so that they can be representative to "others". Suffice is to think of the challenging evolution of the so-called relational theories before reaching more precise statements on this "relationality", that also specify at theoretical level how the mind works in "relational" processes.

It had been realised for some time that a "good relationship" is not established by the good words that pass between the individuals, but by something affective which transits, conveyed "inside" the words but which does not belong to them; empathy has been spoken of, or the passage from unconscious to unconscious, the concept of countertransference was extended so much till invalidating its name ("counter"), and it was nevertheless acquired that what is effective for the change of the patient concerns the "good internal dispositions" of the analyst, which "pass" to the patient, beyond any interpretation. It was understood that the personality, or to put it better, the analyst unconscious structure is the factor at the centre of the therapeutic change. These events were called "non-specific factors of the treatment", with an arrogant expression with respect to the narcissism of the verbal interpretative activity, but it was necessary to wait decades for the explanation (by an analyst who had resigned from the IPA) of "something more than interpretation" (Stern & BCPSG, 1998) (perhaps too sarcastic a saying in relation to the Institution) to have some success and interest in psychoanalysis by neuroscientists (neuropsychoanalysis) like Kandel, Siegel, and Damasio, as well as the psychophysiology of Bucci (1997), had to be rekindled, But this interest is not reciprocal (Merciai, 2013; Mercia & Cannella, 2014) and by some authors who had remained in the IPA no longer by criticism of Freudian metapsychology, as in the

1970s in America, but with more courageous assertions new metapsy-chologies are proposed (Chuster, 2000; Fulgencio, 2006; Jimenez, 2007).

Finally, a favourable social event was added to the efforts that had grown up in the shadow of the Institution: the decline in adult patients[36] and the psychoanalysts turning more and more to the psychotherapy of children–parents–families. All this directed a large part of today's psychoanalysts, aware of the necessary practices, towards these patients (the practices made use of contributions which were not only psychoanalytic[37]) to transfer there the new experience. In this new way of performing clinical psychoanalysis, the theories however remained implicit, within the operability.

In this difficult evolution, only some authors, of those who had remained members of the IPA, were able to assert themselves: I am referring to Fonagy and to his School, with particular reference to the "daring" declarations against the concepts of Freudian metapsychology. The clinical evolution has become imposed, albeit slowly, fostering reflections which could invest the theory. The horizon is therefore open-ing up and gives us reason for hope. The Institution, which in the face of practical evidence seemed to stay silent, reacted with an attitude that still continues, in denying space in its official publications for works that are "too" theoretical, giving importance to those focused on clinical practice, which is also in complete evolution, or even revolution.

Here the observations on what makes up the efficacy of the relation-ship have become increasingly important; non-verbal communication, in the positive as in the negative. From the observations on how non-verbal communication in babies and in children organises, optimally or pathologically, their psychic development, and depending on the men-tal structure of their caregivers (as we have pointed out), non-verbal communication between the analyst and the analysand has been increasingly studied. The "something more" is not at all "more": it is the essence of change. Psychoanalysis is no longer "the talking cure" (Imbasciati, 2010d).

In the child we have evidence of how non-verbal communication is constructive or pathogenic, in conformity with being attuned or not (*cf.* the concept of "attunement", Stern, 1987) of the toing and froing of messages delivered by non-verbal communication. It is this communi-cation in the first months of the baby's life that lays the foundations for its mental structure and this will condition all its further psychic devel-opment. The neurosciences confirm this by highlighting the structuring of the neural networks (Schore, 2003a, 2003b) which form what was called brain maturing (attributed erroneously in the past to the genome). This structuring continues even in the adult and depends on the right emotional level at neural level, which means "pure" emotions which unconsciously transit between two individuals in non-verbal "dialogues", which is perhaps also conveyed by words, but not for what they denote.[38]

Two questions of research arise here, which are a current object of interest: the first relates to the fact that non-verbal communication is automatic and to a great extent unaware, therefore it eludes the cognitive reflection of the classic analysis based on verbalisation, but this communication accentuates the unaware emotions which run between the analyst and the analysand. The classic concepts of transference and countertransference are extended; it is about the communication between unconscious and consciousness. This had already been observed in clinical psychoanalysis some time ago, but having discovered that it is transmitted through non-verbal communication raised the problem of how it is made up and by what it is conveyed. How can it be analysed in its components and how can it be controlled for therapeutic purposes or for confused and pathogenic ambitions?

The second question consists of how to identify the meanings that this communication transmits and by which compound sensory units they are conveyed: it is a semiotic problem of coding and decoding signifiers conveying respective and precise meanings. This is where the key of the "how" and in part of the "why" non-verbal communication is the structuring essence of the psychoanalytic relationship lies. Which meanings, through which codes of signifiers, conveyed by which sensory compositions, are learned with a structuring effect? Negatively or positively?

The two problems, of psychophysiology and semiotics, refer to a third one, neurological, which concerns the fulcrum of the "why". How does the brain, of the analyst and of the analysand, work, in emitting the above meanings on reciprocal vehicles of a sensory semiotics? The neurosciences in their most recent developments of neuropsychoanalysis and in particular on the system of mirror-neurons approach us here.

In the solution or at the least the composition of the three themes, there lies the possibility of using our new metapsychology. The reference to the hard sciences is the tribute that we can make today to the genius of Freud for the invention of his metapsychology.

Both infant observation and even more infant research have explored spontaneous, expressive, automatic, unaware and apparently casual non-verbal communication which runs in the interactions (therefore in the behaviour) along the visual, sound, tactile, motor, olfactory and visceral channels and its structuring, possible therapeutic, value. From here the opportune considerations for the analysis of adults; the problem in these considerations is to understand in full the content of such "corporal" communication which easily eludes the possibilities of consciousnessisation, including of the analyst. A problem arises here upstream: the training of analysts (Imbasciati, 2013a).

A relative osmosis between infant research and infant psychoanalysis and between these and the neurosciences which have dealt with the affective mother/baby regulation/disregulation (Schore, 2003a, 2003b) has clarified, confirmed and detailed many developmental passages intuited and described by psychoanalysts but further and more specific studies are required. Many concepts, derived from the integrations which are still on-going of the various sciences are making changes in psychoanalysis. There is talk of new paradigms (Jiménez, 2006), perhaps concealing behind this expression the term of "new metapsychology". In particular, the very concept of consciousness has been modified, no longer understood as a dichotomy (consciousness yes/consciousness no: conscious/unconscious) or as a natural quality possessed to the same extent by all individuals and constant in time, but as the continuum of an ability which is possessed at different levels individually and variable in the same individual depending on the time and the relational context. This is found in analysis as a variable ability to use the interpretation, beyond the adequacy of the verbal formulation, both of the analyst and of the patient; "timing" and "temperature" have been talked of at various gradual levels depending on the time and the "temperature" of the relationship of that analyst at that time. It is however consciousness understood as a possible and variable epiphenomenon of unaware mental work.

Repressed unconscious and unrepressed unconscious have been talked of (Mancia, 2009): modestly from my point of view, to reconcile an opportunistic continuity with the Freudian structure. In a more articulated way, represented/representable unconscious and unrepresented/unrepresentable unconscious have been talked of (Colombo, 2008) and these concepts are being linked with what we know from the neurosciences about the formation of implicit memories. What is known as

Wilma Bucci's Multiple Code Theory (1997; 2001; 2007a, 2007b; 2009) deserves attention in this context, as it integrates psychoanalysis, cognitive sciences and neurosciences. The author distinguishes a symbolic unconscious and a non-symbolic unconscious (sub-symbolic) or, to put it better, two systems, one which can be connected with some possibility of representation, verbal and non-verbal, and which can therefore have to do with the consciousness, and the other, which cannot be represented (Bucci, 2009; Moccia & Solano, 2009) connected with the body and the structure of implicit memories, absolutely outside the possibility of being outlined through words and perhaps not even forms of any consciousness. A process, called referential, would connect—to a greater or lesser extent—the two systems: this is alleged to be the system responsible for a meaning that cannot be represented, contained and hidden within a representable form, for example visual or sound forms, can have or not a mutative effect on the whole functioning of the mind. We could discern in this last process an explanation of "resistance".

In the framework of the change in course in current psychoanalysis (Moccia & Solano, 2009), it would not make sense to explain the unconscious thinking of defence mechanisms: the mind is essentially unconscious and only a small part of its continuous work is processed in a conscious form. What was conceptualised as "defences" can be explained differently, as an obstacle or, better still, as a "filter" to this process; not defences "against" the unconscious, but particularities of those connections (neural networks) that can allow a given transmission of the unconscious work "towards" some transformed form of consciousness; Schore would say of the work of the right brain towards the left. It does not make sense to presuppose a "*vis a fronte*" by the Ego against a "*vis a tergo*" of the unconscious, but only the natural flowing of the continuous mnestic transformations, amongst which there are also less unconscious, or conscious forms (Imbasciati, 2006b). The pathology or the optimal nature of the functioning of the mind is thus believed to lie in the quality of this processing, and therefore in the structures that control it. In this framework, the criticism that has been made against an excessive identification of the consciousness with language appears justified, without having sufficiently asked on what the consciousness itself represents.

In this context of changes, some aspects of the classic setting have also been questioned, such as the couch, preferring on the other hand the *vis-à-vis* as the means for effective communication and interpretations

(Jiménez, 2006; Benecke & Krause, 2005). Cahn (2002) has entitled one of his recent books "The end of the couch?" (!). Stern and his group (BCPSG: Boston Change Process Study Group, 2005, 2007, 2008; BCPSG, 2011) strenuously maintain that therapeutic changes have little to do with a verbalisation that fosters introspection. The neural structure that carries out certain dysfunctional mental functions[39] in those patients that precisely for this reason improvement is desired, can be modified, not so much by the assimilation of verbalised meanings transmitted by the words of the interpretation, but by the assimilation of meanings which are not verbalised nor can they be verbalised, but are more primitive, pre-verbal and we could say non-symbolic (and not simply sub-symbolic) incarnated in the body, delivered by non-verbal signifiers. This is affective communication, from unconscious to unconscious, which becomes clear in current clinical psychoanalysis but at theoretical level, it has not been adequately "explained". This is the experience, described by Siegel and by Damasio (2010) of "being one's body" or the emotional self of the continuous activity of toing and froing of the brain with the body and in particular with the viscera (Porges, 2011).

Enormous problems open up here, in view of different training for future psychoanalysts that can use non-verbal communication in a therapeutic instead of a pathogenic way. These problems cannot be solved without the aid of the experimental sciences and technologies that other psychological sciences, for example those derived from attachment theory, have already tried and tested. The pride of Freud's great-grandchildren will have to be overcome.[40]

Valid scientists, neuroscientists aware of the progress in clinical psychoanalysis, are re-evaluating psychoanalysis, but this remains a matter of the scientific élite, conducted moreover more by scientists of other disciplines than by psychoanalysts. In the collective imagination, there remains an image formed about one hundred years ago. As at popular level, the other sciences are much better known than psychoanalysis, and are easier to get to know. Psychoanalysis appears very unreliable, scientifically speaking, as though it were a literary product or an old legend. The problem of the social image appears urgent (Imbasciati, 2012d). A new metapsychology, to be offered for a simpler and easier comprehension than the more classic promotion of clinical psychoanalysis—this is where the mediating function of the neurosciences comes into the picture—formulated in terms that are accessible to scientists in other fields, could promote a better image of the psychoanalytic science, which is, on the other hand, penalised and obscured by the ignorance of the enormous progress that this science has nevertheless achieved.

We would have to overcome the anguish of the psychoanalytic Institution (in the meaning of Jacques, 1955): lose the veneration for the master. This does not mean losing the legacy of Freud, or ignoring his genius: do we deny Galileo's genius today? It is an institutionalised anguish of separation and as such is difficult to identify, which prevents the Institutions themselves from promoting the studies that can encourage the new metapsychologies which, although isolated in the silence of the Institutions, have been formulated. Is such an achievement possible in the community? Or rather, of the community.

It is this anguish, so evasively unconscious as it is exclusive to the community, that induces a majority of psychoanalysts to avoid keeping up to date, especially drawing on the other sciences of the mind: first of all on the basic methodology that informs experimental psychology, the discipline officially called General Psychology which is taught (or should be taught: Imbasciati, 2013d) in the universities and which Psychology graduates ought to know and cultivate; in particular and as a consequence for all that research which speak of the unconscious in non-psychoanalytic language (Eagleman, 2012); and in the second equally fundamental place, in the neurosciences, with their neurophysiological foundations of molecular biology. These are two groups of sciences focused on research. Then there are, as here and elsewhere, those that are more focused on the "treatment", cognitive sciences, developments based on attachment theory, infant research and others. The above avoidance is encouraged by the spirit of the institution. The future of psychoanalysis is at stake. Freud had declared that he felt more of a scientist than a doctor, i.e., interested in the treatment. But Freud has been replaced by his icon.

CHAPTER SEVEN

The Institution: doctrine and ideology

The holy theory

Clinical psychoanalysis today has changed enormously and a process of integration with respect to the other psychological sciences (in particular developmental, neonatal, and infant psychology, attachment theory) and the neurosciences (Fonagy, 1999, 2001, 2005; Fonagy & Target, 1997; Stern & BCPSG, 2008; Siegel, 1999, 2012; Schore, 2003a, 2003b; Kandel, 2005; Damasio, 1999; Imbasciati, 2005b, 2012a, 2012c, 2013b) is under way. However, an adequate theoretical reformulation (Imbasciati, 2013a, 2013b, 2013c, 2013d) has not corresponded to this change. Psychoanalysis is a clinical science: "clinical" does not mean "to treat" (*cf.* Chapter Three) but to investigate the mind using a clinical method. The scientific nature of the "clinical method" requires investigating not simply on the single case and on any single result of treatment, but on how to extract from all the cases "treated", or better modified, a general theory of the functioning of the system on which work has been done. This is the difference that distinguishes the scientist from the craftsman. Therefore, general theories have to be inferred from the clinical practice: if it is a science and not craftsmanship, and if the clinical practice progresses and changes, this means that underlying these there are new and different theories which it should therefore be possible to extract and formulate. Psychoanalysis is not only a technique of therapy, but, as Freud underlined (1923a), an investigation of the functioning of the mind: his *On Metapsychology* (Freud, 1915) was an attempt, one hundred years ago, to explain the mind and in particular the unconscious mind, with the help of the sciences of the time (Imbasciati, 2011a). The part that definitely is explanatory is made up of the first two articles: it is here that Freud outlines a theory that explains the general functioning of the mind and it is this that people today still identify as "Freud's theory". In this synthetic expression at the level of popular culture, a part is identified as the whole, a metonymy, as the part that is formulated at explanatory level (the Energy-drive Theory), to which Freud refers throughout his work, is taken as representative of every other description and also as a single and partial explanation; and it is thus assumed precisely as it is an "explanation".

If today "we do clinical psychoanalysis" in a very different way with respect to Freud's time, it means that implicitly a different explanatory theory is assumed on the general functioning of the mind. We only have to think of the so-called "revolutions" of psychoanalysis, the first one by Klein and the second by Bion or to the simpler opposition between a relational theory and an endogenous one on the formation of the mind. Other and different theories on the functioning of the mind are (or are alleged to be) available today, but they do not appear to have been very successful with the "people of psychoanalysis". At present there is an enormous gap between the clinical investigation, with its discoveries and its changes, and the theoretical organisation of psychoanalysis (Imbasciati, 2012a, 2013c); this seems to have stayed anchored to Freud's Energy-drive Theory.

The fact is explicitly denied in the Institution, but psychoanalysts still talk about drives, repression and the unconscious today, referring to Freudian metapsychology, and they speak about it not out of mere historical memory but to support their clinical work, as though they were suitable concepts to explain how the mind works just as they use terms and concepts taken from current clinical psychoanalysis without worrying about a comparison and possible contradiction with the previous ones. What are the reasons that motivate these inaccuracies, almost confusions, with the psychoanalysts for whom it is so important to define psychoanalysis a science?

THE INSTITUTION: DOCTRINE AND IDEOLOGY   183

This chapter intends to indicate some doctrinal aspects, which appear from habits and scientific production specific to the psychoanalytic Institutions, in particular Italian, and their internal Organisation, which hinders an explicit reformulation of a general theory on mental functioning, although implicit in current psychoanalytic practice: this would have as a consequence an equally explicit abandonment of that part of the theorisation which Freud could not do one hundred years ago.

Underlying this difficulty, an ideology, of a religious type, can be glimpsed, so there is a need for a holy icon, of an image of the master, and of "his" psychoanalysis: the one outlined very figuratively in his *On Metapsychology*, the "witch" as the later Freud (1933a) said softly and which, just like a witch, has fascinated generations of psychoanalysts.

At the basis of this attitude of the community, an anguish of losing the "father", or rather of being able to lose him if the cult is abandoned, that has not been sufficiently worked through, can be glimpsed. An ideology, as such hidden in the community, simplifies (Imbasciati, 2013d, 2014d) the distinction between the method, invented by Freud and the discoveries that this method allowed him, as well as a finer distinction between the discoveries of that time and all the subsequent "discoveries" his posteriors could make from the subsequent, present-day developments, derived from that method. This saves a difficult distinction between the method and the discoveries, and of both from the mere conceptual inventions, which throughout the history of psychoanalysis have followed on in the attempt to explain the functioning of the human mind as the method progressed. Typical of any ideology is a reductionist simplification of a series of concepts and propositions which otherwise would impose laborious distinctions, clarifications and further study; this way, the ideology saves effort and the pain of thought, and lends itself to being considered as a solid support of identity.

The epistemological confusion which we find in psychoanalysis can be attributed, in my opinion, to unaware dynamics, which act in the institutional community, as described in the work by Elliot Jacques (Jacques, 1955), giving rise to rituals and rules of the organisation[1] which are used to cover up deep anguishes. There is also a secondary advantage: sparing psychoanalysts the scientific endeavour necessary to bring out from current clinical practice better theoretical formulations; and an easy temptation is also offered by reifying Freud's conceptual inventions, as though they were discoveries, by presentifying them in the tangible hydraulic (Meltzer, 1981) drives mechanism: the icon to be venerated. What had only been a hypothesis becomes an incontrovertible discovery.

A fulcrum of such a mechanism lies in omitting the otherwise indispensable specification of what "theory" means, implemented through the indiscriminate use of this term. In this way, it is difficult to distinguish what was theoretical speculation in Freud, as such hypothetical and explanatory, from all the rest of his work, which allowed the many discoveries (which remain as such) about how the mind which governs humans' lives works, but that are not to be confused with his conceptual inventions (*cf.* Chapter Six).

The term "theory" has multiple and different meanings, both in Italian and in English and other languages. In Italian, the Devoto-Oli dictionary (1995) says: "1. Systematic formulation of general principles relative to a science art or branch of knowledge, and also of the deductions that can be obtained from those principles purely by logic", followed by examples and then, with graphic reference, "extensively: way of thinking, personal opinion" followed by examples; "2. A long procession" of people, animals or objects.

The English dictionary (Collins, 1994) seems to be even more precise and gives the following six meanings: "1. A system of rules, procedures and assumptions, used to produce a result; 2. Abstract knowledge or reasoning; 3. A speculative or conjectural view or idea; 4. An idea or hypothetical situation; 5. A set of hypotheses related by logical or mathematical arguments to explain and predict a wide variety of connected phenomena in general terms; 6. A non-technical name for "hypothesis". Here again it is a question of a great variability of meaning: if we want to refer to a science, we have to consider meaning no. 5, which corresponds to the Italian no. 1. As for the English no. 1, which can be applied to a technique but also to a science, it indicates what can be called "method" with a more precise term.

These definitions show how the meaning of the term "theory" can be multi-faceted: if it is used extensively, the term can take on many meanings that are different from one another. Such a use seems to be recurrent in psychoanalytic literature; this polysemy prevents clearly identifying which theory can be said to characterise psychoanalytic science in full today. Psychoanalysis wants to be a science that with its specific method aims to investigate how the human mind originates, develops and functions, not only in its thousand individual clinical variants, but also in

THE INSTITUTION: DOCTRINE AND IDEOLOGY 185

the more general procedural lines that characterise each human being. In current psychoanalysis, very developed in the clinical practice, the accent has shifted on its therapeutic effect, and we forget that Freud considered this "secondary" to the investigation on the general functioning of the mind (Imbasciati, 1983a). This investigation was uttered by Freud (1923) as the essence of psychoanalytic science; and it is in this sense of generalisation, that the theories characterising a given science are formulated. In psychoanalysis, if the clinical practice (investigation into the mind of individuals or even of groups) progresses, it ought to be essential to update the theories that concern the general objective; to identify the functioning of the mind beyond the individual variations.

Freud formulated a general theory of the functioning of the mind by hypothesising an explanation of his discoveries with the scientific cognitions of his time: this is what was defined the Energy-drive Theory, presented in his *On Metapsychology* (1915). This theory characterised psychoanalysis for one hundred years and still does despite the fact that the general scientific panorama and the knowledge acquired by psychoanalysis has changed. A theory, if understood in the meaning applicable to a science, as Freud understood it, necessarily has to have a hypothetical character: theories are therefore subject to being changed in time, to the extent that a given science develops in the method and in the discoveries that come from the application of the development of the method. Throughout this evolution, an extensive and imprecise use of the term "theory" may obscure the need to clarify the new theories which are triggered off by the progress of that specific discipline with the relative progressive discoveries.

In psychoanalysis, the indiscriminate use of the term "theory" has prevented a clear formulation of the theory that characterises it in its current state. If the term "theory" is used in its extensive meaning, what is called theory may be multiplied infinitely, so that we may lose sight of which new theory is the one which characterises that discipline for a much wider public. Such hindrance is acting in psychoanalysis, where the indiscriminate (extensive) use of the term "theory", by obscuring the importance of considering which theory most characterises nowadays psychoanalysis, and above all how a theory has to be formulated in a comprehensible way for everybody, has been used to configure an icon to venerate.

I use the words "has been used" as I am referring to the action of the Institution on the Organisation, i.e., the defensive effects that the unconscious anguishes of a community produce in the Organisation. In psychoanalysis (let us think of when "psychoanalytic movement" was defined), the terminological inaccuracies that we are describing were used—precisely—as a defence to preserve, through habits and rites of the Organisation, the members of the Institution from being perturbed by conscious feelings of loss and abandonment. The institutionalisation (Schoeck, 1974) of the anguishes in the customs, rites, languages and concepts of the Organisation makes the anguishes and the defences even more unconscious, so that it is difficult for the community to work them through. The defences take the form of convictions, the theories of truth and ideology is formed.

The extensive use of the term "theory" has fostered ways of understanding the Energy-drive Theory in a metaphorical way, with the most varied nuances, thus keeping its reference even amongst today's analysts. This use confuses the clinical level, where a possible metaphor can help the "comprehension" of the analyst of what is happening in and with his patient, with an effective theory plan, in relation to a general theory of mental functioning. The proper meaning that has to be given to "theory" and to an updated theory that can characterise present-day psychoanalysis, is lost sight of (*cf.* Chapter Six).

The confusion between the clinical level and the theoretical one is thus fostered by the ambiguous use of the term "theory". "Freud's theory" thus becomes equivalent to "Freud's way of thinking" just as "theory" is extensively used to mean the "way of thinking" of many subsequent authors. This use of the term fosters keeping theories which otherwise would be declared superseded. Such an ambiguity betrays, in my opinion, Freud's intention announced in 1923.

Freud himself considered his theory hypothetical and he considered metapsychology with caution: ironically he called it "the witch" (1933a) and elsewhere "our mythology" (1933b). Freud's intention, in the ambition of qualifying psychoanalysis as a science before the world, gave its results precisely with his metapsychology: if we wish to follow him, his intention has to be confirmed by a new one. updated and different theory. Collective unconscious anguishes of losing have to be worked through, so that anguishes and defences of the Institution mitigate their effect on the defences implemented by the Organisation.

As psychoanalysis at clinical and methodological level has unquestionably evolved, if we want to identify and clearly formulate new theories which characterise it, we have to return to precise meanings

THE INSTITUTION: DOCTRINE AND IDEOLOGY   187

of the dictionary (no. 1 in the Italian one and no. 5 in the English one). Keeping to that meaning, we therefore have to consider if the theory that Freud formulated with the intention of explaining how the human mind could work, i.e., metapsychology, is still valid, if it still explains the clinical discoveries that have been made, or of it has to be left in the historical archive of psychoanalysis. This may in my opinion be fostered by abandoning the hesitations connected with the confused use of the term "theory": when this defence is dissolved, it will perhaps be possible to allow working through the anguishes of the institutional community, so that the institutionalised religious veneration of the icon of the master, which conceals and is concealed by the icon of the "holy theory", can also be dissolved.

"Theory" and confusions

Many psychoanalysts consider the above distinctions and clarifications on what can be understood by "theory" useless, and sometimes they arrogantly consider them traits of obsessiveness: they maintain that it is possible to understand one another without such fussiness. This may be true amongst psychoanalysts, but what about the others? Are they scotomised by their narcissistic—which is also institutional—pride? In psychoanalytic literature as well, authoritative articles have spoken of a babel of languages and many multiple theories, with consequent internal difficulties amongst psychoanalysts, as well as external one in relation to those who cannot go in a through study of the subject (Wallerstein, 1988).

It is possible for a science to have more than one theory. However, if the term "theory" is not made clear, the multiplicity becomes infinite. You only have to think about the extensive Italian use of the term or the second English meaning. The need for specifications in this regard is not, in my opinion, given sufficient consideration by psychoanalysts. A certain veiled opposition to the opportunity that in psychoanalysis, theoretical clarifications and the above expressed distinctions, often with an ostracism at collective level are necessary, more than at the level of argued objections. "Analysts understand each other anyway!" appears to be a pale objection. This sentence, which I have heard on several occasions from colleagues, hides a narcissism that comes from an institutionalised[2] ideology. Typical of the ideology is avoiding going into depth in a discussion and rather isolating, or ignoring, those who bring innovation: those who are "different", in the Greek etymon, become "heretics", as in the semantic halo which the latter term took on in the history of Christianity, but who can no longer be burned today. They are to be avoided; exclusion and intolerance are submerged in the institutional unconscious (Agazzi, 1992; Imbasciati, 2014c), whilst at apparent level indifference is deployed. Some psychoanalysts maintain that to do a good analysis (as is effectively done in present-day clinical psychoanalysis), the analyst at work must not have any theory in mind; from this statement, they shift to state that it is superfluous to discuss the theory. In my opinion, a good theory is necessary, in clinical psychoanalysis as well, with all due caution: but we have to consider that a theory, which has become a standard doctrinal obligation whilst in reality it is no longer congruent with clinical psychoanalysis, can really damage the analyst in a session with the patient. All the more so if this theory remains implicit. However, it may be, at the level of progress of a science, theory is indispensable. In the arguments of individuals who advocate the indifference of the theory, and relative specifications, there clearly appears, in my opinion, an attitude (understood in the definition given to it in Social Psychology): only those who belong to the "noble" ranks of psychoanalysts who "make up the numbers" which form the best known psychoanalytic Institutions have exact knowledge; while all the others, psychoanalysts and psychoanalytic psychotherapists[3] who are outside it, do not count, even though it would be opportune that what is meant when referring to theories could be clarified precisely for them; and then by clarifying an updated theory; this would be all the more opportune, for all "ordinary people" when they hear "the theory of psychoanalysis".

Ideologies are expressed at level of the unconscious collective thought; often disowned at the level of individuals, they take the form of a climate, almost an "enactment"[4] within a community, embodied in its procedures, regulations, habits, type of literature. It is difficult for the individual members of that community to admit a collective unconscious (and again I recall Jacques); far more remote than any individual unconscious, implicit in the relational interweaving of the interactions that characterise that specific community. There is an ideology hidden by "institutionalisation" (Schoek, 1974) of feelings and attitudes, which can therefore not be recognised.

Such an ideology hinders the development of a scientific methodology, correctly appropriate for a given science. If we want to describe

THE INSTITUTION: DOCTRINE AND IDEOLOGY   189

psychoanalysis as a science, with respect to the other sciences, I believe it would be necessary, first of all, to define the term "theory" in the strictest sense, keeping to the first meaning given in the Italian dictionary and the fifth one in the English dictionary and, in the second place, specifying an updated theory. In psychoanalytic literature, particularly Italian and even more in the current language of psychoanalysts, the term is used extensively; the expression "X's theory" with the name of a specific author is paradigmatic. Here theory usually refers to "the way of thinking".

This has given rise to a language which we could call "psychoanalystical" (= Italian *"psicoanalitichese"*) which has appeared in recent years in a great deal of literature, in particular in Italian, which aims to become typical of present-day psychoanalytic science; a "proper" article (or a book), that can be accepted in the official assembly and consensus of colleagues, has to obey a predetermined pattern. This is made up of two elements: a clinical case and a review of the literature that is relevant to the case described. This prototype (same type?) is called "theoretical-clinical work" where the hyphen may be taken as a symbol of the indiscriminate and therefore confused use of the term "theory".

The relevance required for the review of literature also ought to be relevant to a general theory, as each individual patient can be similar to although not the same as another: in actual fact, the review ends up by consisting of a relatively long list of quotations by some foreign authors on the crest of the wave, variously commented on by Italian colleagues well known in the establishment, which is reduced to quotations, not of theory (if not certain at least probable), but of a list of metaphors and expressions that have been used each time by the former and even more by the latter to illustrate clinical difficulties, situations of malaise and impasses between the analyst and analysand, more or less similar (at their discretion) to those which are illustrated in the case presented: "ways of thinking", more than effective theory of various analysts on similar problems.

The more the quotations have highly imaginative labels, the more successful the article is. I think that underlying this type of appreciation there is the fantasy and perhaps the idea that all those metaphors are explanations of the difficulties encountered in clinical practice by that case: the metaphor is reified. The writer has the sudden satisfaction of being able to show that he has understood and explained the difficulties of the case. Psychoanalystical language thus shows the competence of an analyst and every institutional "scientific" journal thinks that this way it proves the competence of its members.

Theory as someone's way of thinking, therefore: usually about the difficulty of doing analysis. It is true that the analyst works with the emotions, his own unconscious ones, to understand something about the unconscious emotions of the patient—the success of an analysis lies in the absolutely unaware transmission of "good" emotions between the analyst and patient—and that it is difficult to become aware of this and very difficult to illustrate this with words (we are in the realm of the ineffable, of the non-verbal and of implicit memory) but slightly more inflexible thought could perhaps be as useful with respect to the wandering fantasising of one's "free" associations in the intention of building up an explanation of that something that is taking place. It should be borne in mind that the functions involved in that analyst with that patient at that time are one matter, another matter is the necessary level of abstraction that allows a reference to a "theory" that can be communicated in terms of conscious logic.

The human being reaches knowledge as, in the development of the structure of his mind in contact with others (from the start of life: Siegel, 1999), he is able to distinguish an external reality with respect to his body, and then with respect to an incipient self, and therefore to what is being structured in this self, in what at various levels we call thought or memory, imagination, desire, motivation or something else. This takes place first in the acquisition of the organisation of perceptive processes (up to adult perception: *cf.* analysis of perception, Imbasciati, 1998, Chapter Three), corporal and external, and then in the progressive acquisition of the capacity to process and configure increasingly complex representations, both referred to the exterior and to one's interiority. At the end of the latter, a long and complex process, reflective capacities (Siegel, 1999; Imbasciati, Dabrassi, & Cena, 2011, Chapters Ten & Twelve) are acquired. In relation to external reality, the sensory afferences, as processed by the structures which the mind has built, give adults an operatively effective picture of the world that surrounds them and of the world in which the self acts. This ability to observe the various aspects of reality allows describing them to others; usually through language and the conceptual mental operations, which can organise their comprehension. This is a first level of knowledge (of the external world): each individual describes to himself the external world and then he tries to communicate this description to other people.

THE INSTITUTION: DOCTRINE AND IDEOLOGY   191

The mind, in order to orient itself in this "world", seeks out all the possible connections between the various events and phenomena which are "observed". This makes them more intelligible in some way. At a further level, by observing the succession of phenomena and events, the reasons for them is sought, how they can come about, in which way, for which causes, and why they come about, through which more hidden events, motives and agents. The distinction is outlined here between the description and the hypothesis of interpretation with which we try to "explain" or better "explicate" what has been described; how and possibly why. The distinction between description and explanation is as old as it is fundamental: *post hoc* rather than *propter hoc*. In English there is a distinction between *how* and a more advanced *"how well"*, corresponding to different levels of our Italian *"how"*, from *why*: the real why the things that have been observed and described take place. This "why" appears as the ultimate limit of human knowledge, which can always be accomplished, has been accomplished and to be accomplished, an asymptote that can never be reached in its complete sense, and therefore referred to hypotheses which from scientific become philosophical, metaphysical, and religious (Imbasciati, 1994, 1998, 2013a).

Along this journey of knowledge with progressive levels, we use instruments, the first of which is the mind itself of the knowing subject, which invents concepts and words, as well as advanced technological instruments to express what is thought to happen in the phenomena observed. For psychoanalysis, the clinical practice and its evolution (setting, personal analysis and training of the psychoanalyst, important and innovative clinical descriptions) can be assimilated with the invention of instruments, as occurs in other sciences. At the first level of the cognitive process, it is about seeing how what is thought to have been observed—possibly "discovered" if not previously observed by anyone—can be described. After that, connections are sought between the various facts observed and described; in psychoanalysis between the psychic events that have followed on one another in the observation of an adequately equipped analyst. These hypotheses nevertheless are always of a hypothetical nature, as they are attempts to go from descriptions of sequences of events (*post hoc*) to explanations of a causal type (*propter hoc*). A series of hypotheses can be organised to form a theory, but it has to be distinguished as such with respect to the "discovery" or "invention". Elsewhere I have schematically illustrated this cognitive procedure (Imbasciati, 1994, Chapter Four).

192 MINDBRAIN, PSYCHOANALYTIC INSTITUTIONS, AND PSYCHOANALYSTS

In psychoanalysis, if we want to continue with the intention stated by Freud in the light of all the subsequent clinical discoveries and developments of the method, we should identify that general theory of the functioning of the mind that better characterises the current vertex of this discipline in the explanation of the human mind. One hundred years after the formulation of metapsychology, as Freud could construct at the time, having recognised the great development of clinical psychoanalysis, we can no longer consider the Freudian theory as it were an actual one. Moreover, any theory always has a hypothetical nature as it is relative to the state of the art, at a given time, of methods, observational instruments, observations of events and "discoveries". Theory is an invention, not a discovery, unless it is deified, as seems to have been the case for the "holy metapsychology" of Freud.[5]

Invention and discovery

The assumption that guarantees, or would guarantee, the "scientific nature" of a "cognition" appears to be the knowing mind: it therefore has to be presumed as having an "objective" ability. If this objectivity can be reasonably posited with regard to an inanimate reality external to the subject, this objectivity, philosophically questionable in its absolute sense, may however be posited if it is limited to the confirmation of an operative efficiency. When knowledge addresses the human mind, however, the problem of objectivity is further complicated. It is also complicated enormously if we consider psychoanalysis with its first and fundamental discovery; the mind works at unconscious levels and gives unreliable conscious results.

The mind of the scientist who wants to investigate the functioning of the human mind, if he is right in suspecting that the conscious introspection with which an individual describes himself does not say everything[6] (or perhaps he is not telling the truth) and if he does not drift into ideology or into a religion, he finds himself facing a paradox: he has to investigate an unknown object through an instrument—his own mind—which itself is to be assumed as unknown in its functioning. So he has to investigate his own mind at the same time. This is what Freud did: the task was revealed in the years after Freud as progressively more complex and at the same time fundamental: the history of the institution of personal analysis in the training of the future analyst appears extremely laborious and is still evolving. The queries and the

THE INSTITUTION: DOCTRINE AND IDEOLOGY   193

suspicions on what is unknown, that is, can be hidden in the human mind, is turned into queries and suspicions on how one's own instrument works, one's own mind in the investigation and in the comprehension of what can happen beyond what appears to one's consciousness. Supposing that beyond conscious introspection of an observed subject there hides an unknown and different mind, means assuming that, in the investigating mind as well, an equally unknown functioning makes the observation of the other's mind appear to the investigator quite different from how it effectively functions. The complication focuses on the fact that, not only the observed object is hidden from being understood by observation (of oneself and of others) but the observing mind is subject to the limit—enormous as has been gradually discovered—of being not known, therefore occult in its observing function, which invalidates the results which "appear" to the observer. "Objectivity" would therefore not exist, in what psychoanalysis observes.

In actual fact, the positivist conception of objectivity crumbles. Many epistemologists (Agazzi, 2006) maintain that the criteria of operative efficacy and consensuality between experts exist, that can guarantee "sufficient" objectivity. With psychoanalysis, having rightly suspected that conscious introspection is not sufficient, indeed fallacious in telling us how the mind works, the myth of consciousnessism, implied and dominant in the whole of Western tradition, crumbles. What can be done to obtain sufficient reliability about knowing the mind?[7]

The departure from this vicious circle was allowed by the gradual invention of the method: free associations, continued and constant presence of the analyst, (fluctuating) attention to dreams and to everything that to common sense seems casual and insignificant, and other rules that were gradually added to build up to setting, external and above all internal of the analyst. The degree of "success" of the personal analysis of the individual analyst was increasingly clear here. All this can be compared with the result obtained with the patients of that analyst, which acts as a check.

The road was long and complicated, with a laboriousness which still continues in the posterity of Freud.

The greatest difficulty appeared not only in using the above method in the patient, but in excogitating how this (or something else? Or developing it?) could be applied to the analyst himself, so that his mind did not cause him to make any too many oversights. One of the accusations levelled against psychoanalysis is that what the analyst

194 MINDBRAIN, PSYCHOANALYTIC INSTITUTIONS, AND PSYCHOANALYSTS

reports observing nevertheless passes through his capacities for consciousness; and these, as ascertained for the patients, are, although to a lesser extent and different, always fallacious in him as well. This is remedied by the analyst's training to pick up every possible nuance of his feelings with regard to or on contact with the patient: this was called countertransference training. The history of this development of the method was complicated and laborious; there is an enormous amount of literature on the training of the future analyst. The progressive "discovery" of this path was the increasingly greater observation of how every emotional state (of the analyst in this case), felt or not, could influence or even "produce" what at the conscious level was thought was being observed in the unconscious processes of the patient.

The problem however did not end here. In the past few decades, psychoanalysts have realised that even by perfecting the training of the psychoanalyst to understand his own emotional states and those of others, what passes between the patient and himself still passes through language, verbalisation: the "talking cure". The verbal filter, however, still entails the fallaciousness of a consciousness with respect to the emotional state: a major obstacle is thus identified, which is added to the already low possibility of the albeit various levels of consciousness of human beings, even though they are trained.

Today the talking cure is doubted (Imbasciati, 2010d) because it has been increasingly observed (and confirmed by psychological and neurological experimentation today) that what changes the patient is a passage from unconscious to unconscious, which passes above all in the interactions more than in the words, through non-verbal, automatic reciprocal communication and which completely escapes the subjects; something linked by the implicit memory and perhaps mediated by the system of mirror-neurons. In current psychoanalysis, the implicit memory is increasingly considered as the matrix of the unconscious, perhaps quite simply the unconscious. Psychoanalysts are getting ready to recover what experimental psychology discovered fifty years ago about the implicit memory and integrate it today with neurosciences. This is bringing psychoanalysis closer to the other sciences of the mind. The very conception of the unconscious is changing (Siegel, 1999; Imbasciati, 2013d, 2014b). There is a current orientation no longer towards "studying the unconscious" but how a possible consciousness is formed and in what form.

The consideration of the education that an analyst requires (to follow Freud he ought to be a scientist in the first place, Imbasciati, 1983a) so

THE INSTITUTION: DOCTRINE AND IDEOLOGY   195

that his mind is "psychoanalytically equipped", but not only in the only way that goes through the verbalisation of associations and interpretations, is therefore about to change. New scenarios are opening up for the training of psychoanalysts. Non-verbal communication passes through the ability of the individual analyst to feel his own somatic states, in order to be able to grasp and understand what it is the meaning of what happens, not only the somatic states of the patient, but also something of what takes place in his own somatic state. How can a psychoanalyst be trained to feel his own—the finest ones, I mean—corporal states? And how can what the analyst has felt, or deciphered, so that he has expressed it or acted it out, be correlated with something that has modified the patient? The history of the method, in psychoanalysis, is waiting for new revolutionary developments with respect to the talking cure.[8]

Returning to what extent psychoanalysts are for the time being trained, in the use of their capacity for consciousness, in this field as well, it appears very opportune to clarify some concepts which regulate what takes place in the passages that lead to formulating theories. Analysts often take these passages as understood, automatic and almost natural, with the result that the term theory becomes general.

To adequately describe "what" we presume or perceive it has taken place in some way, linguistic terms are needed, including those invented to render abstract concepts: if the investigated object is new, i.e., not yet known, it is probable that abstract concepts and metaphors of ordinary language are not sufficient. New terms and concepts therefore have to be invented. To give some banal examples, the term "microbe" was invented in medicine and "cell" in biology. The words were invented to indicate concepts that did not exist before, as the "things", then discovered, were unknown. The invention was necessary to describe what was being discovered using certain instruments, in this case the microscope. The invention concerns in the first instance invention of concepts, which act as instruments, and these enter into the rules which make up the method of a science, and this method gradually becomes complex and refined, thus allowing new discoveries and hence new inventions. These lead to new hypotheses which can be formulated when verifying and testing the utility of the conceptual and technological instruments and which are used to invent more new instruments. The conceptual instruments can thus attain a sufficiently coherent set of hypotheses, the most probable ones, which can in this way make up a "theory". It will be used to make that cognitive method which characterises a certain science advance, until it is replaced by another better theory, i.e., more useful for the progress of that science.

In this procedure, the description, gradually enriched by the refinement of the method and by the conceptual instruments which better describe what the method has progressively allowed identifying and observing, tends to hypothesise connections between the events observed i.e., it tends towards an "explanation" of the sequences or coincidences of the events that have been discovered. These hypotheses take the form of theories, more or less generalised, which interpret how and why the events observed can take place. In this progressive formulation of theoretical hypotheses, a possible explanation can usually be seen, but which usually gives a glimpse of another further one: in other words, we realise that a hypothesis that appeared explanatory of the phenomena was only a "how" and not a real "why". This "ultimate why" is often revealed to be only an asymptote, to which every science aims, at times with recourse to other sciences as is currently the case of psychoanalysis in relation to neurosciences. The theories can therefore oscillate between the pole of the description, coining, i.e., inventing, new terms and concepts suitable for a better description, and those of the explanation, or better, of an attempt at explanation through the invention of theories that can "explain"; we thus have descriptive theories and explanatory theories. The theory in any case is always a hypothesis, which can be replaced by a better one, with the progress of that science and its method, and it is, however, always a temporary "invention", not a discovery.

The distinction between invention and discovery, which may appear obvious, does not always come to the light, indeed, in psychoanalysis: inventions, if authoritative, are taken as discoveries. We hear "Freud discovered drives". In this way, authoritative conceptual inventions are respected, as though they were unalterable cornerstones, but this hinders, or even prevents, better theories being sought, which can lead to new instruments and to new discoveries and therefore to the progress of this science. This took place for many of Freud's conceptual inventions. The ideology starts on this basis, of confusion between inventions and discoveries, as I try to illustrate below.

The "theory" is the terminal of a series of hypotheses connected organically between one another, invented to give a better comprehensible form to what has been observed. This corresponds to the meanings that in dictionaries indicate what I have defined theory in the

THE INSTITUTION: DOCTRINE AND IDEOLOGY   197

strictest sense; understood in this sense, a theory allows to identify completely the characterisation of a science which progress, is given by its method, throughout its progressive development. Theories are to invent new instruments, i.e., to perfect the method and this means discovering something that before could not be observed or understood. This is the "discovery", to be distinguished from the invention, and from the method and from the theory, which in its turn may allow improving the method.

Method, theory, doctrine

A science is not characterised so much by its object of study but by its method: it is the method which with its predicates "cuts out" the object, i.e., defines it (Agazzi, 2004, 2012). The same real object studied with methods which are very different from one another is configured in as many different "objects". For example, a cathedral, or any building, is a different object if studied from the point of view of Architecture rather than that of Building Science or by History or Economics or Mineralogy (of the materials) or by Anthropology and so on; the same plant is a different object if studied from the point of view of Botany rather than that of Agriculture or Economics. The object "man" can be configured very differently by multiple different sciences. The "mind" is configured as a different object if studied by philosophical reflection, or by the introspection of the individual, or by behavioural observation, or by psychological experimentation or by neurobiology or by psychoanalysis. Each science has a method of its own, which configures its "object": the same object can therefore appear different as it is seen from a different vertex. Some vertexes are "closer" to one another and can be easily integrated, others less so: however, they can be considered equally valid, even though they appear different, if they do not contradict one another. This is a general principle, called "consilience" (Wilson, 1998): if the data offered by a given vertex of a specific method contradict those of another, one or other of the sets of data has to be deemed false, or at least has to be dropped. This principle has to be taken into consideration for theories, in particular for psychoanalytic ones.

Today Freud's metapsychology seems to contradict what current clinical psychoanalysis implies, as well as the other sciences of the mind. Today a psychoanalysis without the Freudian theory is necessary (Imbasciati, 2010c, 2013b, 2013d), without the fear of demolishing Freud's whole work which remains fundamental, if the theory is detached from it without misunderstanding the theory itself.[9]

The specific object of psychoanalysis comes from its specific method. Invented by Freud, it has been gradually enriched, until it defines the object in a progressively different way, With Freud and for many decades, the object of psychoanalysis was, and still is, the unconscious, even though with more recent developments it can be outlined as "the capacity for consciousness" (Imbasciati, 2005b, 2012a, 2014a; Cena & Imbasciati, 2014). The study of the consciousness is, on the other hand, the most up to date horizon in the neurosciences (Damasio, 1999).

The epistemological distinctions illustrated so far are necessary to characterise a given knowledge as "science". Psychoanalysis, after the first attempts to de detached from medical practice, was qualified as an autonomous science (Freud, 1923) and as such has made a great deal of progress. Today's psychoanalysts, qualified by their specific scientific associations, pay great attention to the scientific validity of their subject and the scientific character of their work, and they write about this in the works they produce in abundance. However, if we look at this very carefully, we can see how this scientific nature is concentrated in the efficiency of operating "psychoanalytically" on the individual patients, so that an improvement takes place; i.e., on the efficacy of psychoanalysis as a treatment. This is however only the second characteristic of the three Freud had already identified. The first, which indicated the method, concerned the investigation on how the human mind works, which implies the formulation of a general theory, whilst the third indicated the "contents" (= the "objects") of the "new scientific discipline" (Freud, 1923, p. 437). It should be noted how the master in all his work privileged the investigation into the functioning of the mind, more than the treatment.[10] The scientific character that psychoanalysts intend therefore appears somewhat reductive; when they speak, and today they increasingly do so, of "scientific research", they mean the efficacy of the treatment, the change of the structure of a patient in relation to the various qualities, or techniques, of the work of the analyst in the relationship with that patient; but, overlooking some elementary epistemological principles of a scientific nature, in the first place the due distinctions between method and theory as well as between invention and discovery, they also overlook the fact that emphasis on efficacy without the presupposition of an adequate "investigation" into the general functioning of the mind entails considerable difficulties.

If the above distinctions are not specified, which proceed from a correct epistemology, the inventions taken for discoveries may crystallise the theories and the real discoveries cannot be adequately exploited to perfect the method, and lead to new discoveries with which to invent new theories; whilst old theories, taken for discoveries, are of little use for improving the method. A science slows down, when it is harnessed or even immobilised, in a thousand discussions in which each person describes the same things with different words each time.

Psychoanalysts ought to be "scientists" in the most complete sense, scholars of their "objects" and not simple professionals, if they want to make their (and our) science advance, without remaining with the limits of a noble but perhaps extemporary craftsmanship. Outside a bitter hyperbole, I could pontificate—please forgive me—that Freud has to be imitated by superseding him, rather than stopping to worship him (Imbasciati, 2011a).

The competence that analysts acquire in the ponderous training of the psychoanalytic institutions which come under the best known and most accredited organisations for their severity, and in the subsequent continuing training fortunately imposed on them by the same, is usually excellent as far as clinical psychoanalysis is concerned, but defective on the epistemological level and on that of scientific methodology, and consequently on the theoretical level so that these defects can invalidate or diminish clinical competence (Imbasciati, 2013b, 2013c). In particular, a lack of distinction between discovery and invention generates confusion, as theoretical inventions are reified as though they were discoveries.

The method, and the relative techniques, cannot be called "discoveries", i.e., existing before they were known, because knowledge of them is the result of invention and the invention can change in time and improve, whilst the discovery remains what it is and can, if anything, be "discovered" more completely. This is relatively established as far as the method is concerned, which therefore and for this reason is in continuous progress and transformation (despite the fears indicated earlier) but as far as distinguishing between a theoretical concept and a real discovered event is concerned, it may be forgotten that concepts are not real "things", but descriptive or explanatory inventions, For instance, Freud is said to have discovered drives and repression: easily under this indiscriminate and current linguistic use of the terms "to discover" and "discovery" there is aligned the idea (not really conscious but equally cogent) that drives really exist; forgetting that the Freudian *trieb* was a conceptual invention of the explanatory type that Freud formulated to better describe and understand how man was led to certain actions (Imbasciati, 2010a, 2011b). This misrecognition may lead to the indiscriminate use of recourse to drives to explain events that otherwise could be more correctly comprehensible. In the same way, there is thought "to be" repression, forgetting that Freud's discovery was that of observing how difficult it was for patients to assimilate the meaning of what Freud offered with the interpretation, i.e., it was the discovery of the "resistance" (*widerstand*): it was to explain thus that Freud, assuming that *trieb* would have had to give rise to consciousness, presupposed the opposing *verdrangung*, backward thrust (= repression) (Imbasciati, 2013d, *cf.* also Chapter Six). On the other hand, it was inconceivable for Freud, considering his conception of memory, that something that had been conscious, was no longer so afterwards.

Misunderstandings of this type, which are subterranean rather than explicit, occur not only in psychoanalysis, but in all psychological sciences (Salvini, 2005, 2012). It is a drift, almost natural for how the structural base of the mind works, to the reification of concepts; it is easier to have in mind representations of concrete things than abstract representations, even more so if complex like scientific concepts. It is the process that philosophers indicated by the name of "hypostasis". A certain hypostasis of his own sexual feelings operated in Freud, when he gave the Latin term "libido" a more general and simultaneously biological connotation: from here he arrived at the concept of *trieb*, with which he built up all this theory of energy-drive, extending it to an explanation of all psychic functioning (Imbasciati, 1994, 2005a). Perhaps the process of hypostasis is to make something easier to understand, and perhaps that helped Freud in his "*zu erraten*" (to conjecture after the session) and so helped him to further theorise, to better try to understand the human mind. But it has to be borne in mind that this is a hypothesis, a conceptual, temporary invention, which is used to find a better one. Freud was cautious, I believe, in curbing his tendency to hypostasis, as he treated his theory as mythology: the witch (Freud, 1933a, p. 190; 1933b, p. 300).

However, this was not the case for many of those who came after him.

THE INSTITUTION: DOCTRINE AND IDEOLOGY   201

One example which in my opinion is paradigmatic of the reification of theoretical concepts is the one which can be glimpsed in the systematisation of psychoanalytic theory by David Rapaport (1951, 1953, 1960, 1977). His clarification of the drive investment in a quantitative sense, with the concept of cathexis, i.e., of a "charge" which would invest, more or less, the individual representations of objects (objects defined such as "objects of the drive" according to the classic description that Freud gave of them in *On Metapsychology*) easily suggests, at least at phantasmatic level, a concrete object, a charge of the electric or biochemical type, as Freud had moreover hoped, but cautiously postponed to those coming after him (Freud, 1895, p. 200; 1905a [1901], p. 113f; 1905b, p. 168f, 214f, 218f; 1906, p. 277f; 1914, p. 78; 1915, p. 125; 1915–1917, p. 320; 1931, p. 240; 1933a, p. 96). The quantitative accentuation and the very coining of the term "cathexis", with an esoteric flavour (as moreover "drive" with respect to a common *trieb*) easily suggest the hypothesis of the libido as a flow of concrete energy, the drive as hydraulic pressure (Meltzer, 1981). The specification of the "economic model" easily suggests that the mind is like a set of communicating vases. Whether objecting or not that Rapaport only used analogies seems to ignore the emotional bases of conscious thought, as neurosciences have shown today, as well as the continuum that exists between the unconscious and consciousness and the facility with which the mind draws on it with "less symbolised" representation, with the boundless imagination with which the child that is in us thinks. If experts can understand one another (always?) the same is not true for "outsiders". How do they conceive of drives and cathexes?

The Freudian theory is thus reified and the concepts, from Freud all the way down the chain of those who came after him, are transformed into "images", or rather into icons which—repression is a typical example—lend themselves to being worshipped ·(Imbasciati, 2013a) and to being the altar of a religiosity that covers anguishes from loss. In the rites of the Organisation, these icons cannot be profaned by removing their veil: the iconostasis of the altar of the Orthodox rite.[11] The "phantasmatic of the theory" (Imbasciati, 1999) enters the formation of the identity of the psychoanalyst and we must not forget that this identity is essentially unconscious. It is, however, precisely this which acts at the level of the institution. The Mystery is celebrated behind the iconostasis: in other words, the imprecision due to the declared double

202 MINDBRAIN, PSYCHOANALYTIC INSTITUTIONS, AND PSYCHOANALYSTS

sense, phantasmatic and conscious, of the concepts of the "theory" takes hold in the souls of the faithful, like the presence of God hidden in the mystery of the sacred representation.

The theory becomes doctrine.

Ideology

A science, as such, progresses, evolves and changes aspect. A science that is immobile becomes a doctrine. This axiom—which can be endorsed by all epistemologists and philosophers of science—presupposes a clear epistemological distinction on what, for each science, the method is, on what discoveries are and, lastly, what invention is, in other words, the theories that characterise it.

The discoveries remain and the theories change; the application and the development of the method lead to new discoveries which are connected through suitable theories, often new ones, On each new discovery the connections have to be hypothesised: this is the theory, or better, the theories, that therefore have to change. A theory is a conceptual invention, an instrument to understand the new discoveries, to refine the method, to make a science progress: an instrument which is therefore provisional, as well as hypothetical.

However, theories are often confused with discoveries. A theory is never a sequence of events to be considered "discovered", i.e., a sequence of facts ascertained in their casual nexuses; on the contrary, a new discovery can revolutionise all the science to which it belongs. "True" theories do not exist: if what is hypothesised is ascertained, that theory is no longer theory but becomes a "discovery". Inversely, if a theory is considered immutable without what has been hypothesised being ascertained, it is confused with a discovery; the science of which it is the herald then loses its character as a science and becomes a doctrine. This is an unaware drift and a collective process into which a scientific community can fall.

At times psychoanalysts may be heard saying "Freud's doctrine": is this a lapsus? What does the use of the expression "Freud's doctrine" unconsciously express?

It is not always easy in psychoanalysis to distinguish what is method rather than theory or what discovery is. Freud, in "Two encyclopaedia articles" (1923) outlined a distinction, moreover subsequently blurred when he speaks of the inseparable junktim which would characterise

THE INSTITUTION: DOCTRINE AND IDEOLOGY   203

this science (Freud, 1923). On the other hand, epistemology, which deals with these distinctions in the definition of science, has also developed since Freud's times.

What, in psychoanalysis, can be defined "theory"? The interwoven method/discoveries/theories cannot easily be disentangled. Yet Freud has given us a very clear example of "theory", a work which everybody still recognises today as forming an obvious example of "theory", writing in his *On Metapsychology* (1915): the first two essays postulate the Energy-drive Theory, which for a long time remained, by antonomasia, "Freud's theory", except to then use the term "theory" indiscriminately.

Why does Freud's metapsychology, from so many other elements of Freud's work, seem so clearly "theory" to us? The evidence is given by the fact that his metapsychology is an explicative theory and not a descriptive one; this is why it was successful. However, it was only one theory and the best and most plausible one at that time. In Freud's time, the discovery of what he called the unconscious, showed a very different psychology beyond the psychology of that time: this is the reason for the term "meta", equivalent to "beyond". Above all though, in the face of the difficulty to master the method that would have allowed verifying these discoveries, or in the face of the obvious marvel and mistrust of all the scientists of the period, who had been used for centuries to another psychology, an explanation was necessary in a comprehensible theoretical hypothesis. The "why" there existed unconscious psychic processes had to be found; thus the first paragraph of the third essay in *On Metapsychology* is entitled "Justification of the unconscious". If "justifying" was deemed opportune, it was obviously assumed that the psychic processes had to be conscious. An explanation about this justification was necessary, about why there were also unconscious processes: Freud used his ingenuosity to work them out.

Resuming the ideas outlined in *Three Essays on the Theory of Sexuality* (Freud, 1905b), and extending them (Imbasciati, 2005a), from the description of what is subjectively felt about certain impulses—sexual ones being paradigmatic—Freud goes on to hypothesise an explanation for them: a drive of a biological type, he called *trieb*: a general word in German, the questionable translation of which into other languages has given rise to esoteric connotations which have contributed to considering it a "discovery". About this "push", defined "psychobiological" (in actual fact very poorly defined this way), Freud hoped that the biochemical substratum would be discovered. This, after a hundred years, has not happened.

This *trieb* is not a discovery; it is a hypothesised concept, i.e., invented to explain the clinical detection—the description—of tendencies, impulses, motivations not recognised by patients, the importance of which in sexuality was made a paradigm by Freud to explain all other human conduct (Imbasciati, 2005a).

Why did Freud imagine—invent—this explanatory concept? In the logic of the supremacy of the consciousness, an explanation of the unconscious appeared as cogent. Freud worked it out by following the cognitions and the convictions of the time: he thought that these pushes (*trieb*) should have reached in some way the consciousness (unanimously considered the most essential part of the mind) in the form of affects and deemed that the affects must have been conscious by definition, as an unconscious affect could not have been conceived at the time (Pulver, 1971: "Can affects be unconscious"). The affect had to be the "psychic representative" of the drive, to represent it to the unconscious mind.

Shortly afterwards, Freud stated the endeavour that was to characterise psychoanalysis: "*Wo Es war soll Ich warden*", "Where Id was, there Ego shall be" (Freud, 1933a, p. 190): an endeavour compared to draining the *Zwiderzee*. He therefore thought that the *trieb*, at least with the help of analysis, should have reached the conscious mind; therefore although he had discovered the unconscious, he still thought that the consciousness was the centre of the mind. Today, we think something completely different. The mind is essentially unconscious and the neurosciences confirm this (Siegel, 1999; Schore, 2003a, 2003b; Damasio, 1999).

On the other hand, Freud observed that the patients showed difficulty (or even opposition) to becoming aware of what he was interpreting to them. This is resistance (*Widerstand*). Faithful to the idea that everything sooner or later should have flowed into the consciousness, in the face of observing resistance, Freud had to invent an explanation for it: he postulated an obstacle, an opposition of a contrary force, the *Verdrangung*, the "backward thrust", poorly translated as "repression".

Repression is still considered today a "discovery" but it is only the theoretical hypothesis consequent to the idea that the *trieb* had to push towards the consciousness. In other words, the *trieb* having been invented, as an hypostatically explication of what was observed in subjectivity (first sexual and then generalised) and having discovered

THE INSTITUTION: DOCTRINE AND IDEOLOGY   205

the phenomenon of resistance as an obstacle towards the consciousness, the *countertrieb* so to speak, *Verdrangung*, repression, had to be invented. At the basis of this conceptual concatenation, necessary to give an explication to the observation, there was an ideology of the period; the mind *had* to be conscious. A victim of this ideology,[12] that shows the strength of the community, Freud could not exploit his discovery of the unconscious to the full.

Freud therefore invented the theory. I believe that many analysts will protest at this sentence. Don't they know what "to invent" means? Or do they confuse the use (chiefly in Italian) of this verb with "improvise", with any fancy that comes into the mind? Or does their possible protest hide an "implicit" considering the "Freudian theory" as a "discovery"? Then it would be another case of reification.

Resistance, an observed clinical event, therefore discovered, is thus confused with a hypothesis about its explication: a theoretical element is confused with a discovery. The theory had to be invented, considering the a priori presupposition of the ideology, i.e., the idea of a conscious Ego nevertheless at the centre of the mind. Resistance had to be explained by this presupposition. The concatenation of these two inventions explains the difficult progression that Freud was able to make along his knowledge about the human mind. We also may understand the hypothetical nature of his theory, about which he realised too.

Today, we do not need to "justify" the unconscious, because we know that the mind is essentially unconscious and that only a very small part of it, sometimes, and in any case transformed, is translated into consciousness, whilst a large part of it can never become conscious, but remains implicit memory. All the functioning of the mind, of the brain-mind, remains well beyond any awareness. Conversely, other discoveries, with the contribution of neurosciences, act as presuppositions whereby it is possible to hypothesise other better theories on the construction and functioning of the mind (Imbasciati, 2013b).

In Freud's time, all this geography of the mind was yet to be discovered and therefore, because of the conviction of the time that the consciousness was the centre, the "sun" of the mind, the unconscious had to be justified before clinical practice. To do so, it was not sufficient to describe the unconscious processes which could be deducted from clinical practice, but they had to be "explicated" especially because there was difficulty (resistance) in realising them. Freud had to explain to his incredulous contemporaries, by using models from the hard sciences, how this unconscious may exist. The whole energy-drive structure of metapsychology, with the reference to endocrinology, to the physics of the communicating vases, to thermodynamics (all concepts that at that time were known), was linked to the discoveries of other strong sciences, so that it could be easily understood by his contemporaries. The fact that, then as today, what was formulated in metapsychology clearly appears as a "theory" proceeds from being an explicative theory. An "explication" (= why) completes the concept of theory.

In this way, metapsychology marked the success for the promotion of psychoanalysis in the world.

Will it have been this success which means that the Energy-drive Theory of Freudian metapsychology is still considered valid today, by many psychoanalysts and even more so at institutional level, even though its assumptions are no longer topical? And even though at institutional level it is asserted that it is to be understood today only at a metaphorical level. Today, the concept of repression, which is a mere concept invented as a consequence of the invention of the drive, is still considered a discovery, confusing it with the discovery of resistance. I do not think that this was the reason for keeping the Energy-drive Theory, as rather the defensive institutionalisation of the anguishes of loss.

The reification of repression, which has been done at the level of the psychoanalytic Institutions, is still alive in the community soul and in its deep identity; it has become the icon which conceals the fact that Freud has been dead for seventy-five years and that his *On Metapsychology* was written one hundred years ago. At individual level, perhaps no psychoanalyst will recognise himself in these statements, but this is exactly where the power of the collective unconscious lies, institutionalised in what can be defined ideology, incognisable to the soul of the individual. The collective excellently conceals the irrationality of beliefs and therefore prevents its recognition; the veneration of the master, of rather the anguish that his image may be lost, leaving us without an inheritance, is part of these beliefs. Why do other more updated metapsychologies not circulate today? (Chuster, 1999; Imbasciati, 2002a, 2002b, 2007b, 2007c, 2010a; Fulgencio, 2008). Above all, why, if they have been proposed, do they not "circulate"? (Imbasciati, 2013a). The inheritance of Freud lies in the method and in his brilliance in finding an explication—explicative theory—for his discoveries: it lies in the genius of the intention, not in the content that it produced, i.e., in what could be imagined with the means of the time. Moreover, the

THE INSTITUTION: DOCTRINE AND IDEOLOGY   207

later Freud, ironically calling his metapsychology "witch", perhaps realised, without confessing it, that his invention had to be changed (Imbasciati, 2013b).

The ideology that permeates the Institutions proceeds from deep anguishes and relative defences, as we have tried to identify in reference to psychoanalytic-social studies. In my opinion, these anguishes are reinforced today by the increased professional difficulties. Patients are different compared to the past: they are "difficult" patients, no longer neurotic, but borderline, psychotic, psychosomatic, with disorganised Attachment styles or, at any rate, "serious" patients. They are also patients with (economic, work, study, life) difficulties for the regularity required by analysis, which imposes on the analyst an emotional load which at times is very difficult to bear. All this can, at a deep level, intensify anguishes of loss of identity and a tension towards some anchoring in the institutional community and tradition. Dealing with patients with these characteristics can easily lead to seeking shelter in an institutional ideology. This is, in my opinion, a further motivation for keeping the icon of sacred metapsychology. The force of the unconscious emotions is stronger than the recognition of how greatly this image, contradicted today at scientific level, is therefore counterproductive for the popular image of psychoanalysis (Imbasciati, 2011b, 2012a, 2012c, 2013b, 2013c). Furthermore, in times of crisis, when fewer and fewer patients are turning to psychoanalysis.

The situation today is very critical for the future of psychoanalysis: someone (Kernberg, 2011) speaks of "suicide of psychoanalysis" if the Organisation does not change. In their devotion to Freud, psychoanalysts have overlooked one of the most scientific aspects of his intentions: investigating the functioning of the mind, not simply trying to modify it, as in clinical practice, but theorising explanatory hypotheses which guide clinical psychoanalysis taking it from the empirical, artisanal attempt to a conceptual scientific vision (Freud, 1923). To characterise a science, the operative verification is not sufficient: it can confirm, if anything, the technique, but, to characterise a science, a set of skills of abstraction and methodological competences are necessary which allow going back from the particular to the general, from the individual patient to the mental functioning not limited to the latter's. To do so, it is necessary to know how to theorise. Correct epistemology is necessary for theory, so that theory is not mistaken for discovery, in order that with new discoveries, better theories are sought.

Psychoanalysts (and I am referring in particular to the most "classic" Italian Institutions) have scotomised the importance of theory: their publications seem almost to find it repulsive. If an article does not have detailed clinical cases, its importance is not considered. Those referees who read a theoretical work are unable to understand it. The religious ideology has led to reducing the scientific nature to operative verification alone: clinical practice; for which different theoretical principles are haphazardly invoked each time, as it is not known what is precisely meant by the term "theory". This is the reason for the lack of relative skills in the training of psychoanalysts and their closing up to other sciences: in the past few years the mistrust of neurosciences, which covers up having overlooked and despised for years the earlier contributions of experimental psychology.

Psychoanalysis is thus seeking shelter in a production, deemed scientific, which, as it is concentrated on the professional clinical detail, is reduced to technique; as such it is not very easy to understand for scientists of different sciences, and for ordinary people it is unfavourable compared with other techniques. Psychoanalysis has thus closed up narcissistically into itself and externally it is disqualified. There is a lack of patients, for psychoanalysts, because those who need psychic help turn today to other techniques, or better, to other arts and crafts. The poor definition, the imprecision, the approximation and the confusion that I have tried to describe in this book, have also contributed to forming in the popular image a psychoanalysis/psychotherapy which is basically dictated by human wisdom, rather than scientific methods. This has fostered the proliferation in the past decades of variegated forms of psychological consulting (e.g., counselling or coaching), which want to appear as scientific-professional like the work of a psychoanalyst, but which in actual fact are carried out by totally unqualified people. The poor image of psychoanalysis arrives here.

How can we get out of this critical situation? Many years ago, Fornari (1978) proposed the psychoanalysis of the Institutions, with the relative therapy for "ill" Institutions. The development of this course of study came to an end with the premature death of the scholar. The psychoanalytic Institutions was horrified[13] when it was proposed to refer it to our own Institutions. Perhaps today the situation is more mature, driven by the rarefaction of patients for psychoanalysts ("there's no work") and the competition of many other psychotherapists. Or perhaps time has allowed the community's deep anguishes of identity/loss to be

THE INSTITUTION: DOCTRINE AND IDEOLOGY 209

worn off. Some authoritative voices, inside the IPA, are being raised to sponsor the contact and collaboration of the psychoanalytic organisations with the Organisations of other sciences (Universities, Hospitals, Research Centres), especially if these concern the mind (Kernberg, 2011). The appeal appears cogent today in relation to the neurosciences and quite a few favourable orientations are appearing: however, often these are in conflict with a mistrust, which is generated by the insinuation in the institutional spirit of a substantial contempt for the formative importance of experimental psychology, which in turn was generated by the many decades of marginalisation of those psychoanalysts who as well as being psychoanalysts cultivated other sciences, in other institutions (*cf.* note 3). Generations of candidates have been trained in this spirit, sometimes forgetting their previous training (Imbasciati, 2012d).

The proposal to promote the collaboration of the psychoanalytic organisations with the Organisations that deal with other sciences, although authoritative, underline the need to eliminate particular organisational systems: but without confronting the deep reasons that have generated them as defences, which still maintain them.

After all, the contents of this chapter also target the defences, although underlining that unconscious motives support them. These are my propositions too, for the epistemological improvement of the concepts and theories that are still dominant. I deem harmful for the image of psychoanalysis as a science a targeting only defences. This is basically the easiest way, which can be followed with the diffusion of ideas that can be verbalised for the consciousness, whilst the analysis of the institutional unconscious would require work and consensus that can certainly not be reduced to the contribution of a single scholar. Perhaps another way can be reached by this one, if the perplexities of the Institution at being analysed are taken into consideration.

NOTES

Introduction

1. Kernberg, O. "Suicide prevention for psychoanalytic institutes and societies", *Journal of American Psychoanalytical Association*, 2011, 60: 707–719; Zepf, S., & Gerlach, A. "Commentary on Kernberg's suicide prevention for psychoanalytic institutes and societies", *Ibidem*, 2012, 61: 771–786.

Chapter One

1. Thomas Aquinas, with Scholasticism, and the relative concepts on the soul, the spirit rather than the flesh, cognition rather than affection, us to be remembered (Imbasciati, 2007a).
2. At that time the university competitive examination was for the sole role of Full Professor.
3. The IPA has training and organisational rules with which all the different societies in various countries comply, each of which can give itself rules of its own on condition that they come within those of the IPA. Each new national society which is founded must be under the direct

212 NOTES

control of an IPA Commission, which oversees the seriousness of the training of the new analysts, for a few decades.

4. As he was half-Jewish, Musatti was removed from the chair of Padua, although he was not otherwise persecuted; he was Jewish only through his father and therefore he was not Jewish for the Jews.

5. As in the time of Freud, the first psychoanalysts were not obliged to undergo a personal analysis. Like Freud, Musatti, who was not analysed, analysed the first Italian psychoanalysts, assisted by Servadio and Perrotti in Rome.

6. Musatti was an active Socialist supporting the Communists, according to the system of the political parties at the time. Gemelli, obviously, as a Catholic in the 1950s and 1960s, could only be anti-Communist.

7. In 1966, the examining board was made up of Musatti, Massucco Costa, Ancona, and Marzi: according to the system of the time, the board had to pass three candidates (the trio). That trio was made up of only two candidates: Ferradini was made to withdraw and Giovanni Carlo Zapparoli was excluded to a great scandal. Both academic pupils of Musatti and with a good training, they were also psychoanalysts. Obtaining the call for a second chair in Musatti's university was not something an everyday occurrence; the position was not filled and the chair was lost. Great gossip continued for years over the occult reasons for this event (Imbasciati, 2013a).

8. One of the presidents of the SPI, even in 2000, specified that the organisational offices of the SPI had to be assigned to those who were *only* psychoanalysts: the "pure"!

9. After training, with which it is possible to become an Associate member of the SPI, there are two other higher "ranks": Full Member and Training Analist (=Didact).

10. I recall the fundamental distinction made by Jacques (1955) between Organisation and Institution.

11. For example, the expulsion of Jacques Lacan.

12. I emphasise here again the distinction between Institution and Organisation, according to the description of Elliott Jacques (1955).

13. The German bombing of London halted the "trial" that orthodoxy was building up against the Kleinian concepts.

14. At present psychologists make up ninety per cent of the SPI members.

15. Some SPI members think completely naturally that General Psychology is psychoanalysis.

NOTES   213

Chapter Two

1. The insinuation that abstract terms (i.e., the words and concepts) corresponded to precise entities, by an unconscious process of reification, played a part in this confusion.
2. Yet Freud (1923) defined the therapeutic effect as secondary, with respect to the aims of psychoanalysis! (Imbasciati, 2005b).
3. The old medical idea of *noxa* that alters *physis*.
4. Psychoanalysts consider this statement as a "rationalisation" to avoid the thorny difficulty of how to identify and study affects.
5. Some neuroscientists maintain that even feeling of being the author of one's actions is misleading: the brain has already decided on that action before the awareness of having wanted to do it was formed (Wegner, 2003; Merciai & Cannella, 2009).

Chapter Three

1. The substantive that generalises the affects appears all the more explicit in revealing the underlying conviction that the emotional sphere was a sort of disease that could affect the mind. The etymology (*ad-fecto* = *ad factum*) reveals an unconscious underlying thought.
2. This term, which I have used since 1980, was subsequently chosen by Schachter (1996) with the same meaning and then used by others.
3. Since alexithymia has been defined as the inability to feel and identify emotions, I have called antilexithymic abilities (Cena, Imbasciati, & Baldoni, 2010; Imbasciati, Dabrassi, & Cena, 2011) those functions with which, conversely, emotional relations and regulations of reciprocal understanding can be established.
4. Logopaths = incapable of expressing thought.

Chapter Four

1. Experiments on tennis players are still well-known: the brain decides how to go for the ball which arrives before the player even sees it and therefore can decide how to move.
2. The concept of engram must not be thought of as that of symbol, i.e., as an image that portrays or represents another, or even less as its meaning in psychoanalysis, but in its more extensive use, as in any semiotic process, including extra-human.

214   NOTES

Chapter Six

1. Organisation as distinct from Institution (Jacques, 1955).

2. We have to remember that consciousness is not a natural endowment possessed by everyone in the same way: nor is it dichotomic. Using the term "consciousness" may be equivocal: the consciousness is a continuum, from zero to an (infinite) point of full lucidity. It is therefore better to speak of "capacity for consciousness". Each person has their quantum of capacity for consciousness, their quality of their consciousness and this ability, as well as varying from one person to another, in the same person varies depending on the moment and on the relational context. We have evidence of this in the evolution of analysis along the analytic relationship, in the flow of the various sessions, where the ability to realise something that seemed "understood" varies, is reduced, disappears, and returns. For these variations, having recourse to the concept relative to the mechanism of repression is, at the very least, insufficient. (Imbasciati, 2005a, 2005b, 2006a, 2006b, 2006c).

3. I emphasise how this expression, still in use, presupposes a very restrictive idea of consciousness, of spiritualist philosophical heritage, totally incoherent with what we know today about this capacity: see the previous note.

4. We could recall the early works by Musatti.

5. An enormous amount of literature has flourished on *Nachträglichkeit* or *après-coup* as the French have translated it, aimed at discovering the "mysterious" affective reasons that are believed to have produced the "surprising" change of a recollection. The reasons for the change can certainly be seen under the affective conceptualisation, however the great surprise and great literature proceed from the ignorance that the memory is always changing: it is plastic, as for decades experimental psychology had defined and how today the neurosciences pick up again the concept and the term (Alberini, 2012). The work of the brain that changes it is, like all neuronal processes, unconscious and of an emotional nature: in this (biochemical) characteristic, it is difficult to trace a corresponding event of affects that can be made conscious, such as those which are presumed to give to the result of a change of the conscious recollection. An inadequate knowledge of the processes by which some consciousness (and not "the consciousness") is formed, play a misunderstanding, with respect to how much the brain continuously works.

NOTES 215

6. Panksepp & Biven (2012), considering affects as memory of functions, notes how any "feelings", felt by the individual to a greater or lesser extent, make up forms of consciousness.

7. "Public image" is not to be misunderstood with the image amongst professionals; as at times I have heard: social image as the image amongst the members of a psychoanalytical Society (social=Society).

8. I recall the meaning given to the term by Jacques (1955).

9. It is not a coincidence that Freud called his *trieb*, Libido (Imbasciati, 2005a).

10. Article 3, section M, IPA Rules: "The term 'psychoanalysis' refers to a theory of personality structure and function and to a specific psychotherapeutic technique. This body of knowledge is based on and derived from the fundamental psychological discoveries made by Sigmund Freud."

11. Various formulations have been put forward (Chuster, 1999; Fulgencio, 2005), which have remained isolated and buried in the ideological implications that continue to permeate the psychoanalytic organisations, which form the institutions in the sense of Jacques (1955).

12. Kernberg (2011) predicts that the ambiguity and isolationism of psychoanalysts can lead to the "suicide" of the psychoanalytic institutions. Others comment that ambiguity and isolationism cannot be eliminated without a definite clarification on theory (Zepf & Gerlach, 2012).

13. In the third essay of Freud's *On Metapsychology* (1915, p. 52), he curiously implies that not all people necessarily have a consciousness which is the same as his own. However, this idea is not developed and for decades everyone still believed that the consciousness was a natural endowment and therefore the same for everyone.

14. At the time it was thought that language, in various languages, was also a natural prerogative of man; it was thought that language had given rise to inter-human communication and from here to socialisation "I communicate because I speak", was the axiom. Today the anthropologists have inverted it: "first I communicate, then I speak". The tendency to communication and socialisation is primary, it is natural of homo sapiens as for almost all mammals.

15. An emotion is a form of awareness, common to all animals (Panksepp & Biven, 2012).

16. The adjective "unconscious", indicating what is not conscious, implicitly considers the latter primary, as is fitting to the whole of Western tradition, which considered the human mind as though it were

216   NOTES

conscious. Today, knowing how the mind is primarily and principally outside consciousness, we should find another adjective, the negation of which would indicate what is transformed into that particular psychic event to which we have given the presumptuous substantive of "consciousness".

17. Is the SPI a "scientific" society? Or only a School of highly advanced professional training?

18. I recall authoritarian statements by authoritative colleagues in the Società Psicoanalitica Italiana.

19. Perceptive orders: for instance, what is perceived as "visual" from what is perceived as auditory and so on.

20. Remember that it is always well beyond any consciousness.

21. Perception is a term which should be reserved for an event of some level of completeness, or consciousness, as in the adult and is generally referred to the perceptions of external reality through the organisation of the sensorialities.

22. This distinction, as well as the need for the various sciences to be integrated, are often ignored by many psychoanalysts, especially when they are immersed in the atmosphere of their institutions, which implicitly claim that it is only psychoanalysis that can understand the human mind, whilst the other sciences are superfluous. Institutional ideology conveniently covers up scientific ignorance.

23. Infant psychoanalysts have assimilated the empiricist (learning) and relational conception of learning, however, their contribution to the general corpus of psychoanalysis has not yet been completely assimilated, and above all it has not led to the explanations of new and different theories with respect to the classic tradition.

24. Let us think of to what extent psychoanalysts indulged themselves in hypothesising the causes of *Nachträglichkeit*, of amnesia, of trauma, without considering its explanation according to the continuous physiological change of the mnestic trace. Today, biochemistry, which governs every change of neural networks at every new experience, gives us the "explication".

25. We could also say that it is possible to learn how to destroy oneself. Beyond the irony of a superficial discourse, there can be learning (vital events? Traumatic ones?) which cancel previous learning, i.e., which destroy the possibility of "new thoughts" or even cancel the precious thought abilities possessed.

26. Panksepp, (2012), in describing the evolution of animals, in particular from reptiles to mammals, points out the importance of the nuclei of

NOTES 217

the median line of the brain trunk, as being responsible for the basic emotional systems, the ones that ensure survival of the lower animals and which, ascending the zoological scale from primates to man, are outclassed by learning, especially cortical. Should we therefore hypothesise that the foetus and the baby function according to these basic emotional systems only: like reptiles?

27. A similar process, of cancellation of what could have become thought, is described by Bion; here I wanted to hypothesise an explanation in terms of destruction of engrams at neural level.

28. It has to be remembered that perception, as studied by experimental psychology (*cf.* Imbasciati, 1998b, Chapter 3.2), is absolutely not an automatic and simple process, but presupposes a whole series of previous acquisitions by learning.

29. The analysis of perceptive processes, in the sense of experimental psychology (Imbasciati & Purghè, 1981) and as a series of progressive organisations of the afferents to reach effective perception (Imbasciati, 1986, vol. 2 Chapter 1, 1994, Chapters 14 & 15, 1998b Chapter 3) provides the most suitable model for exemplifying the path of transformation of a physical physiological event—afferences—in a psychic organisation: perception. In other words, from sensory to thought, as Bion intuited with more abstract concepts.

30. It is in the relationality and from its type that all the learning, on which all the functions which are gradually built up and which then construct the mind, take place.

31. Curiously enough, the Bionian concept of "lie" can be recalled here.

32. Perhaps we should speak about innate primitive engrams, of epigenetically inherited neural circuits (brain trunk?)

33. It could be thought that the refusal of many colleagues to compare psychoanalysis with experimental psychology and neurosciences, although argued in different ways, may, underneath it all, be a rationalisation against realising their ignorance, and a remedy to spare themselves the effort of overcoming it: this is another aspect of the ideology of the psychoanalytic institutions.

34. This section is based on an article rejected by the journal of the SPI and published in Argonauti. The decisive argument for the rejection was "a lot is said about the image of psychoanalysis but in the end the author does not tell us what it is" (!!!).

35. In the training required for future analysts of the IPA, there does not appear to be any room for training that goes beyond excellent craftsmanship, neglecting a basic and methodological scientific training, as

218   NOTES

well as of the other psychological sciences, which have informed us so greatly on the functioning of the mind.

36. Due to socioeconomic events or due to a decline of psychoanalysis?

37. The psychoanalytic institutions, somewhat rigid for the "classic" clinical psychoanalysis of adults, were tolerant towards what was slightly contemptuously considered "application" of psychoanalysis, to children, parents, as well as to groups. This official under-estimation was healthy precisely to change the dual psychoanalysis of adults.

38. Reference is made to the distinction between denotation/connotation.

39. As mentioned at the end of the previous section, the discovery that neurological maturing is due to the relational learning of the baby and that similarly the intimate relations between adults, such as the analytic one, also modify the neural networks (Imbasciati, Dabrassi, & Cena, 2011) fully justifies the reference that can be made in psychoanalysis to the neurosciences regarding the mutative effect of the analysis, i.e., the therapeutic effect of the Relationship.

40. Cesare Musatti, in an ironic booklet written towards the end of his life, proclaimed he was a great-grandson of Julius Caesar.

Chapter Seven

1. Jacques distinguished "institution" from "organisation": the manifest characteristic of the latter contains implicit meanings, which would connote the hidden spirit (ideology?) of the collective unconscious of the group of people effectively belonging to a given organisation, within which they implicitly agree with and express, we would say "live" what makes up the "Institution". The institution encloses the collective unconscious, which acts despite what has been officially announced by the Institution, in the Organisation orienting it against the explicitly declared claims.

2. Institutionalised means belonging to a collective unconscious and therefore inaccessible to the individual consciousness of those who "feel" they belong to the Institution.

3. Authoritative colleagues of the SPI establishment have publicly maintained that the institutional positions ought to be reserved for those who *only* exercise the psychoanalytic profession and do not have a simultaneous psychological or psychiatric activity, in a hospital or university. Is this a pronouncement in favour of the "pure" race? Or a proud perching

on the nobility of being descended from Freud and in a spirit of loyalty which covers the deep anguishes of loss of the institutional collective?

4. This is a term used in psychoanalysis to indicate how the thread of an implicit thought may be recognised in sequences of interpersonal interactions. The concept is however much more complex than can be reductively shown here.

5. I believe that all analysts, taken individually, deny having deified Freud's metapsychology, but this is the conscious thought of the individual, not the implicit spirit of the collective unconscious of the Institution which is expressed in the Organisation. The distinction made by Jacques is recalled here once again.

6. The School of Wurzburg (Külpe, 1883) maintained the possibility of investigating the mind by experimentally organising the conscious introspection of the individuals.

7. The beginnings of neurosciences had fuelled the idea that it was possible to abandon using the instrument "mind" to study how it works, but the most authoritative neuroscientists at present (we can mention Kandel, Siegel, Schore, Damasio and Gallese, 2011, 2006) say that psychoanalysis is indispensable: the interpersonal relationship structures the brain and to modify its functioning in a therapeutic sense it is necessary to know how interpersonal relationship work and what they consist of: we must therefore have recourse to instruments developed by psychoanalysis (Imbasciati, 2013c, 2013d; Cena & Imbasciati, 2014), but these ought to be further perfected. What correspondence does what can be described in the psychoanalytic "relationship" have in the structuring of the neural networks which form the mutative efficacy of the relationship itself?

8. Perhaps psychoanalysts will have to draw on experimental psychology, which to date has been marginalised and despised as extraneous to psychoanalysis.

9. It is not easy to overcome the sense of sacrilege that this scientific effort arouses in the Institution. One of my books, which was recklessly entitled "Psychoanalysis without Freudian theory" was immediately removed from the institutional notice-board which was regularly updated in the premises of the organisation.

10. Freud, who liked to define himself a scientist and assert his new science, said that he never "really felt a doctor" and that the therapeutic effect of psychoanalysis was "secondary" compared to the investigation, i.e., to

220 NOTES

the research on mental functioning (*cf*. Imbasciati, 1983a). In this framework, psychoanalysis can, in my opinion, be qualified as a cognitive and self-cognitive science, more than as a therapy.

11. In the rite of the Byzantine Church, the most important part of the Mass is celebrated by the priest behind a barrier of sacred images which conceals him from the view of the faithful, thus asserting the Mystery of the Eucharist, the nature of which, as is fitting for a mystery, is "hidden".

12. The relationship and the difference between prejudice and ideology, is discussed: a fundamental difference lies, in my opinion, in the power, or even in the incoercibility of the belief inside the community. This is why I speak of ideology, drawing confirmation from what happened after Freud (Imbasciati, 2014b).

13. I was a protagonist in the 1980s, together with other colleagues, of a turbulent episode in a SPI assembly following the proposal to proceed with a regular and scientific analysis of our institution, conducted obviously with the due methods that at that time some organisations, especially in industry, were testing to measure the spirit of their Institutions. It was inconceivable that the community of psychoanalysts were to be treated like a "patient"!

REFERENCES

Agazzi, E. (1976). Criteri epistemologici fondamentali delle discipline psicologiche. In: G. Siri (Ed.), *Problemi epistemologici della psicologia*. Milano: Vita e Pensiero, 1976.

Agazzi, E. (1992). *Il bene e il male e la scienza*. Milano: Rusconi.

Agazzi, E. (2004). Epistemologia delle scienze psicologiche. In: M. Giordano (Ed.), Seminario Gruppo Analitico Nazionale. Milano: FrancoAngeli, 2006.

Agazzi, E. (2012). *Ragioni e Limiti del Formalismo*. Milano: FrancoAngeli.

Alberini, C. (2012). Memoria, traccia fragile e dinamica. In: Cena L. & Imbasciati A., *Neuroscienze e teoria psicoanalitica*. Milano: Springer, 2014.

Alberini, A. (2013). *Memory Reconsolidation*. New York: Elsevier.

Amadei, G. (2005). *Come Si ammala la Mente*. Bologna: Il Mulino.

Ammanniti, M., & Gallese, V. (2014). *The birth of Intersubjectivity. Psychodynamics, Neurobiology, and the Self* (The Norton Series on Interpersonal Neurobiology). New York: Norton & Co.

Antiseri, D. (1981). *Teoria Unificata del Metodo*. Padova: Liviana.

APA (American Psychoanalytic Association) (2006). Panel 20.1.2006 *On Consciousness*.

Baron-Cohen, S., Target-Flussberg, H., & Cohen, D. J. (1993). *Understanding Other Minds: Perspectives from Autism*. New York: Oxford University Press.

222 REFERENCES

Bateson, G. (1972). *Steps to an Ecology of Mind; Collected Essays in Anthropology, Psychiatry, Evolution and Epistemology.* San Francisco: Chandler.

BCPSG (Boston Change Process Study Group) (2011), *Change in Psychotherapy.* New York: Norton.

Beebe, B., & Lachmann, F. M. (2002). *Infant Research and Adult Treatment.* Hillsdale NJ: Analytic Press.

Benecke, C., & Krause, R. (2005). Facial affective relationship offers of patients with panic disorder. *Psychotherapy Research, 15*: 178–188.

Bick, E. (1964). Note sull'osservazione del lattante nell'addestramento psicoanalitico. In: V. Bonaminio & A. Iaccarino (Eds.), *L'Osservazione Diretta del Bambino,* Torino: Boringhieri, 1986.

Bion, W. R. (1962). *Learning from Experience.* London: Heinemann.

Bion, W. R. (1963). *Elements of Psycho-Analysis.* London: Heinemann.

Bion, W. R. (1965). *Transformations.* London: Heinemann.

Bion, W. R. (1970). *Attention and Interpretation.* London: Tavistock Publications.

Blandino, G. (2012). *Cent'anni di Psicologia Scientifica e Professionale,* Torino: Ananke.

Bornstein, R. F. (2001). The impending death of psychoanalysis. *Psychoanalytic Psychology, 18*: 2–20.

Brosio, C. (2015). Come funziona la mente. *Rivista di psicoanalisi, LXI, 1*: 265–272.

Bucci, W. (1997). *Psychoanalysis and Cognitive Science: A Multiple Code Theory.* New York: Guilford.

Bucci, W. (2001). Pathways of Emotional Communication. *Psychoanalytic Inquiry, 20*: 40–70.

Bucci, W. (2007a). New perspectives on the multiple code theory: The role of bodily experience in emotional organization. In: F. S. Anderson (Ed.), *Bodies in treatment: The Unspoken Dimension* (pp. 51–77). Hillsdale, NJ: The Analytic Press.

Bucci, W. (2007b). Dissociation from the perspective of Multiple Code Theory. *Contemporary psychoanalysis, 43*: 165–184, 305–326.

Bucci, W. (2009). Lo spettro dei processi dissociativi per la relazione terapeutica. In: G. Moccia & L. Solano (Eds.), *Psicoanalisi e neuroscienze.* Milano: FrancoAngeli.

Cahn, R. (2002). *La fin du divan.* Paris: Odile Jacob.

Casadio, L. (2010). *Tra Bateson e Bion.* Torino: Antigone.

Cena, L., & Imbasciati, A. (2014). *Neuroscienze e Psicoanalisi: Verso una Nuova Teoria della Mente.* Milano: Springer Verlag.

Cena, L., Imbasciati, A., & Baldoni, F. (2010). *La Relazione Genitori/Bambino.* Milano: Springer.

Cena, L., Imbasciati, A., & Baldoni, F. (2012). *Prendersi Cura dei Bambini e dei loro Genitori.* Milano: Springer.

REFERENCES   223

Chuster, A. (1999). *W.R. Bion Novas Leituras*. Rio de Janeiro: Companhia de Freud Editoria.

Collins, (1994). *Collins English Dictionary*. 3rd edition. Glasgow: Harper Collins.

Colombo, D. (2008). What Use is Consciousness? A clinical neuroscience roundtable. *Journal of the American Psychoanalytic Association, 56*: 1, 273–280.

Conrotto, F. (2006). Statuto epistemologico della psicoanalisi e "sapere" metapsicologico. In: F. Conrotto (Ed.), *Statuto epistemologico della psicoanalisi e metapsicologia*, Roma: Borla, 2006.

Damasio, A. (1994). *Descartes' Error: Emotion, Reason, and the Human Brain*. New York: Quill.

Damasio, A. (1999). *The Feeling of What Happens*. London: Heinemann.

Dennet, D. (1991). *Consciousness Explained*. Boston: Little & Brown.

Devoto, G., & Oli, G. C. (1995). *Dizionario della lingua italiana*, Firenze: Le Monnier.

Eagleman, D. (2011). *Incognito: The Secret Life of the Brain*. New York: Pantheon.

Ebbinghaus, H. (1885). *Memory*. New York: Dover.

Edelmann, G. (1989). *The Remembered Present*. New York: Basic Books.

Fabozzi, P., & Ortu, F. (1996). *Al di là della Metapsicologia*, Roma: Il Pensiero Scientifico.

Fairbairn, W. R. D. (1952). *Psychoanalytic Studies on Personality*. London: Tavistock.

Ferro, A. (2011). Making the best of a bad job: faire de la recherché dans le bureau d'analyse. Psychanalyse en Europe. *FEP Bulletin, 65*: 30–35.

Fonagy, P. (1999). Memory and therapeutic action. *International Journal of Psycho-analysis, 80*: 215–223.

Fonagy, P. (2001). *Attachment Theory and Psychoanalysis*. New York: The Other Press.

Fonagy, P. (2003). *Regolazione affettiva, mentalizzazione e sviluppo del Sé*. (Italian collection) Milano: Cortina.

Fonagy, P. (2005). Psychotherapy meets neuroscience. *Psychiatric Bulletin, 28*: 357–359.

Fonagy, P., & Target, M. (1997). Attachment and Reflective function. *Child & Psychiatry*, 679–700.

Fonagy P., Gergely G., Jurist E.L., & Target M. (2003). Affect Regulation, Mentalization and Development of the Self, Other press, New York.

Fonagy, P., & Target, M. (2001). *Attaccamento e funzione riflessiva* (Italian collection), Milano: Cortina.

Foresti, G. B. (2013). "More than" or "More about"? Breve e incompleta storia delle ipotesi sull'interpretazione psicoanalitica. *Rivista di Psicoanalisi, 3*: 645–663.

224 REFERENCES

Fornari, F. (1978). *Psicoanalisi e Istituzioni*. Firenze: Le Monnier.

Freud, S. (1895). *Entwurf einer Psychologie*. *Studies on Hysteria*. *S. E., vol. 2*.

Freud, S. (1905a). *Drei Ablandlungen zur Sexualtheorie*. *Three essays on the theory of Sexuality*. *S. E., vol. 7*.

Freud, S. (1905b [1901]). *Bruchstück einer Hysterie-Analyse*. *Fragment of an analysis of a case of Hysteria*. *S. E., vol. 7*.

Freud, S. (1906). *Meine Ausichten über die Rolle der Sexualität in der Ätiologie der Neurosen*. *My views on the part played by Sexuality in the Aetiology of the Neuroses*. *S. E., vol. 7*.

Freud, S. (1914). *Zur Einführung des Narzißmus*. *On Narcissism: an introduction*. *S. E., vol. 14*.

Freud, S. (1915). *Metapsychologie*. *On Metapsychology*. *S. E., vol. 14*.

Freud, S. (1915–1917). *Vorlesungen zur Einführung in die Psychoanalyse*. *Introductory Lectures on Psychoanalysis*. *S. E., vol. 20*.

Freud, S. (1920). *Jenseits des Lustprinzips*. *Beyond the Pleasure Principle*. *S. E., vol. 18*.

Freud, S. (1923). *Handwörterbuch der Sexualwissenschaft*. *Two Encyclopaedia articles*, *S. E., vol. 19*.

Freud, S. (1926). *Die Frage der Laienanalyse*. *The Question of Lay Analysis*. *S. E., vol. 20*.

Freud, S. (1931). *Über die weibliche Sexualität*. *On the feminine Sexuality*. *S. E., vol. 20*.

Freud, S. (1933a). *Neue Folge der Vorlesungen zur Einführung in die Psychoanalyse*. *New Introductory Lectures on Psychoanalysis*. *S. E., vol. 22*.

Freud, S. (1933b). *Warum Krieg? Why war? S. E., vol. 22*.

Freud, S. (1937c). *Die endliche und die unendliche Analyse*. *Analysis terminable an interminable*. *S. E., vol. 23*.

Fulgencio, L. (2008). *O Metodo Especulativo em Freud*. Rio de Janeiro: EDUC Editoria.

Gallese, V. (2006). Corpo vivo, simulazione incarnata e intersoggettività. In: M. Cappuccio (Ed.), *Neurofenomenologia*. Milano: Mondadori.

Gallese, V. (2011). Neurosciences and phenomenology. *Phenomenology and Mind, 1*: 33–48.

Gallese, V. (2012). Tra neuroni e esperienza: genesi della soggettiviyà e della intersoggettività. In: L. Cena & A. Imbasciati, *Neuroscienze e teoria psicoanalitica*, Milano: Springer, 2014.

Gilbert, P. (1989). *Human nature and suffering*. London: Erlbaum.

Gill, M. M. (1976). Metapsychology is not psychology. In: M. M. Gill & P. S. Holtzmann *Psychology versus Metapsychology*, New York: International Universities Press.

Gill, M. M., & Holtzmann, P. S. (1976). *Psychology versus Metapsychology*, New York: International Universities Press.

REFERENCES   225

Guntrip, H. (1961). *Personality Structure and Human Interaction*. New York: International Universities Press.

Heard, E., & Martienssen, R. (2014). Transgenerational Epigenetic Inheritance: Myths and Mechanisms. *Cell, 157*: 95–109.

Holt, R. R. (1965). A review of Freud's biological assumptions and their influence on the theory. In: N. S. Greenfield & W. C. Lewis (Eds.), *Psychoanalysis and Contemporary Science*. New York: McMillan, 1969.

Holt, R. R. (1972). Freud's mechanistic and humanistic image of man. In: R. R. Holt & E. Peterfreund, *Psychoanalysis and Contemporary Science*. New York: McMillan.

Holt, R. R. (1981). Death and transfiguration of metapsychology. *International Review of Psychoanalysis, 8*: 129–143.

Holt, R. R., & Peterfreund, E. (1972). *Psychoanalysis and Contemporary Science*. New York: McMillan.

Holt, R. R., & Peterfreund, E. (1976). Drive or Wish? A reconsideration of the psychoanalytic theory of motivation. In: M. M. Gill & P. S. Holtzmann, *Psychology versus Metapsychology*, New York: International Universities Press.

Ianniruberto, A., & Tajani, E. (1981). Ultrasonic study of movements. *Seminars in Perinatology, 5*: 175–181.

Imbasciati, A. (1978). *Principi Introduttivi della Psicoanalisi*. Milano: FrancoAngeli.

Imbasciati, A. (1983a). Strutture protomentali nell'atteggiamento terapeutico e in quello conoscitivo. *Psicologia Clinica, 2*: 11–41.

Imbasciati, A. (1983b). *Sviluppo Psicosessuale e Sviluppo Cognitivo*. Roma: Il Pensiero Scientifico Imbasciati, A. (1984). *Fondamenti psicoanalitici della Psicologia Clinica*, Utet Libreria (De Agostini), Torino.

Imbasciati, A. (1986). *Istituzioni di Psicologia*, two volumes, Torino: Utet.

Imbasciati, A. (1989a). *La Consapevolezza*. Roma: Borla.

Imbasciati, A. (1989b). Toward a psychoanalytic model of cognitive processes: Representation, perception, memory. *International Review of Psychoanalysis, 16*: 2, 223–236.

Imbasciati, A. (1991). *Affetto e rappresentazione*, Franco Angeli, Milano.

Imbasciati, A. (1993). *Psicologia Medica: Ambiguità dei Medici Italiani e Fondazione Scientifica della Disciplina*. Padua-Napoli: Liviana/Gnocchi.

Imbasciati, A. (1994). *Fondamenti Psicoanalitici della Psicologia Clinica*, Torino: Utet Libreria (De Agostini).

Imbasciati, A. (1997). Uma teorìa psicanalitica explicativa: a teoria do protomental. *Revista de Psicanálise da Sociedade Psicoanalitica do Porto Alegre, 4, 3*: 409–423.

Imbasciati, A. (1998a). Le protomental: une théorie psychanalytique explicative. *Cliniques Méditerranéennes, 57–58*: 243–257.

226 REFERENCES

Imbasciati, A. (1998b). *Nascita e Costuzione della Mente*, Torino: Utet Libreria (De Agostini).

Imbasciati, A. (1998c). Una teoría psicoanalítica explicativa: la teoría del protomental. *Psicoanalisis* (Asociación Psicoanalitica de Buenos Aires), *20(1)*: 35–54.

Imbasciati, A. (1998d). *Afeto e Representação*. São Paulo: Editoria 3G.

Imbasciati, A. (1999). Identità dell'analista e fantasma della teoria. *Rivista di Psicoanalisi, 45, 1*: 95–105.

Imbasciati, A. (2001a). Quale inconscio? La costruzione dei processi di simbolizzazione. *Psichiatria e Psicoterapia Analitica, 20, 2*: 125–142.

Imbasciati, A. (2001b). The Unconscious as Symbolopoiesis. *The Psychoanalytic Review, 88*: 837–873.

Imbasciati, A. (2001c). Que Inconciente? *Revista de Psicanálisi da Sociedade Psicanalitica do Porto Alegre, 8, 1*: 65–88.

Imbasciati, A. (2001d). Una proposta per una teoria esplicativa in psicoanalisi. *Rivista di Psicoanalisi, 50, 2*: 351–372.

Imbasciati, A. (2002a). *An explanatory theory for psychoanalysis, International Forum of Psychoanalysis, 11, 3*: 173–183.

Imbasciati, A. (2002b). A psychoanalyst's reflections on rereading a cognitivist: towards an explanatory theory of relationship. *The Psychoanalytic Review, 89* (5): 595–663.

Imbasciati, A. (2002c). Una lettura psicoanalitica sulle scienze cognitive. *Psichiatria e Psicoterapia analitica, 21, 3*: 199–216.

Imbasciati, A. (2004). Una proposta per una teoria esplicativa in psicoanalisi. *Rivista di psicoanalisi, 50, 2*: 351–372.

Imbasciati, A. (2005a). *Freud e la Sessualità: le Conclusioni Sbagliate di un Percorso Geniale*. Milano: FrancoAngeli.

Imbasciati, A. (2005b). *Psicoanalisi e Cognitivismo*. Roma: Armando.

Imbasciati, A. (2006a). *Constructing a Mind. A New Base for Psychoanalytic Theory*. London: Brunner-Routledge.

Imbasciati, A. (2006b). *Il Sistema Protomentale*. Milano: LED.

Imbasciati, A. (2006c). Uma explicação da gênese do trauma no quadro da Teoria do Protomental. *Revista de Psicanálise da Sociedade Psicanaltica do Porto Alegre, XIII*: 75–102.

Imbasciati, A. (2007a). Medici e psicologi: e perché non altri? *Psicologia Toscana, XIII, 1*: 7–14.

Imbasciati, A. (2007b). Nuove metapsicologie. *Psychofenia, X, 16*: 143–163.

Imbasciati, A. (2007c). Neurosciences et Psychanalyse: pour une nouvelle metapsychologie. *Revue Française de Psychanalyse, LXXI, 2*: 455–477.

Imbasciati, A. (2008a). Clinica e Psicologia Clinica: breve storia di qualche equivoco. *Giornale Italiano di Psicologia, XXXV, I*: 13–35.

Imbasciati, A. (2008b). *La Mente Medica*. Milano: Springer.

REFERENCES 227

Imbasciati, A. (2010a). Towards new metapsychologies. *Psychoanalytic Review, 97, 1*: 73–90.

Imbasciati, A. (2010b). Psicoanalisi senza teoria freudiana. *Giornale Italiano di Psicologia, XXXVII, 4*: 737–749.

Imbasciati, A. (2010c). Pacienties "dificeis" e comunicação não verbal: mudanças em psicanálise. *Revista de Psicanálise da Sociedade Psicanalitica do Porto Alegre, XVII, 3*: 463–498.

Imbasciati, A. (2010d). Qualche interrogativo sulla talking cure. *Psichiatria e Psicoterapia, 29*: 247–261.

Imbasciati, A. (2010e). Lo sviluppo della psicoanalisi al di là della teoria di Freud. *Psychofenia III, 23*: 89–113.

Imbasciati, A. (2011a). The Meaning of a Metapsychology as an Instrument for "Explaining". *Journal of the American Academy of Psychoanalysis and Dynamic Psychiatry, 39, 4*: 643–671.

Imbasciati, A. (2011b). La clinica psicoanalitica e l'assetto teorico della psicoanalisi: qual è l'immagine pubblica della psicoanalisi? *Rivistapsicologiaclinica.it, 2*: 97–109.

Imbasciati, A. (2012a). Cambiamenti nella clinica psicoanalitica, assetto teorico della psicoanalisi e immagine della psocianalisi. *Psychofenia, 26*: 15–38.

Imbasciati, A. (2012b). Nascita, morte e transfigurazione della Psicologia Clinica italiana. In: G. Blandino (Ed.), *Cent'anni di psicologia scientifica e professionale*, Ananke, 2012.

Imbasciati, A. (2012c). Qual è l'oggetto della psicoanalisi attuale? *Psychofenia, 27, XV*: 99–116.

Imbasciati, A. (2012d). Una "immagine" per la psicoanalisi: la necessità di teoria. *Rivistadipsicologia.it, 2*: 9–16.

Imbasciati, A. (2013a). Psicoanalisi senza teoria freudiana. Roma: Borla.

Imbasciati, A. (2013b). *Dalla Strega di Freud alla Nuova Metapsicologia: Come Funziona la Mente*. Milano: FrancoAngeli.

Imbasciati, A. (2013c). Gli psicoanalisti han paura di Nonna Teoria. In: Imbasciati A., *Psicoanalisi senza teoria freudiana*. Roma: Borla, 2013.

Imbasciati, A. (2013d). L'invenzione della metapsicologia come strumento per spiegare l'inconscio ai contemporanei: quelli di Freud o i nostri?", Centro Milanese di Psicoanalisi, 10/3/2013.

Imbasciati, A. (2013e). *Baron fottuto, Studenti fottuti: Memorie sull'Università Italiana*, Milano: Ferrari Sinibaldi.

Imbasciati, A. (2013f). Quale Immagine per la Psicoanalisi? Il Gap tra Teoria e Clinica. *Gli Argonauti, 136*: 61–80.

Imbasciati, A. (2014a). Commento alla relazione di Cristina Alberini. In: L. Cena & A. Imbasciati, *Neuroscienze e teoria psicoanalitica*. Milano: Springer, 2014.

228 REFERENCES

Imbasciati, A. (2014b). Psicoanalisi e ideologia: Teoria e dottrina. In: A. Imbasciati & L. Longhin (Eds.), *Psicoanalisi, Ideologia, Epistemologia.* Roma: Aracne.

Imbasciati, A. (2014c). Our future mind: epochal developments of Perinatal Clinical Psychology. *Journal of Child Health and Nutrition, Sept. 2014, 1*: 11–27.

Imbasciati, A. (2014d). "O objecto da psicanálise mudou", *Revista de Psicanálise da Sociedade Psicoanalitica do Porto Alegre, 1*: 11–27.

Imbasciati, A. (2014e). Una nuova metapsicologia congruente con le neuroscienze. In: A. Cena & A. Imbasciati, *Neuroscienze e Teoria Psicoanaltica,* Milano: Springer, 2014.

Imbasciati, A. (2014f). Ideologia e Scienza: riflessioni di uno psicoanalista. In: A. Imbasciati & L. Longhin (Eds.), *Psicoanalisi, Ideologia, Epistemologia.* Roma: Aracne.

Imbasciati, A., & Buizza, C. (2011). *L'Emozione Sessuale.* Napoli: Liguori.

Imbasciati, A., & Calorio, D. (1981). *Il Protomentale.* Torinio: Boringhieri.

Imbasciati, A., & Cena, L. (2010). *Il bambino e i suoi care-giver,* Roma: Borla.

Imbasciati, A., & Cena, L. (2015). *Psicologia Clinia Perinatale, Vol. 1, Neonato e radici della salute mentale; Vol. 2 Genitorialità e origini della mente del bambino.* Milano: FrancoAngeli.

Imbasciati, A., & Longhin, L. (2014). *Psicologia, ideologia e epistemologia.* Roma: Aracne.

Imbasciati, A., & Margiotta, M. (2005). *Compendio di Psicologia per gli operatori sanitari,* Padua: Piccin.

Imbasciati, A., & Purghé, F. (1981). *Psicologia dei processi visivi.* Roma: Il Pensiero Scientifico.

Imbasciati, A., Cristini, C., Dabrassi, F., & Buizza, C. (2008). *Psicoterapie: orientamenti e scuole. Scienza, misconoscenza e caos nell'artigianato delle psicoterapie,* Torino: CSE Centro Scientifico Editore, taken over by Milan: EdiErmes.

Imbasciati, A., Dabrassi, F., & Cena, L. (2007). *Psicologia Clinica Perinatale,* Padua: Piccin.

Imbasciati, A., Dabrassi, F., & Cena, L. (2011). *Psicologia Clinica Perinatale per il futuro individuo. Un uomo transgenerazionale,* Torino: Espress Edizioni.

Jacques, E. (1955). Social systems as a defence against persecutory and depressive anxiety. In: M. Klein, P. Heimann, & R. Money-Kyrle (Eds.), *New Directions in Psycho-Analysis.* London: Tavistock, 1955.

Jaynes, J. (1976). *The Origin of Consciousness in the Breakdown of the Bicameral Mind.* New York: Houghton Mifflin.

Jiménez, J. P. (2006). After pluralism: towards a new integrated psychoanalytic paradigm. *International Journal of Psychoanalysis, 87*: 1487–1509.

Kandel, E. (1998). *Principles of Neural Science.* New York: Elsevier.

Kandel, E. (1999). Biology and the future of psychoanalysis. *American Journal of Psychiatry, 156*: 505–524.

REFERENCES   229

Kandel, E. (2005). *Psychoanalysis and the New Biology of Mind*. Washington-London: Psychiatric Publishing Inc., Washington-London.

Kaplan, K., & Solms, M. (2000). *Clinical Studies in Neuropsychoanalysis*. London: Karnac.

Katz, D. (1944). *Gestalt Psychologie*. Basel: Benno & Schwabe.

Kaufmann, L. (1974). *Sight and Mind*. New York: Oxford University Press.

Kernberg, O. (2011). Suicide Prevention for Psychoanalytic Institutes and Societies. *Journal of the American Psychoanalytic Association, 60/4*: 707–719.

Klein, G. (1976). *Psychoanalytic Theory*. New York: International Universities Press.

Köhler, W. (1929). *Gestalt Psychologie. Gestalt Psychology*. Liveright, *1970*.

Külpe, O. (1883). *Grundriss der Psychologie*. Leipzig-Wurzburg: Verlag Engelmann.

Le Doux, J. (2002). *Synaptic Self*. New York: Viking.

Lichtenberg, J. (1989). *Psychoanalysis and Motivation*. Hillsdale NJ: The Analytic Press.

Liotti, G. (1994). *La Dimensione Interpersonale della Coscienza*, Roma: NIS.

Liotti, G. (2001). *Le opere della coscienza*. Milano: Cortina.

Lombardo, G. P. (2014). *Storia della Psicologia Clinica*. Roma: Alpes.

Mancia, M. (1998). *Sogno, conscienza, memoria*. Roma: Borla.

Mancia, M. (2004a). *Sentire le parole*. Torino: Bollati.

Mancia, M. (2004b). Conoscenza, sogno, memoria: possibili contaminazioni neuro psicoanalitiche. *Psiche, 12, 1*: 75–84.

Mancia, M., & Longhin, L. (1998). *Temi e Problem in Psicoanalisi*. Torino: Bollati.

Meltzer, D. (1981). The Kleinian expansion of Freud's metapsychology. *International Journal of Psychoanalysis, 62*: 177–187.

Merciai, S. (2013). Cavarsela alla meno peggio. In: L. Cena & A. Imbasciati, *Neuroscienze e teoria psicoanalitica*. Milano: Springer Verlag.

Merciai, S., & Cannella, B. (2009). *Psicoanalisi nelle terre di confine*. Milano: Cortina.

Moccia, G., & Solano, L. (2009). *Psicoanalisi e neuroscienze*. Milano: FrancoAngeli.

Panksepp, J., & Bevin, L. (2012). *The Archaeology of Mind*. New York: Norton.

Pera, C. (1980). Apologia del metodo, Bari, Laterza.

Pert, C. (1997). *Molecules of emotion: why you feel the way you feel*. New York: Scribner.

Peterfreund, E. (1971). *Information, Systems and Psychoanalysis*. Psychological Issues, Vol. VII, Monograph 25/26. New York: International Universities Press.

Peterfreund, E. (1972). *Psychoanalysis and Contemporary Science*. New York: McMillan.

230 REFERENCES

Porcelli, P. (2014). Regolazione emotiva, rappresentazione del Sé e somatizzazione. In: G. Northoff, M. Farinelli, R. Chattat, & F. Baldoni (Eds.), *La plasticità del Sé*. Bologna: Il Mulino.

Porges, S. (2011). *The Polyvagal Theory*. New York: Norton.

Pulver, S. E. (1971). Can Affect be unconscious? *International Journal of Psychoanalysis, 52*: 347–354.

Rapaport, D. (1951). *Organization and Pathology of Thought*. New York: Columbia University Press.

Rapaport, D. (1953). On the psychoanalytic theory of affects. In: R. P. Knight & C. R. Friedman (Ed.), *Psychoanalytic Psychiatry and Psychology: Clinical and Theoretical Papers*. New York: International Universities Press, 1954.

Rapaport, D. (1960). *The Structure of Psychoanalytic Theory. Psychological Issues, Vol. 2, Monograph 6*. New York: International Universities Press.

Rapaport, D. (1977). *Il modello concettuale della Psicoanalisi/Italian collection works 1942–1960*, Milano: Feltrinelli.

Riolo, F. (2005). Ricordare, ripetere, rielaborare: un lascito di Freud alla psicoanalisi futura. *Colloquio SPI Italo-Argentina*, Bologna, 2005.

Riva-Crugnola, C. (2007). *Il bambino e le sue relazioni*. Milano: Cortina.

Salvini, A. (2005). *Psicologia Clinica*. Padova: Upsel-Domeneghini.

Salvini, A. (2012). L'evoluzione epistemologica delle psicoterapie e il loro riflesso sulla psicoanalisi. Contributo epistemico da parte delle psicoterapie postmoderne. In: Imbasciati A., *Psicoanalisi senza Teoria Freudiana*. Roma: Borla, 2013.

Salvini, A., & Bottini, R. (2011). *Il nostro inquilino segreto*. Firenze: Ponte alle Grazie.

Schacter, D. (1996). *Searching for Memory: The Brain, the Mind and the Past*. New York: Basic Books.

Schäfer, R. (1975). Psychoanalysis without Psychodynamics. *International Journal of Pyschoanalysis, 5*: 41–58.

Schoeck, H. (1966). *Der Neid. Eine Theorie der Gesellschaft*. Frieburg-München: Verlag Karl Alber.

Schore, A. N. (2003a). *Affect Regulation and the Repair of the Self*. New York: Norton.

Schore, A. N. (2003b). *Affect Disregulation and the Disorders of the Self*. New York: Norton.

Seung, S. (2012). *Connectome*. New York: Houghton Mifflin Harcourt.

Siegel, D. (1999). *The Developing Mind*. New York: Guilford Press.

Siegel, D. (2012). *Pocket Guide to Interpersonal Neurobiology*. New York: Norton.

Solms, M., & Turnbull, O. (2002). *The Brain and the Inner World: An Introduction to the Neuroscience of Subjective Experience*. London: Karnac.

REFERENCES 231

Stern, D. (2010). *Forms of Vitality*. New York: Oxford University Press.

Stern, D., & BPCSG (1998). Non-interpretive mechanisms in psychoanalytic therapy: The "something more" than interpretation. *International Journal of Psycho-Analysis 79*: 903–921.

Stern, D., & BPCSG (2005). The something more than interpretation revisited. *Journal of the American Psychoanalytic Association, 53, 3*: 693–729.

Stern, D., & BPCSG (2007). The foundational level of psychodynamic meaning. *International Journal of Psychoanalysis, 88*: 843–860.

Stern, D., & BPCSG (2008). Forms of relational meaning. Issues in the relations between the implicit and the reflective verbal domains. *Psychoanalytic Dialogues, 18*: 125–202.

Turchi, G., & Perno, A. (1999). *Modello medico e psicopatologia come interrogative*. Padova: Upsel-Domenighini.

Vallino, D., & Maccio, M. (2004). *Essere neonati*. Roma: Borla.

Vassalli, G. (2001). The birth of psychoanalysis from the spirit of technique. *International Journal of Psychoanalysis, 83, 3*: 25.

Vassalli, G. (2006). Transformations epistémologiques de la psychoanalyse. *Bulletin FEP, 60*: 42–51.

Vassalli, G. (2007). Vers la formation d'une théorie psychanalytique. *Symposium de la Société Suisse de Psychanalyse*, September 2007, Yverdon.

Wallerstein, R. (1988). One Psychoanalysis or many? *International Journal of Psychoanalysis, 69*: 5–21.

Wallerstein, R. (1990). Psychoanalysis: the common ground. *International Journal of Psychoanalysis, 71*: 3–20.

Wallerstein, R. (2005). Will psychoanalytic pluralism be an enduring state of our discipline? *Internat. J., 86*: 623–626.

Wegner, D. M. (2003). The Mind's best trick: how we experience conscious will. *Trends in Cognitive Sciences, 7, 2*: 65–69.

Westen, D. (1999). The scientific status of unconscious processes: is Freud really dead? *Journal of the American Psychoanalytic Association, 47, 4*: 1061–1106.

Wilson, O. (1998). *The Unity of Knowledge*. New York: Alfred Knopf.

Zepf, S., & Gerlach, A. (2012). Commentary on Kernberg's "Suicide Prevention for Psychoanalytic Institutes and Societies". *Journal of the American Psychoanalytic Association, 61*: 771–786.

INDEX

active learning, 21
affect, 76–77, 129, 141
  in adult, 142
  cognition and, 24–27
  internal product, 143–144
  protoaffect, 141
  to thought, 148
affective communication, 79
affective neurosciences, x
affectivity, 17, 38 *see also*: mental
    functions
afferences, 139, 140
Agazzi, E., 122, 188, 193, 197
Alberini, A., 115, 157, 158
Alberini, C., 22, 79, 214
alexithymia, 213
Amadei, G., 103
Ammanniti, M., 2, 78
anomaly, 43
Antiseri, D., 172
Aquinas, T., 17, 211
attachment theory, 43, 79, 87, 149, 170,
    207 *see also*: mind, origins of

developments, 46, 48, 57, 112
Augustine of Ippona, 17

Baldoni, F., 54, 67, 70, 81, 132, 213
Baron-Cohen, S., 2
Bateson, G., 130
Beebe, B., 76
Benecke, C., 179
Bevin, L., 22, 75, 127, 156, 215
Bick, E., 43, 149
Bion, W. R., 21, 46, 134, 166
  in cognitive processes, 134–135, 136
Blandino, G., 9
Bornstein, R. F., 114
Boston Change Process Study Group
    (BCPSG), 179
Bowlby, J., 24
  school of, 76
brain, 16, 17, 18, 29, 102, 126 *see also*:
    neuropsychic development;
    mind; mind, origins of
  active learning, 21
  affective communication, 79

234   INDEX

affectivity, 38
consciousness, 83
and decision making, 63–68
development of, 74
emotions, 22
experience of, 78–83
final outcome of adult brain, 67
functions of mind's activities, 18
hippocampus, 104
infant psychoanalysis, 79
intelligence, 31
learning and, 64
learning baby brain, 46–49
-machine, 33
maturing, 80, 176
memory, 21–22, 102
mental functions, 18, 33, 73
mental life, 30
mind and, 73–78
/mind problem, 19
mind/brain relationships, 37
mind independent of, 35–39
neural connections, 76
neural networks, 74, 126
psychosomatic, 40
self, 82
sensory systems, 74
structure and functioning, 43
Brosio, C., 150, 178
Bucci, W., 26, 51, 174
Buizza, C., 112

Cahn, R., 179
Calorio, D., 50, 141, 143, 159
Cannella, B., 41, 64, 83, 114, 115, 174, 213
Casadio, L., 130
cathexis, 201
Cena, L., 19, 26, 38, 41, 43, 44, 46, 47, 54,
57, 64, 67, 69, 78, 81, 126, 132,
150, 190
cerebral maturing, 56 see also: mind,
origins of
Chuster, A., 175, 206, 215
clinical psychology, 83–84, 170–171,
181 see also: Perinatal Clinical
Psychology

cognition, 15, 19, 24
affect and, 24–27
and affectivity, 17
cognitive processes, 127
archaic layers of mind, 134
Bion's work, 134–135, 136
experimental psychology, 133
function memory, 137
Klein's work, 136–137
Köhler's theory of isomorphism,
133
psychoanalysis of, 132–138
representation, 137
sensoriality, 136
unconscious, 133
cognitive sciences, 13
psychoanalysis and, 13–17
Cohen, D. J., 2
collective imagination, 179
Collins, 184
Colombo, D., 117, 177
connectomes, 37
consciousness, 14, 24, 25–26, 70, 83,
115, 124, 214 see also: mind,
origins of; neuropsychic
development
illusion of, 35–39
and omnipotence, 39–42
unconscious and ability for,
126–132
consciousnessism, 2, 62, 68, 99, 118,
119, 193
consilience, 197
countertransference, 163, 172, 174, 176
see also: transference
training, 194

Dabrassi, F., 26, 43, 44, 46, 47, 54, 57, 69,
81, 126, 132, 190
Damasio, A., 17, 20, 22, 26, 40, 50,
62, 63, 75, 77, 127, 174,
181, 219
Dennet, D., 105, 127
Descartes, 17–21
Devoto, G., 184
dichotomic, 18

INDEX 235

drive(s), 16, 23, 70, 93, 97, 106, 115, 135–137, 157–158, 173, 200–201
dynamic unconscious, 104

Eagleman, D., 63, 180
Ebbinghaus, H., 101
Edelmann, G., 20, 105, 127
embodied simulation model, 69 *see also*: neuropsychic development
emotions, 22, 47, 215
Energy-drive Theory, x, 25, 90, 92, 98, 108, 105, 110, 182, 185, 200, 203
  with concept of investment, 101
  functioning of mind, 149, 185, 186
  inside to outside, 136
  metapsychology, 108, 110, 206
  Oedipus and, 25
engram, 50, 70, 153, 213, 214 *see also*: neuropsychic development
  acquisition of, 161
  drive, 157–158
  formulation of metapsychology, 154
  function trace, 154, 156–157
  learning, 155
  memory, 154
  mirror-system, 156
  progressive, 161
  subjectivity, 155–156
epigenetics, 37, 79
evolution of animals, 216–217
experimental psychology, 3, 133
    see also: psychology
explanatory hypothesis, 144
external object, 151

Fabozzi, P., 98
Fairbairn, W. R. D., 92, 93, 141, 167
fascist climate, 3
Fechner, G., 3
feelings, 15, 16
  and cognition, 17
  as conscious events, 16
  in small children, 17
Ferradini, F., 212
Ferro, A., 105

Fonagy, P., 57, 115, 128, 181
Foresti, G. B., 125
Fornari, F., 208
free will, 16, 64
Freudian innovation, 13
Freudian theory, 89–92, 172 *see also*: Energy-drive Theory
  psychoanalysis, 90
  unconscious, 90
  words, 91
Freud, S., 16, 92–96, 98 *see also*: Energy-drive Theory
  about brain, 16
  doctrine of, 202
  and early psychoanalytic science, 122
  feelings, 16
  intention, 96–101
  and memory, 101–105
  metapsychology, 92, 100, 167
  neurophysiology, 93
  psychoanalytic process, 98
  repressed unconscious, 104
  repression, 105
  resistance, 105, 127
  therapeutic effect, 213
  unconscious, 105
Fulgencio, L., 175, 215
function
  memory, 137
  trace, 154

Gallese, V., 2, 69, 78, 155, 219
Gemelli, 5, 212
genetics, 32
Gergely, G., 57
Gerlach, A., 215
Gilbert, P., 126
Gill, M. M., 96
Grünbaum, A., 6
Guntrip, H., 93, 141

hallucination in babies, 143
Heard, E., 64
Helmholtz, H. von, 3
hippocampus, 104

236 INDEX

Holt, R. R., 93, 173
Hook, S., 6

Ianniruberto, A., 43
Imbasciati, A., 3, 5, 7, 9, 13, 17, 18, 19,
    21, 22, 24, 26, 32, 38, 39, 41, 43,
    44, 46, 50, 54, 57, 63, 64, 67, 69,
    81, 102, 105, 126, 132, 141, 143,
    144, 146, 150, 172, 173, 181,
    190, 200, 217
implicit memory, 104, 152
implicit semantic halo, 115
ineffable, 130
infant psychoanalysis, 79
infant psychoanalysts, 216
Institution(s), 24, 89, 91, 112, 119, 167,
    168, 173, 174, 175, 180, 182,
    183, 185, 186, 188, 206–209,
    212, 214, 215, 216, 218, 219,
    220 see also: Organisation(s)
institutionalised, 218
intelligence, 17, 31
internal objects, 151
internal product, 143–144
internal working models (IWM), 69, 76
International Psychoanalytical
    Association (IPA), 4, 14, 23
    psychoanalysis, 215
    training and organisational rules,
    211
intrapsychic permeability, 165
intuition, 31
isolationism, 23
    of psychoanalysis, 25
    of psychoanalysts, 21–24

Jacques, E., 24, 119, 180, 183, 212, 215
Jaynes, J., 129, 161
Jiménez, J. P., 175, 177, 179
Jurist, E. L., 57

Kandel, E., 127, 174, 181, 219
Kaplan, K., 127
Katz, D., 101
Kaufmann, L., 133, 151
Kernberg, O., 207, 209, 211, 215

K function, 145
Klein, G., 96, 173
Klein, M., theories, 136–137, 143–145,
    151, 153, 160
knowledge, 14
Köhler theory of isomorphism, 133,
    137
Krause, R., 179
Külpe, O., 22, 97, 118, 219

Lachmann, F. M., 76
learning, 42, 76, 155, 216
Le Doux, J., 35
libido, 92–93, 97, 167, 200, 201, 215
Lichtenberg, J., 97, 120
Liotti, G., 24, 39, 77, 124
logopaths, 57, 213
Lombardo, G. P., 3
Longhin, L., 19, 22, 25, 103

Mancia, M., 103, 126, 177
Margiotta, M., 43
Martienssen, R., 64
maturing, 68, 80 see also: neuropsychic
    development
Meltzer, D., 115, 117, 136, 184, 201
memory, 21, 51, 74–75, 154 see also:
    brain; mind
    bodily, 75
    at continuous work, 104
    dynamic unconscious, 104
    Freud and, 101–105
    function, 137
    implicit, 75, 104, 152
    Pert's theory, 103
    primary, 75
    principle of constancy, 101
    repression, 104
    unconscious and, 104
    visceral, 75–76
    which cannot be recalled, 76
mental faculties, 17–18
mental functions, 18, 33, 73
    in foetus-child relationships, 21
    Peterfreund, 94
mental life, 30

INDEX 237

Merciai, S., 41, 64, 83, 114, 115, 149, 174, 213
metapsychology, 70, 149–153, 166–169
  see also: neuropsychic development
  criticisms of, 92
  external object, 151
  formulation of new, 154
  Freudian and Holt, 93
  Gill, 96
  implicit memory, 152
  internal objects, 151
  memory and perception, 153
  neurophysiology, 149
  neuropsychophysiological explication, 149
  perception, 150–151
  Protomental Theory, 150
  theorised by Freud, 167
  unconscious psychic processes, 97
metapsychology congruent with neuroscience, 89
  affect, 141–144
  engram, 153–158
  beyond Freud, 92–96
  Freud and memory, 101–105
  Freud's intention, 96–101
  hallucination in babies, 143
  icon of Freudian theory, 89–92
  image of psychoanalysis, 169–173
  new metapsychology, 149–153, 166–169
  non-verbal communication and psychoanalysis, 173–180
  object of psychoanalysis, 121–126
  origin of mind, 158–162
  perception, 138–141
  protomental system, 144–149
  psychoanalysis of cognitive processes, 132–138
  psychoanalytic process, 98
  repression, 114–121
  symbolopoiesis of mindbrain, 162–166
  theory and clinical practice, 105–111
  theory in psychoanalysis, 111–114

unconscious and ability for consciousness, 126–132
mind, 15, 16, 29, 48 *see also*: mind, origins of
  affective-emotive, 36
  affects, 76–77
  archaic layers of, 134
  and brain, 73–78
  brain/mind problem, 19
  development, 47
  between feeling/cognition, 22
  independent of brain, 35–39
  individuals and, 19–20
  learning, 76
  memories, 74–75
  mind/brain relationships, 37
  normal functions, 36
  origin, 152
  psyche, 77
  psychic pathology, 78
  remembering, 75
  thinking, 75
mind, origins of, 29, 158–162 *see also*: mindbrain
  anomaly, 43
  cerebral maturing, 56
  clinical Kleinian intuitions, 159
  consciousness, 161
  consciousness and illusion of omnipotence, 39–42
  developments of attachment theory, 48
  function trace, 158
  infant observation, 42–46
  learning, 42
  learning baby brain, 46–49
  mind/brain relationships, 37
  mind independent of brain, 35–39
  naive organicism, 29–35
  neurobiological illusion, 34
  neurophysiology, 31
  neuroscience contribution, 49–51
  organicist conception, 33, 37
  paranoid-schizoid metabolism, 160
  perinatal period care, 57
  progressive engrams, 161

238 INDEX

transgenerational effect, 56–57
transgenerationality and
intervention point, 55
mindbrain, x, 51 *see also*: mind, origins
of; neuropsychic development
and civilisation, 51–57
conscious and unconscious, 165
construction, 68–71
and future of civilisation, 51–57
intrapsychic permeability, 165
maturing, 68
symbolopoiesis of, 162–166
transgenerationality, 65
mirror-system, 156
Moccia, G., 178
Multiple Code Theory, 178
Musatti, C. L., 5, 212

neural connections, 76
neural networks, 74, 126
neurophysiology, 31, 149 *see also*: mind,
origins of
genetics, 32
localising research, 31–32
neuropsychic development, 59
brain and decision making, 63–68
consciousness, 70
consciousnessism, 68
embodied simulation model, 69
engrams, 70
learning and brain, 64
metapsychology, 70
mindbrain and
transgenerationality, 65
mindbrain construction, 68–71
philosophy of free will, 64
preconceptions and prejudices,
59–63
Protomental Theory, 69
role of relationship, 68
neuropsychoanalysis *see* neurosciences
neurosciences, x, 10, 20, 21, 79, 93
see also: mind, origins of
brain, 126
concept of representation, 50
contribution, 49–51

engram, 50
integration with epigenetic studies,
22
memory, 51
neurological maturing, 49
Protomental Theory, 50
scientists, 51
nociception, 139, 141, 160, 166
non-verbal communication (NVC), 127,
173–180, 195
brain maturing, 176
in child, 175
collective imagination, 179
countertransference, 174
infant research and infant
psychoanalysis, 177
non-specific factors of treatment,
174
referential process, 178
repressed unconscious and
unrepressed unconscious, 177
Wilma Bucci's Multiple Code
Theory, 177–178
normal functions, 36

Oli, G. C., 184
organicism, 29–35 *see also*: mind,
origins of
organicist conception, 33, 37
Organisation(s), 7, 24, 91, 183, 185–186,
201, 207, 209, 212, 214, 218,
219 *see also*: Institution(s)
Ortu, F., 98
Ossicini, A., 9

Panksepp, J., 10, 22, 75, 127, 156, 216
paranoid-schizoid metabolism, 145–147,
160
parent(s), 46, 53–57, 81–83, 85–88,
Pera, C., 172
perception, 138, 150–151, 216, 217
afferences, 139, 140
capacity for, 139
heterothermal, 140
neural organisation, 140
nociception, 139

INDEX 239

processes analysis, 217
valence, 141
Perinatal Clinical Psychology, 81
   care system based on, 85–86
   clinical psychology, 83–84
   identified patient, 85
   multidisciplinarity, 87
   pathogenic transgenerational
      circuit, 86–87
   transgenerational effect, 85
   and transgenerationality, 83–88
Perno, A., 32, 84
Pert's theory, 103
Peterfreund, E., 93, 94, 173
polyvagal theory of Porges, 139, 160,
   166
Popper, K., 6
Porcelli, P., 2
Porges, S., 76, 156, 179
   polyvagal theory of, 139, 160, 166
preconscious, 128
prejudice and ideology, 220
protoaffect, 141
protomental system, 144–149
   affect to thought, 148
   afferences, 145
   anger, 145
   explanatory hypothesis, 144
   intrapsychic permeability, 147
   K function, 145
   paranoid-schizoid metabolism,
      145–147
Protomental Theory, 50, 69, 144,
   150 *see also*: neuropsychic
   development
psyche, 14, 15, 16, 38, 47
psychiatry, 3
psychic, 16, 38
   functioning, 100
   pathology, 78
   representations of drives, 16
psychoanalysis, x, 1, 13, 90, 181, 215
   active and personal conception of
      experience, 21
   clinical psychoanalysis, 170–171
   of cognitive processes, 132–138

and cognitive sciences, 13–17
consciousness, 124
debate against, 6
drive theory, 173
emotions in cognitive processes, 20
evolution of, 16, 123
Freud and early psychoanalytic
   science, 122
Freudian theory, 172
fundamental notions, 15
historical development, 1–5
image in comprehension, 169–173
infant, 79
isolationism of, 15, 21–24, 25
in Italy, 5–7
libido, 97
non-verbal communication and
   psychoanalysis, 173–180
object of, 121–126
persecution of Jewish, 23
psychoanalysis without
   psychodynamics, 96
psychologists, 7–11
SPI, 7
as study of affectivity, 16
substance, 15
theory in, 111–114, 171–172
unconscious, 124
psychoanalysts, 10
psychoanalytic doctrine and ideology,
   181 *see also*: Energy-drive
   Theory
   cathexis, 201
   consilience, 197
   countertransference training, 194
   Freud's doctrine, 202
   Freud's metapsychology, 197, 203
   Freud's theory, 182
   holy theory, 181–187
   ideology, 202–209
   invention and discovery, 192–197
   method, theory, doctrine,
      197–202
   non-verbal communication, 195
   and organisations of other sciences,
      209

240 INDEX

repression, 201, 204, 206
suicide of psychoanalysis, 207, 215
talking cure, 194
theoretical-clinical work, 189
theory, 184
theory and confusions, 187–192
trieb, 204
X's theory, 189
psychoanalytic process, 98
psychological sciences, 1, 15
psychologists, 7–11
psychology, 1, 14
 antonomasia psychology of consciousness, 4
 consciousness, 14
 Freudian innovation, 13
 scientific, 1
psychosomatic, 40
psychotherapy, 8–10, 170–171
Pulver, S. E., 16, 94, 204
Purghé, F., 144, 217

Rapaport, D., 115, 201
reciprocal dialogue, 132
"Remembering, repeating and working through", 102, 116
representation, concept of, 50, 137
repressed unconscious/non-repressed unconscious, 104
repression, 104, 105, 114–121, 127, 201, 204, 206
 consciousness, 115
 drive model, 117
 Freud and, 120–121
 Freudian concepts, 116
 implicit semantic halo, 115
 resistance, 115, 119
 unconscious, 115, 118
resistance, 105, 115, 127
Riolo, F., 102
Riva-Crugnola, C., 171

Salvini, A., 83
Schacter, D., 213

Schäfer, R., 96, 173
Schoeck, H., 119, 186, 188
School of psychotherapy, 9
School of Wurzburg, 219
Schore, A. N., 78, 26, 36, 37, 38, 43, 105, 121, 176, 177, 181, 219
science, 197, 202
 of mind, 1
scientific psychology, 1
self, 82
sensoriality, 139
sensory systems, 74
Seung, S., 35, 63
shrink, 2
Siegel, D., 22, 40, 78, 105, 127, 138, 174, 181, 190, 219
Società Psicoanalitica Italiana (SPI), 5
Solano, L., 178
Solms, M., 127
Stern, D., 26, 41, 124, 125, 132, 174, 175, 181
subjectivity, 128, 155–156
symbolopoiesis, 164

Tajani, E., 43
talking cure, 194
Target, M., 57, 115, 128, 181
Target-Flussberg, H., 2
theory, 90, 130, 171–172, 184 *see also*:
  Energy-drive Theory
 Babel of languages, 107
 and clinical practice, 105–111
 explanation of mental facts, 109–110
 hypothesis of explanation, 109
 of mind, 2
 One Theory, 111
 in psychoanalysis, 111–114
 terms and concepts, 110
thinking, 75
transcriptome, 37
transference, 116, 125, 172, 176 *see also*:
  countertransference
transgenerational effect, 56–57, 85
  see also: mind, origins of

INDEX   241

transgenerationality *see also*: mind,
    origins of
  from grandfathers to
    grandchildren, 81
  and intervention point, 55
  and Perinatal Clinical Psychology,
    83–88
Turchi, G., 32, 84
Turnbull, O., 127

unconscious, x, 25, 90, 105, 115, 124,
    133
  and ability for consciousness,
    126–132
  ineffable, 130
  preconscious, 128
  reciprocal dialogue, 132
  repression, 127
  subjectivity, 128
  Wilson's principle of consilience, 131

Vallino, D., 126
Vassalli, G., 98, 129
Vienna Psychoanalytic Society, 4 *see*
    International Psychoanalytical
    Association (IPA)

Wallerstein, R., 107, 187
Weber, E. H., 3
Wednesday group, 4
Wegner, D. M., 41, 64, 213
Westen, D., 99, 173
Wilma Bucci's Multiple Code Theory,
    177–178
Wilson, O., 149, 197
  principle of consilience, 131
words, 91
Wundt, W., 3

Zapparoli, G. C., 212
Zepf, S., 215